Edward A. Mabry
The University of Wisconsin at Milwaukee

Richard E. Barnes
The Executive Committee
and
The University of Wisconsin at Milwaukee

Prentice-Hall, Inc., Englewood Cliffs, New Jersey 07632

the DYNAMICS *of* SMALL GROUP COMMUNICATION

Library of Congress Cataloging in Publication Data
Mabry, Edward A
  The dynamics of small group communication.

  Includes bibliographies and indexes.
  1. Communication in small groups.   I. Barnes,
Richard E., joint author.   II. Title.
HM133.M2   301.18'5   79-22108
ISBN 0-13-222000-8

© 1980 by Prentice-Hall, Inc., Englewood Cliffs, N.J. 07632

PRINTED IN THE UNITED STATES OF AMERICA

10 9 8 7 6 5 4 3 2 1

editorial production/supervision: CATHIE MICK MAHAR
interior design: LINDA CONWAY
cover design: INFIELD/D'ASTOLFO ASSOCIATES
manufacturing buyer: HARRY P. BAISLEY

PRENTICE-HALL INTERNATIONAL, INC., *London*
PRENTICE-HALL OF AUSTRALIA PTY. LIMITED, *Sydney*
PRENTICE-HALL OF CANADA, LTD., *Toronto*
PRENTICE-HALL OF INDIA PRIVATE LIMITED, *New Delhi*
PRENTICE-HALL OF JAPAN, INC., *Tokyo*
PRENTICE-HALL OF SOUTHEAST ASIA PTE. LTD., *Singapore*
WHITEHALL BOOKS LIMITED, *Wellington, New Zealand*

to

ANN, ROANNE, STACY AND SHAUN

CONTENTS

PREFACE

Small group behavior has obvious ties to communication, social psychology, and sociology. Considerable information can also be found in the journals and texts of other academic disciplines and schools like business administration, education, linguistics, and social welfare. This text integrates certain explanations and perceptions about small group interaction that cut across diverse disciplinary perspectives. It would be unreasonable to expect that a single text, or set of authors, could effectively summarize and synthesize all relevant knowledge about small groups. We relied heavily on some perspectives and, unfortunately, probably slighted or overlooked others. Our decisions have been consistent with a basic objective of illustrating the inseparable relationship between communication and human involvement in small groups.

We view the book as appropriate for both introductory and advanced classes in small group communication or small group behavior. The contents have been used successfully in both our introductory, freshman-sophomore level, and advanced, junior-senior level, group communication courses. Finding the "optimum" student level for a text is never easy, and numerous assumptions must be made. We, for example, do not assume students in our introductory courses have had any background in communication or small group behavior. We do assume they are serious-minded students and generally possess average intellectual capabilities. Our classes are oriented toward experiential learning through classroom simulation exercises and field experiences supplemented by text and lecture materials. We believe this book can be integrated into that or other formats.

Throughout the book we have employed examples about groups in business, industrial, and other organizational settings. Our students have found it helpful to apply group behavior to such career settings. Many group memberships are embedded in organizational environments, and there appears to be increasing interest in communication as it relates to business and industry.

We have elected to avoid many of the "humanistic" prescriptions commonly offered in introductory textbooks. There is ample evidence to suggest that situational constraints often make prescriptions inappropriate. Why, for example, should all group members be encouraged to participate if not all have something worthwhile to contribute? Why should an elected leader adopt a democratic style of leadership if members express a need to be controlled or time constraints do not permit an open exchange of opinions?

One of the few prescriptions we do offer is that students can become more effective group members if they act as participant-observers. Groups need to examine themselves in terms of task accomplishments *and* as complex sets of human relationships requiring monitoring and feedback. For classroom and laboratory purposes, paper and pencil self-assessment instruments are useful. For many "real life" group situations, however, such methods may be impractical. If an instructor can instill the importance of monitoring group processes, feeding back observations, and openly discussing group functions, students will be more effective as participants and groups can be more productive and personally satisfying. We believe the role of participant-observer is more than just a skill or technique. It is a mental set or attitude regarding appropriate group behavior. Beginning students should be satisfied with just developing a desire to adopt such techniques and using them to facilitate their participation as group members. Advanced students should be able to use participant-observation techniques as a research methodology.

All authors have biases about their subject matter and we are not exceptions. We have alluded to a few of them already. The merging of our biases has led us to examine small group communication as a process whereby separate individuals, with unique personalities, attitudes, and competencies, are integrated into functioning social units many people call *systems*. Thus, we approached this project with a specific purpose: to demonstrate how communicative behavior operates in the formation, maintenance, and change of small group-systems. Our desire to touch upon diverse sets of information about small groups has sometimes dictated we not talk about communication *per se*. Without interactive relationships, however, various combinations of people would only be unorganized assemblies occupying common spaces. Communication is the key ingredient in all small group activity. These are our biases and this text's predominant themes.

We are indebted to a number of people for helping us through various stages of text development. Dean Hewes, Cliff Kelly, and Gary Schulman read various drafts of the manuscript and contributed many helpful ideas. Our special thanks to go John Busch and Cathie Mahar for their many contributions. Ann Mabry typed numerous rough and "final" drafts, helped with the editing chores, and managed *not* to divorce her husband. Finally, our students were helpful critics and necessary respondents for our ideas.

Edward A. Mabry
Richard E. Barnes

The purpose of a text's introductory chapter is to familiarize readers with basic concepts, definitions, and the approach, or "slant," its authors have toward their subject matter. Chapter 1 contains our definitions for basic concepts like small group and communication. In addition, we explain a model that sorts out the multitude of human and environmental factors associated with small group action. We use this model to organize the remaining parts of the text.

INTRODUCTION

Part
One

Chapter

Three people stand at a bus stop talking with each other. A surgical team performs a major operation. Department heads of a large company meet. Two couples go out together on a Saturday evening. A motorcycle gang cruises around the city. At first glance, these different sets of people appear to have nothing in common and, in most respects, they probably don't. However, there is one important commonality all these people share—each set constitutes what is usually called a *group*. Specifically, these diverse sets of people may be thought of as "small" groups. Exploring human relationships, and the role communication plays in those relationships across various group situations, is the major concern of this text.

Most groups have either professional or social reasons for existing. While these two types of groups accomplish tangibly different outcomes for their members, they nonetheless have goals and objectives that frame the rationale for their existence. Most of us have familiar images of highly structured groups such as factory production teams, office units that perform interrelated jobs, and decisionmaking groups in

1 *a framework for understanding small group processes*

government organizations. Hospital surgical teams, student study groups, and civic activities groups also fit into this category of *task oriented* groups. Social groups (or *cathectic oriented* groups) run the gamut from Friday night drinking partners, bowling teams, and travel tours to juvenile gangs, athletic teams, and families.

DEFINING SMALL GROUP COMMUNICATION

Two important bodies of thought are involved in the study of small group communication. On the one hand, there is the study of small group behavior in general; there are literally thousands of research articles and books dealing with this topic. On the other hand, there is the subject of human communication, which has been studied and investigated for thousands of years. Any attempt at defining something called "small group communication" only scratches the surface of two complex study areas. Bear in mind that both terms, "small groups" and "communication," are merely abstract labels behavioral scientists use when referring to complex aspects of human social behavior. No definition can really do justice to the social complexities associated with either term.

We define a *group* as *a network of people who have intentionally invested part of their personal decision making power in the authority of a larger social unit* (called *the group*) *in pursuit of mutually desired but separately unobtainable goals*. This may sound unduly complex, but to say, "some people agree to work together in order to accomplish a common objective," would be an oversimplification. First, it is necessary to recognize that groups exist because people are linked to one another through their actions. The concept *network* implies such linkages. Second, groups cannot remain intact as social units unless people identifying themselves as members are able to control their actions as social participants. This means that the individual must accept some restraints on personal desires and behaviors so the unit can function effectively. Individual control is accomplished by each member *investing authority* with the group to exercise certain controls over personal action as a condition of membership. Last, we all recognize that groups serve some useful purposes for their members— otherwise no compelling reason would exist to join a group and accept restraints on one's individuality. Group membership is stimulated by our needs and desires. The latter statement makes sense even when group membership is determined by employers or other authority figures. A requisite for continued employment may be satisfactory performance as part of work "team." Moreover, successful adaptation to the "social environment" of a work place may require joining friendship groups composed of fellow employees.

The Size of "Small" Groups

Whether we label units of people as "small" or "large" groups is somewhat arbitrary. Generally, a *small* group is said to exist if its members are able to conduct their affairs together in face-to-face interaction. Obviously, most groups use other modes of interaction as well. Telephone conversations and written correspondence are also ways of contacting group members. However, a substantial amount of face-to-face interaction, during which time a group finishes the bulk of its necessary work activities, is an essential and distinctive feature of small group settings.

How a group divides subtasks or responsibilities among members is another clue to its size. A group small enough to function without dividing itself into committees and subcommittees for effective goal attainment would fit our general notion of a small group. A football team, for example, is really an organized assembly of smaller units called "offense," "defense," and "special teams." The local chapter of the P.T.A. usually contains a large body of members, some of whom may also serve on various committees that report to a board of officers or to the membership as a whole.

As yet we have avoided giving a specific number of members for the "ideal" sized small group—and with good reason. Prevailing opinion does not seem to favor a magical number. We can say, with a reasonable degree of confidence, that small groups are composed of at least three members. This minimum number differentiates what we label as a group from situations involving only two people—usually labeled a *dyad*. Many researchers (for example, Bales and Borgatta, 1965; Hare, 1976) have pointed to substantial behavioral differences between dyads and larger social units. Dyad members, for example, seem to use fewer disagreeing or antagonistic messages toward each other than are used in larger units.

The fundamental distinction between dyads and groups containing three or more people, one which may explain many behavioral differences, is the unique demand placed on dyad members for consensus on pertinent decisions or issues. Unlike small groups with three or more members, dyad participants cannot seek "majority" support as a lever in gaining consensus. Dyad members must apply their persuasive skills on each other to act as a social unit (in making decisions, taking a joint approach to some issue, and so on). Unless this happens, dyads dissolve to two individuals acting separately.

While three people may be the minimum necessary for a small group, what is the maximum? Once a group reaches a size where its members are uncomfortable or unable to work effectively as a unit, there is good reason for assuming that the group is too large. We should, however, be careful with this criterion. Many groups with only six or seven members routinely split up to pursue separate task activities. This frequently happens in educational settings when a group decides certain members will work on particular tasks independently (possibly more than one member per task) and then meet to exchange information and collaborate on an overall report.

Just as there are behavioral differences between dyads and larger social units, so too are there differences between groups of various sizes. A partial list of differences gleaned from a number of sources (including Bales and Borgatta, 1965; Hare, 1976; Weick, 1969) indicates that as group size increases: (1) there is less absolute time available for each member to participate, (2) less time available for each member to participate also means there is less time for each member to engage in developing and maintaining relationships with other members, (3) those persons who do talk more than other members become more visible and influential, (4) differences in the frequency of participation are intensified, (5) designated or emerging leaders tend to assume more control over the process and direction of a group, and (6) subgroups (also called *coalitions* or *cliques*) are likely to develop among group members.

While these and other behaviors (by individuals or groups) may be consequences of various group sizes, a crucial question is whether the *differences make a difference*. Weick (1969) argues that size differences become important only to the extent particular group sizes permit opportunities for (or place restrictions on) certain processes in the social organization of a group. Hence, specific sizes like three, five, seven, and nine might facilitate the formation of majority and minority coalitions. Other numbers such as four, six, and eight could make majority control more difficult to obtain because coalitions between members with similar sentiments or attitudes might not lead to a clear majority.

To better appreciate these differences, visualize two groups, one with four members and the other with five. Suppose the groups are composed of friends (for our purposes all female or male) who are trying to decide what to do on Saturday night. In the four person group, two people opt for hitting the local discotheque while the other two favor a rock concert. Just as a dyad is faced with the dilemma of reconciling opposing alternatives, so too must the four person group, composed at this point of two dyads, find a way of overcoming conflicting desires so all four members can act together as a group. Now transfer that dilemma to a five person group. Two members intent on a concert, two on the disco, and a fifth member who prefers going to a movie. Whereas members of our four person group had to work things out among the two coalitions, the five person group has a number of alternatives for resolving their decision problem. Most obvious is the possibility the lone movie buff might be persuaded to favor dancing or a concert. Should this happen, the single altered "vote" becomes a strong lever in moving the whole group to one course of action. Another possibility, though somewhat less likely, is that choosing the third alternative (going to a movie) might emerge as an easy way of avoiding a conflict and obtain support from one or both opposing coalitions. Regardless of the outcome, it should be clear that our hypothetical five person group has the potential to behave somewhat differently than a group of four people.

"Communication" in Small Groups

Now that you have some idea about the nature and size of human collectivities we label small groups, our next definitional chore is trying to assign meaning to the concept *communication*. There is far greater difficulty associated with this definition because there are so many facets to the concept (see Dance, 1967; Smith, 1966). Also, definitions for communication vary with the definer's perspective; some writers focus on describing basic elements or components presumably related to communication while others concentrate on more eclectic descriptions of the term as an abstract symbol.

One of the clearest explications of basic elements in human communication was that given by Berlo (1960). He outlined a model of communication which included four primary elements: *source-encoders, messages, channels,* and *receiver-decoders*. At minimum, communication occurs when a source encodes (puts into some transmittable form a set of words or other stimulus cues) a message (a presumably coherent thought unit or units), transmits that message over some channel (speaks or writes out the message, for example), and the message is received by someone else who decodes the spoken or written language symbols or behavioral cues. It is also important to understand that we are simultaneously acting as encoders and decoders whenever we exchange messages with someone else. The way you understand language symbols or behavioral cues (such as gestures) might not match another person's meanings. Some channels are more effective than others—written messages seem to lose something "in translation" whereas face-to-face interaction involves more potential messages (oral, visual, and so on), but is more complex and seemingly easier to misunderstand.

While Berlo's perspective offers useful insights into what probably happens during attempts to communicate, other writers have tried to define communication as the nature of our relationships with people. In other words, communication is the substance of our social relationships, or social reality. Such a position is a theme vividly expressed by Hawes

(1973). He argues that communication is really a derivation of meanings we extract from enacted behaviors of others in particular social settings and at various points in time. These behavioral enactments are what Berger and Luckmann (1966) call the *routine* elements of our social reality.

Language symbols and other behaviors form a *meaning context* and point of reference for how we interpret the symbols and behaviors of others. When people exchange symbols and behaviors in one another's presence (when they are *enacted*), meaning assessment derives from decisions like "What does it (the symbol or behavior) mean when *I* do it?" "*Who* is enacting the behavior?" "*Where* are we?" "*What* has just happened (or will happen)?" Whenever we are not sure how to interpret a behavior, or there are competing interpretations, we may attempt to clarify and negotiate meaning. When this happens (and it doesn't always happen), a common meaning for that behavior is adopted. Viewed from this perspective, communication is both a means of developing social relationships and part of those relationships that develop.

Clarification and negotiation represent attempts at providing *feedback* about the interpretation of meaning. As a communication concept, feedback is the response a receiver-decoder emits that is contingent upon the meaning assigned to a source-encoder's message. How do we know when a message represents feedback? We don't, unless we can refer to one or more previous messages. The simple greeting, "Hi! How are you?" may evoke, "Fine. What about yourself?" In this instance, feedback is very easy to discern. This might not be the case in a heated argument. Hence, feedback is a component of any communication process and an integral part of meaning interpretation.

As the reader can infer from the discussion so far, communication is not static. We continuously exchange behaviors with others and, in so doing, develop sets of meanings about our relationships. These meanings become part of social routines and are used in deriving new or changed meanings for other behaviors. This perspective leads to the assumption that communicating is a kind of social *process* (Berlo, 1960). To say communication is a process implies that it is dynamic— continuously happening and ever-changing. This makes good sense when we reflect on our own lives and social relationships and consider that they too constantly change.

If everything is changing all the time (if meanings for behavioral enactments continuously change), how do we make sense out of our social world? Changes are rarely radical; commonly shared meanings do not appear and vanish overnight. More importantly, our social lives are relatively homogeneous. Most people we associate with have similar experiences and meanings and methods of working out differences in

meanings. Finally, social realities are anchored in the contexts of space (or place) and time. Even when we make new acquaintances, there are certain expectations we have about their enactments. For example, a group of protesters standing on the steps of a campus administration building might chant, "We want *freedom* now!" and mean something very different from a prison inmate who writes a parole board asking for "freedom." These two distinct uses of the word "freedom" are easily discernable because we understand the difference in social contexts surrounding the word and word user.

We believe a communication can best be thought of as *a social process that involves the simultaneous exchange of symbols or behaviors (translatable into symbols) between two or more people.* By *process* we are implying that symbols and behavior exchanges are continuous and cumulative. Social participants are always reacting to and enacting cues which, in each person's memory, add up to meaningful impressions of relationships. Symbols are equivalent to language. Behaviors other than symbols include what is usually labeled *nonverbal* elements of communication (see Burgoon and Saine, 1978) such as body and facial gestures or movements, vocal expressiveness, uses of distance, and so on. The term *simultaneous* implies that symbols and/or behaviors are always being exchanged regardless of who is supposed to be sending or receiving them. In other words, even if we are "passive" receivers, we are enacting some types of behaviors available to others who may receive, interpret, and react to them.

We say nothing about intent in this definition. Some writers question whether communication takes place unless all parties are consciously trying to reach one another. This issue need not concern us here. That you consciously meant to send a message to someone is less important than your recognition that the party received and interpreted some set of symbols and/or behaviors. When you receive feedback it becomes your responsibility to deal with the meanings a receiver-decoder attaches to a set of stimuli. Success in any human relationship rests on using this capacity for recognizing and adapting to feedback.

THEORETICAL PERSPECTIVES

Suppose you want to develop an energy efficient method for transporting students between campus and home—one that most of them would use. Some research on your part shows that 65 percent of the students ride to campus in cars while the remaining 35 percent use buses or walk. Knowing this, you assume that most students would prefer to use automobile transportation. This assumption leads you to design a car pool strategy. Proud of your creation, you show the plans to a couple of

friends. One looks the idea over and says you're all wrong. Most people wouldn't car pool because they work, and work-school schedule conflicts cancel out most car pool efforts. Your friend goes on to point out that more people would ride buses if routes were laid out differently. Changing bus routes would result in a better plan. The other friend chimes in and says both of you are wrong. Class scheduling is really the problem. Much gasoline would be saved if students could takes classes they wanted without coming to campus every day (maybe coming only two or three days a week). Various methods of transportation scheduling, or alternate forms of transportation, would just be frosting on the cake.

By the end of this conversation you are ready to look for some new friends. Everything would have been fine if they had agreed with your initial assumption. However, your friends made different assumptions which led them to other conclusions. Scholars studying small group behavior have the same problem. They might begin with different assumptions about specific aspects of group processes or the general approach to the study of small groups. The latter are related to matters of focus or emphasis. These different assumptions (or, more specifically, interrelated sets of assumptions) are called *theories*. A theory provides a framework, or set of intellectual boundaries, about sets of assumptions that shape and guide a researcher's actions. Researchers focus their attention on substantiating the accuracy of those assumptions.

We can categorize numerous research theories together on the basis of what assumptions they make in their approaches to studying small groups. We will review four theoretical orientations related to small group research: *field, exchange, interaction,* and *systems* orientations. These four orientations significantly influence the ways researchers investigate small groups. No one orientation has, as yet, provided comprehensive explanations and predictions about all forms of group behavior. Each contributes to the study of communication in small groups by focusing on certain aspects of group behavior to the exclusion of others.

Field Theory

The field theory perspective is based on the following assumption about human behavior: group behavior involves a constant balancing of goals held by each group member, constraints placed on fulfillment of individual goals by group goal(s), and demands placed on the group by its external environment. The bulk of a group's interaction is devoted to settling differences between members about how to function in ways that maximize individual and group goals. Communication in the field theory perspective is a medium or channel through which the group exchanges information intended to regulate the course of the group and to provide for the satisfaction of each member.

Over the past three decades field-theoretical research has investigated a variety of group processes. Among these research efforts has been: (1) the study of how personality and compositions of personalities affect outcomes like group productivity and personal satisfaction with group membership (Haythorn, 1953, 1968), (2) ways varied styles of, and attitudes toward, leadership in small groups influence member behavior and group output (Lewin, et al., 1939; Carter, et al., 1950; Stogdill, 1959; Fiedler, 1958, 1967, 1971), (3) the influence of communication channels on group productivity (Bavelas, 1950; Berkowitz, 1953; Mulder, 1959; Shaw, 1954, 1958), (4) the effects of cooperative or competitive individual goals on group achievement (Deutsch, 1949a, 1949b), (5) how group expectations (or social norms) regulate individual behaviors (Festinger, Schachter and Back, 1950; Schachter, 1951), and (6) the origin and maintenance of personal power and group power structures (French, 1956; French and Raven, 1968).

While field theory has stimulated a substantial amount of research on small group processes, it has dealt only peripherally with the substance of verbal and nonverbal messages exchanged in face-to-face interaction. Typically, laboratory and field studies have focused on relationships between member characteristics (abilities, attitudes, personality) and tangible outcomes of group activity like the amount or quality of work completed, interpersonal reactions to other members, or satisfaction with group outcomes. The principle oversight in this orientation, from the point of view of communication research, has been the limited attention given to learning about the kinds, frequency, duration, and impact of communicative messages exchanged between group members. The responsibility of showing how communication relates to other important aspects of group action is the communication researcher's task.

Exchange Theory

In contrast to field theorists, the *exchange* theorist attempts to explain group behavior in terms of interlocking behavioral transactions, or exchanges, used in building and sustaining social relationships between members. A position advanced by the exchange theorist is that group behavior is best understood by assessing how members develop and nurture consistencies in their interactions with each other. As an interpersonal process, *social* exchange is viewed as activity regulated by *norms* of interpersonal conduct (rules or standards for expected behaviors). Norms develop as members interact and are influenced by other social constraints that define a group's place in larger social contexts (Homans, 1950, 1958, 1961; Kelley and Thibaut, 1954, 1968; Thibaut and Kelley, 1959). This process is similar to the way social communicators arrive at shared meanings for language symbols and behavioral cues.

Exchange theory uses an economic analogy to explain the outcomes of human interaction. Interpersonal relationships are assessed in terms of *reward* and *cost* properties for their participants. The basic premise is that relationships are formed and maintained because people perceive their potential rewards (psycho-social and tangible) as greater than the costs of maintaining the relationships. For example, you might not be particularly attracted to the person sitting across the room (or that person toward you) but it may be to your mutual advantage to study together because that person does well in biology and you do well in chemistry.

Virtually every group membership we maintain can be thought of in the same way—we remain members as long as our rewards outweigh the current and projected costs of group membership. This principle also applies to various internal decisions a group might make. You may not want your best friend elected leader of a group, though he or she desires the position, because you know from past experience this friend would do a poor job. Before you vote, you must weigh the potential cost in risking the loss of friendship against the potential reward of seeing the group have a competent leader. The consequences of your decision, either way, may be so unsettling that you might feel compelled not to participate in the group.

Thibaut and Kelley (1959) describe the dilemma posed in the foregoing example as an instance where your *Comparison Level* (CL) for group membership will not be met. Comparison Levels are judgmental standards for comparing reward/cost ratios you use when deciding to interact with others. In this case, helping to elect your friend would detract from the group's efforts, but not helping would put your friendship in jeopardy. Both alternatives contain costs you do not wish to bear and probably fall short of your CL for group membership. At this point, you must assess your *Comparison Level for Alternatives* (CLalt). The CLalt is a minimum reward/cost outcome you can accept based on a comparison of all possible alternatives. If both of these alternatives fall below your CLalt, you will withdraw from the group.

Variables influencing group behavior come from both *internal* and *external* sources of control (Thibaut and Kelley, 1959; Homans, 1950). The network of relationships in a group may dictate some of the reward and cost properties of group membership. In the previous example, suppose your friend is chosen as group leader. Though the group may be less effective than it would be with strong leadership, you might remain in the group because it contains other friends that you do not see very often. There can be strong motives for participating in groups that do not provide adequate rewards. This happens quite often when people are required to maintain group memberships because of their occupational roles. Such motives can result in group members that have only weak identification with a group and who are not motivated to fully participate as group members.

The interlocking nature of our interpersonal behavior is a particularly important idea to grasp. By "interlocking" we mean that units of activity (communicative messages) are sequentially integrated—one message is at least a partial cause of the next message. The greeting, "Hi, how are you?" triggers the response, "Fine, how are you?" As information processors, we assign meanings to discrete symbolic and behavioral acts and to sequences of messages or behaviors that accumulate over time. Thus, messages exchanged between participants, sequentially combined over time, can have a meaning that transcends the content of any particular message.

The essence of group experience is rooted in the continuity of member interactions over time. Normative expectations for interpersonal conduct emerge as members recognize and evaluate various sequences of behavior. Those receiving positive evaluations are accepted and encouraged while others receiving negative reactions are discouraged. Members' CL's and CLalt's may change in light of group expectations. A person expecting "great things" may become frustrated because a group grows to expect less from its members than that person desires. Conversely, someone else may find the same group exceeding their expectations.

Interaction Theory

Sociologist Robert F. Bales and his colleagues have been responsible for a substantial amount of research about how people communicate with each other in small groups. Bales (1950, 1965, 1970) developed the method of Interaction Process Analysis (IPA) as a technique of categorizing what people in groups say to each other. Bales' work has also contributed to understanding relationships between communicative activity and the development of group *social structures*. A social structure exists when some set of expectations develops between participants in regard to their role relationships and interpersonal reactions. A person's group *role* is determined by his or her actions and the relative value that activity attains in the eyes of other members.

Bales' early research on message acts separated communicative behavior into *task* and *social-emotional* activity. Task activity encompasses asking for and giving information, opinions and suggestions (nonpersonal in nature). Social-emotional activity indicates agreement or disagreement, showing antagonism or solidarity, and showing tension and enjoying tension releases (such as laughing). An early theoretical position advanced by Bales (1950) speculated that decision making groups, meeting over a sustained period of time, seek an equilibrium point that strikes a harmonious balance between task oriented and social-emotional communications.

Bales' assumption that groups strive for equilibrium implies that groups continuously attempt to accommodate both individual needs for influence and workable interpersonal relationships. In a recent restatement of his position, Bales (1970) proposed a three-dimensional model to account for interpersonal behavior in small groups. Each dimension represents a continuum on which people can be positioned according to their behavior as group members. Dominant or submissive behaviors associated with perceived influence and power constitute an *upward-downward* continuum. The extent a person's behavior is directed toward establishing and maintaining interpersonal bonds with others is assessed along a *positive-negative* continuum. The third continuum represents an individual's orientation to how a group should achieve goals and is labeled *forward-backward*. Bales describes goal achievement in terms of conventional or conservative methods (forward) versus novel, untested, or radical methods (backward).

The three-dimensional model provides a simplified way of labeling individual behaviors within a group. It is assumed some type of labeling process is conducted by all group members as they come in contact with each other. Though you may not use the label "upward" to describe someone's dominant behavior, you probably have a label that meaningfully describes such behaviors when you encounter them. One positive aspect of Bales' theory is it narrows the vast range of individual behaviors in groups to a manageable set of significant dimensions with easily identifiable names. He has also gone so far as to create rating instruments to aid in classifying a person's behavior as it is perceived by other group members.

Assessing observable behavioral changes groups, as groups, undergo has received much attention from interactionist researchers (Bales and Strodtbeck, 1951; Bales and Slater, 1955; Heinicke and Bales, 1953; Strodtbeck and Mann, 1956). The study of *group development,* for example, has shown that small groups undergo systematic and predictable shifts in interaction over time. Though the exact number of shifts (phases) and how they unfold depends upon a number of complex measurement factors (c.f., Mabry, 1975a, 1975b), the existence of these growth patterns provides a structure for viewing group interaction and making comparisons between groups.

Systems Theory

Contrasted with the other approaches, systems theory may be thought of as a method for systematically putting together assumptions about relationships between sets of social processes or variables. A "general systems" theory orientation is a perspective on how to construct theories about complex social relationships such as those found in small groups (Monge, 1973). Exchange and interaction orientations contain aspects of systems theory when they address those facets of group dynamics responsible for creating and maintaining ways members relate to one another.

The concept of *social system* is easier to provide examples for than to define in abstract terms. Our definition of a small group could be interchanged, given some modifications, with various definitions of human social systems (cf., Buckley, 1967; Monane, 1967; Monge, 1973). Small groups are, in fact, prototypical social systems that differ from larger human systems (political, military-industrial, or religious institutions or larger bureaucratic organizations) only by the size-determined complexity of relationships between group members. Recall we defined a group as a network of people who have intentionally invested part of their personal decision making power in the authority of a larger social unit (a group) in pursuit of mutually desired and separately unobtainable goals. The important ideas in this definition are *network, individual decision making power*, and *mutuality of goals*. We will review each one of these concepts separately.

Networks. A communication network is formed when people interact with each other—when patterns of talking and behaving develop over time. Communication networks, theoretically and practically, occur when two people interact. Communication networks are linkages of *channels* over which messages are exchanged. When we talk with one another, the auditory sensors of our bodies (ears) pick up the verbal stimuli from the air waves created in verbal expression. Likewise, our eyes are receptors for visual stimuli transmitted through the refraction of light waves. All of our senses combine to help us receive and send messages. In a more abstract way, communication channels are similar to the routes that written messages follow within a large organization. Technically, a channel of communication is established when one person directs a message to another person. But the essence of a communication network is lost when the example of two people is used. Patterns of interaction that emerge between three or more people are rather different and provide vivid examples of the organizing property of networks as they exist in human systems (see, for example, Weick, 1969).

In small face-to-face groups, networks are the maps of communication between participants. These maps can be constructed by observing and analyzing the flow of verbal and nonverbal acts between group members. Inspecting network patterns can show how group members are relating to each other. One form such relationships take is called a *coalition* between members. Coalitions exist when subgroups (or *cliques*) develop in a group. Each subgroup represents an interest faction wishing to influence group outcomes (Caplow, 1959; Gamson, 1961). What a researcher looks for in diagramming communication networks is who talks to whom and how (that is, the content and perceived intent of messages).

The *feedback* members give to each other is carried over network channels and provides a basis for the social bonds that permit groups to remain together and work effectively. A group may find itself in trouble when channels are not conducive to disseminating feedback between members. It then risks disintegration because of productivity loss or disturbances in comparison levels held by group members. Communication networks link, or integrate, people in a small group just as larger aggregates of people are linked together in larger systems.

Individual decision making power. Individuals share power with a group when their actions indicate the group has some effect on their behavior. Often this is implied by group membership and is never overtly tested. On the other hand, when group members do test the power of a group, they risk threats to their self-images (embarrassment or loss of prestige) and the group risks a reduction in its projected image of control and solidarity. A person tests group power by asserting influence to direct or change group action. The risks are great—especially for members already possessing a certain amount of influence or status—because their ability to influence may diminish and shift to other members. When this happens increased competition takes place between members vying for higher status and the unsuccessful challenger must once again compete for the position he or she held.

Power is important to the survival of a group. Individuals must be able to tolerate limitations on their personal ego gratifications, and the "subjugation of ego needs" insures that all members will be ready to reinforce prevailing group norms. This phenomenon of "social control" that we have been describing acts as a *leveling* process between members. Regardless of a member's prestige, there are certain similarities in behavior that all must display. Social control insures an interlocking of mutual expectations between people that creates an identification with the rationale for the group's existence (La Piere, 1954). This happens constantly in groups, notably youth gangs, college fraternities and sororities, and casual friendship groups.

Members occupying leadership positions are subject to two sets of expectations in regard to their behavior. On the one hand, leaders are expected to exemplify group norms. Leader behavior is used by other group members as an anchoring point for their actions. In essence, the leader is a *reference image* for other members to model. On the other hand, leaders are, on occasion, permitted to violate norms without negative repercussions. This can happen when a leader steps out of character but the group rationalizes the "deviant" actions by attaching them to some accepted group objective. The leader of a student study group may be late for a study session before an important exam. However, group members are likely to accept the leader's tardiness assuming the weight of the exam or checking out needed materials at the last minute was at fault. Regardless of the actual reason, they are less likely to apply direct negative feedback to the leader than another member. The term "idiosyncrasy credit" was coined to describe the process of accommodation that takes place when group members permit deviant behaviors by leaders (Hollander, 1958).

Mutuality of group goals. Most groups, outside of occupational settings, form because their members perceive a need to come together. Reasons for group formation can be expressed in terms of shared interests or goals. All groups have some set of objectives that define group existence. These objectives, or goals, represent group members' shared perceptions of what their joint actions should accomplish. Goals bind members together by promoting mutual control over their individual behaviors and focusing group action on desired outcomes.

There should be some correspondence between members' individual desires and a group's goals. Rewarding aspects of membership are not always tied to specific group objectives. You might, for example, join a class study group to get better acquainted with one of its members. To satisfy this desire, however, you must assume certain duties related to the group's specific objectives. You might eventually drop out if it seems that your personal goal will not be a fulfilled. Your CLalt hasn't been attained, and you concentrate on other relationships.

Two types of goal states characterize individual member needs and influence group action. Individual-to-group goal relationships can be thought of as *cooperatively interdependent* or *contriently interdependent*. (Deutsch, 1949a, 1949b). *Cooperatively interdependent* situations are those where pursuing individual or group goals also contribute to attainment of personal goals held by other members. A human relations training group goal for example, might be creating a climate conducive for member experimentation with new forms of interpersonal risk taking. Members may wish to participate in self-disclosure exercises that provide risk taking experiences. The objective is to help them use self-disclosure more frequently and effectively in their daily relationships. This situation is an example of cooperatively interdependent goals. Personal behaviors necessary for maintaining a satisfactory atmosphere for risk taking will inevitably aid in the execution and processing of disclosure as a behavioral goal for each member.

Situations where attaining an individual (or group) goal will impede working on other individual or group goals are called *contriently interdependent*. Once again, assume that a group is working on individual member needs to self-disclose. But this time, assume that one or more members are unable, or unwilling, to help promote this necessary climate of openness and trust. When the group needs supportive behavior, the member or members fail to provide it. The group suffers because there is less interaction between members focusing on desired goals. The difficulty is an inability to translate individual goals into group goals. This lack of correspondence may not lead to group dissolution but will cause some degree of disorganization and difficulty in attaining group objectives. Members may begin to compete with each other to meet their personal objectives.

System integration. Human systems are groups of people interacting with each other for a common purpose(s). They exercise an amount of control over people to gain compliance with rules for working together. The analogy of the small group as a system appears to have merit when social systems are described in this manner. *System integration* is, in fact, the development of purposive behavioral controls in interaction networks established between group members.

How a group functions is also measured by its progress toward goal attainment. The *outputs* of any group or system follow from some type of problem solution process that is generally acceptable to group members. Systems do not, however, need to depend on only one method of goal attainment. Many paths may be used to accomplish the same goal. This "goal path multiplicity" is one significant feature of complex adaptive human systems (Buckley, 1967). Moreover, the tasks groups work on can vary widely with respect to possible courses of action or the extent to which members must coordinate their individual efforts. Even groups that have developed a history of working and interacting together do not approach similar tasks or goals the same way each time they attack them.

To summarize, the formation of interaction networks, the amount of group control individual members accept, and the correspondence between individual and group goals are primary social and psychological factors in the formation and maintenance of human groups. These factors help integrate people who make up a group-system by (1) linking individuals together (through communication networks), (2) promoting stable ways of interacting together (subjugation of individual decision making power) and (3) deciding on objectives for group-system action (mutuality of group goals).

A DYNAMIC MODE OF GROUP FUNCTIONING

A significant barrier to understanding and analyzing group interaction is grasping the ways complex psychological and social processes simultaneously effect group-system integration. It is difficult to conceive, let alone appreciate, the complexity and diversity of small social systems. What really happens when people interact in groups? How much can one individual's behavior affect an entire group? How do members affect each other? What kinds of communicative behaviors help (or hinder) group achievement?

One means of conceptualizing a group-system was suggested by Stogdill (1959). He believed group achievement could be viewed in a linear fashion as a sequence of *inputs, throughputs,* and *outputs*. Group inputs are composed of member characteristics (such as their personalities, attitude, abilities), goal related tasks, and physical and social environment factors associated with places where members interact. The throughputs of a group are those elements of behavior that facilitate or impede progress toward a goal. The primary element of the throughput stage is communication between group members. Simultaneously, as members are involved in communicative exchanges, they also develop positive and negative impressions of one another, new role and status relationships, coalitions, and patterns of influence related to group outcomes. These are elements in group-system integration. They evolve as people communicate and are modified through communication. The output dimension of a group includes both tangible and intangible results of a group work. Tangible results, from the point of goal attainment, can be viewed in terms of whether a group's tasks have been accomplished. Additionally, there are certain tangible and intangible consequences associated with the human aspects of group membership. Group members may experience changes in attitudes, work styles, or other behaviors. Most changes are intangible because they are not easily measured or directly observable.

A model that elaborates on the input-throughput-output sequence initially proposed by Stogdill is presented in Figure 1.1. This model shows relationships between important components in Stogdill's three dimensions. The five components of the model are *Individual Group Members, Task Environment, Integrative Processes, Achievement and Development,* and *Changes in Group Members.*

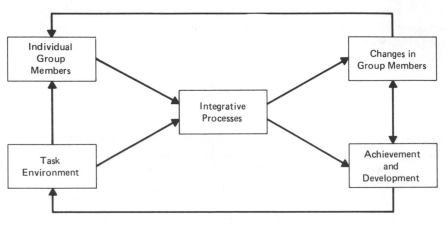

Figure 1.1

Input Components

The input dimension of a group is composed of *Individual Group Members* and the *Task Environment* components. There is a broad constellation of factors one could consider when assessing characteristics of group members. Some factors are more useful than others in understanding why people act as they do. Human personalities, and how we perceive them during interaction, attitudinal biases toward ideas or other people, and our own competencies as communicators have a significant impact on integrative processes and group outputs.

Task Environments are the social and physical contexts where group action takes place. They are comprised of tasks, or action objectives, and individual goals, and the sociophysical settings where tasks are presumably accomplished. Tasks are also generated by social settings. Most occupational groups respond to task demands originating from the operating requirements of an organizational system. Physical attributes of social settings also create demands, or limitations, on how members interact and accomplish task objectives.

There is a distinct sequence associated with how these components affect each other. Groups influence their environments as a result of their achievements and development. These results follow as a consequence of Integrative Processes. A group's ability to meet task demands or change aspects of its social and physical setting depends on its integration as a social unit. The model also shows that Task Environments affect individual members but that individuals have no immediate impact on the Task Environment. Many facets of human tasks and social environments are perceived differently by members of the same group. Therefore, it is only until a group reaches acceptable interpretations about its work and work-place that Task Environment factors have behavioral implications. Members reach these common understandings through interaction and, subsequently, they influence the course of group outcomes.

Integrative Processes

The throughput dimension in the model is labeled *Integrative Processes*. Integrative Processes are inherently social and communicative in nature. They encompass ways group members communicate with each other, communication patterns between members, members' affiliations and coalitions, and norms and roles that develop to control and structure relationships between members. Integrative Processes are components of all groups. Interaction links group members together, and both the communicative content and networks of message exchanges between members indicate the types of linkages that are made. Group roles identify the status of members in networks, and group norms define appropriate and inappropriate behaviors and communicative linkages. The group member that attends irregularly, habitually argues with other members about how tasks should be completed, and keeps a group from applying its full energies to task goals is quite likely to be accorded very little status by other members. Members may quickly adopt a collective attitude about how to communicate with this person, one that corresponds with that member's low status. Members will expect each other to restrict the amount and kinds of interaction they have with the person. Presumably, these norms for interaction and relating to the low status member will prevail until the "deviant" behavior changes.

The Integrative Processes component is an abstraction created to describe the throughput stage as a point of integration for all group components. It might be thought of as a *process construct* in that it subsumes relationships between sets of concepts (for instance, interaction content, channels, norms, roles) that are constantly changing as a result of their relationships to each other. As a component in the model, it represents the way behavioral enactments are formulated into organized images of relationships between group members. This begins with communicative acts which are then structured to formulate impressions of personal affiliations, roles, norms, personal influence or leadership, and so on. These variables are both causes and effects of output components. This can also be viewed as a control function for human relationships: input components are placed together, their effects are mediated and, ultimately, there are tangible and intangible output consequences of their relatedness that act as feedback. The importance accorded to Integrative Processes seems appropriate since it is through communication that human systems, small or large, are created and maintained.

Output Components

Just as input components of a group rely on Integrative Processes, output components also rely on group interaction and integration to give them form and substance. The components we will examine are *Achievement and Development* and *Changes in Group Members.*

Achievement is generally thought of as a tangible outcome of group interaction. Outcomes are usually perceived as goals attained by accomplishing certain tasks. Tasks are quite diverse and range from solving problems or making complex decisions to more tangible jobs, such as assembling a new carburetor. Goals, too, can be quite diverse ranging from earning a living to gaining personal satisfaction from interacting with others. Rewards for goal attainment can be either explicit or implicit, but they must be present. Rewards provide the motivation for members to maintain their affiliations with a group.

In actual practice, task achievement is usually not a dramatic occurrence; it takes place gradually over some period of time. Group *development* represents the stages of integration associated with a group's pursuit of goals. We assess development by observing changes in behaviors, attitudes, roles, and norms over time. We can use these assessments to provide "progress reports" about Integrative Processes.

Members are affected by their work in groups. The *Changes in Group Members* component represents ways interacting with other people can influence us. These changes may relate to attitudinal positions, behavioral styles, acquiring information, and making (or losing) friends and acquaintances. Changes that do occur are, for the most part, psychological in nature. These changes are far less tangible than many goals that motivate group action, and they frequently go unnoticed.

The Achievement and Development and Changes in Group Member components are related to each other and to input components. Input and output relationships are rather straightforward. Personal changes as a consequence of integrative involvement in a group alter a person's initial starting point as an input component. This happens every time a group meets. Therefore, to some extent, this component is always changing. A group's Achievement and Development affect its Task Environment. Sometimes immediately and substantially, other times imperceptibly.

Achievements and development also influence group members. The influence may be through Task Environment relatedness as we discussed earlier. Member changes, however, can be stimulated by group accomplishments or a group's development not immediately tied to Task Environment factors. The student who joined a study group to get acquainted with another member is a good example. Failure to develop those relationships changed the person's decision to remain in the group. This could have come about as the group developed. Perhaps this student's personal goal detracted from efforts to help others study for the class. Failing to meet group norms might have contributed to a breakdown in the relationship building process.

ORGANIZATION OF THE TEXT

You may have realized by now our primary theoretical assumption about small groups is that they constitute social systems of a particular size. The model presented in Figure 1.1 is a useful way of thinking and talking about psychological, social, and communicative processes associated with small group systems. This text is organized to continuously reinforce these assumptions. In the ensuing chapters, the model's components and other important issues about small group communication processes will be discussed. Chapters are arranged in parts specifically dealing with the input, throughput, and output dimension components. They will focus on understanding and analyzing why and how certain behaviors and processes are related, how to recognize them, and how to use your knowledge of their significance for understanding small group action.

REFERENCES

Bales, R.F. 1950. *Interaction process analysis.* Reading, Mass: Addison-Wesley.

Bales, R.F. 1965. The equilibrium problem in small groups. In *Small groups: Studies in social interaction,* rev. ed., eds. A.P. Hare, E.F. Borgatta, and R.F. Bales, pp. 444–476. New York: Knopf.

Bales, R.F. 1970. *Personality and interpersonal behavior.* New York: Holt, Rinehart & Winston.

Bales, R.F. and Borgatta, E.F. 1965. Size of group as a factor in the interaction profile. In *Studies in social interaction,* rev. ed., eds. A.P. Hare, E.F. Borgatta, and R.F. Bales, pp. 495–512. New York: Knopf.

Bales, R.F. and Slater, P.E. 1955. Role differentiation in small decision making groups. In *The family, socialization and interaction process,* eds. T. Parsons and R.F. Bates, pp. 259–306. New York: Free Press.

Bales, R.F. and Strodtbeck, F. 1951. Phases in group problem-solving. *Journal of Abnormal and Social Psychology, 46,* 485–495.

Bavelas, A. 1950. Communication patterns in task-oriented groups. *Journal of the Acoustical Society of America 22,* 725–730.

Berger, P.L. and Luckmann, T. 1966. *The social construction of reality.* New York: Doubleday.

Berkowitz, L. 1953. Sharing leadership in small decision making groups. *Journal of Abnormal and Social Psychology 48, 231*–238.

Berlo, D. 1960. *The process of communication.* New York: Holt, Rinehart & Winston.

Buckley, W. 1967. *Sociology and modern systems theory.* Englewood Cliffs, N.J.: Prentice-Hall, Inc.

Burgoon, J. and Saine, T. 1978. *The unspoken dialogue.* Boston: Houghton Mifflin.

Caplow, T. 1959. Further development of a theory of coalitions in the triad. *American Journal of Sociology 64,* 448–493.

Carter, L., Haythorn, W., Shriver and Lanzetta, J. 1951. The behavior of leaders and other group members. *Journal of Abnormal and Social Psychology 46,* 589–595.

Dance, F.E.X. 1967. Toward a theory of human communication. In *Human communication theory,* ed. F.E.X. Dance. New York: Holt, Rinehart & Winston.

Deutsch, M. 1949a. A theory of co-operation and competition. *Human Relations 2,* 129–152.

Deutsch, M. 1949b. An experimental study of the effects of co-operation and competition upon group process. *Human Relations 2,* 199–232.

Festinger, L., Schachter, S. and Bach, K. 1950. *Social pressures in informal groups.* New York: Harper & Row, Pub.

Fiedler, F. 1958. *Leader attitudes and group effectiveness.* Urbana, Ill.: University of Illinois Press.

Fieldler, F. 1967. *A theory of leadership effectiveness.* New York: McGraw–Hill.

Fieldler, F. 1971. Validation and extension of the contingency model of leadership affectiveness: A review of empirical findings. *Psychological Bulletin 63,* 128–148.

French, J.R.P. 1956. A formal theory of social power. *Psychological Review 63,* 181–194.

French, J.R.P. and Raven, B. 1968. The bases of social power. In *Group dynamics: Research and theory,* 3rd. ed., eds. D. Cartwright and A. Zander, pp. 259–269. New York: Harper and Row, Pub.

Gamson, W.A. 1961. A theory of coalition formation. *American Sociological Review 26,* 373–382.

Hare, A.P. 1976. *Handbook of small group research,* 2nd ed. New York: Free Press.

Hawes, L.C. 1973. Elements of a model for communication processes. *Quarterly Journal of Speech 59,* 11–21.

Haythorn, W. 1953. The influence of individual members on the characteristics of small groups. *Journal of Abnormal and Social Psychology 48,* 276–284.

Haythorn, W. 1968. The composition of groups: A review of the literature. *Acta Psychologica 28,* 97–128.

Heinicke, C. and Bales, R.F. 1953. Developmental trends in the structure of small groups. *Sociometry 16*, 7–38.

Hollander, E.P. 1958. Conformity, status and idiosyncrasy credit. *Psychological Review 65*, 117–127.

Homans, G.C. 1950. *The human group.* New York: Harcourt Brace Jovanovitch.

Homans, G.C. 1958. Social behavior as exchange. *American Journal of Sociology 63*, 597–606.

Homans, G.C. 1961. *Social behavior: Its elementary forms.* New York: Harcourt Brace Jovanovich.

Kelley, H.H. and Thibaut, J.W. 1954. Experimental studies of group problem-solving and process. In *The handbook of social psychology*, vol. 2., ed. G. Lindsey, ch. 21. Reading, Mass.: Addison-Wesley.

Kelley, H.H. and Thibaut, J.W. 1968. Group problem-solving. In *The handbook of social psychology*, 2nd ed., vol. 4., eds. G. Lindsey and E. Aronson, pp. 1–101. Reading, Mass.: Addison-Wesley.

La Piere, R.T. 1954. *A theory of social control.* New York: McGraw-Hill.

Lewin, K., Lippitt, R. and White, R.K. 1939. Patterns of aggressive behavior in experimentally created 'social climates.' *Journal of Social Psychology 10*, 271–299.

Mabry, E.A. 1975a. Sequential structure of interaction in encounter groups. *Human Communication Research 1*, 302–307.

Mabry, E.A. 1975b. Exploratory analysis of a developmental model for task-oriented small groups. *Human Communication Research 2*, 66–74.

Monane, J. 1967. *A sociology of human systems.* New York: Appleton-Century-Crofts.

Monge, P.R. 1973. Theory construction in the study of communication: The system paradigm. *Journal of Communication 23*, 5–16.

Mulder, M. 1959. Group-structure and group-performance. *Acta Psychologica, 16*, 356–402.

Schachter, S. 1951. Deviation, rejection and communication. *Journal of Abnormal and Social Psychology 46*, 241–246.

Shaw, M.E. 1954. Some effects of problem complexity upon problem solution efficiency in different communication nets. *Journal of Abnormal and Social Psychology 48*, 211–217.

Shaw, M.E. 1958. Some effects of irrelevant information upon problem-solving by small groups. *Journal of Social Psychology 47*, 33–37.

Smith, A. 1966. *Communication and culture.* New York: Holt, Rinehart & Winston.

Stogdill, R.M. 1959. *Individual behavior and group achievement.* New York: Oxford University Press.

Strodtbeck, F. and Mann, R.D. 1956. Sex role differentiation in jury deliberations. *Sociometry 19*, 3–11.

Thibaut, J.W. and Kelley, H.H. 1959. *The social psychology of groups.* New York: John Wiley.

Weick, P. 1969. *The social psychology of organizing.* Reading Mass.: Addison-Wesley.

The model presented in Chapter 1 describes small groups as ongoing systems. Human social systems are comprised of various intrapersonal, interpersonal and environmental processes. Components of the model are subsumed under the labels Inputs, Integrative Processes (Throughputs) and Outputs. Chapters in this section focus on Inputs. Chapters 2 and 3 review important intrapersonal variables (personality, attitudes, social competencies). They also assess the ways such variables influence personal behavior in small groups. Our responses to group situations, our communicative interchanges with others, are related to the activation of the variables in particular group contexts. This activation is a "two-way street" for all group members. Individual Member Characteristics produce unique styles of behaving. Each member's behavioral style is perceived and evaluated. This evaluation, in turn, affects behavior. The Task Environment of a group involves the "what" and "where" of group activity. Groups are goal-oriented social entities. All groups have some goal(s) that binds members together. Goals are achieved by accomplishing tasks. Generally, groups operate under certain constraints pertaining to their task work or goal attainment. Chapter 4 reviews tasks, goals, and constraints that may impinge on group action.

GROUP INPUTS

Part
TWO

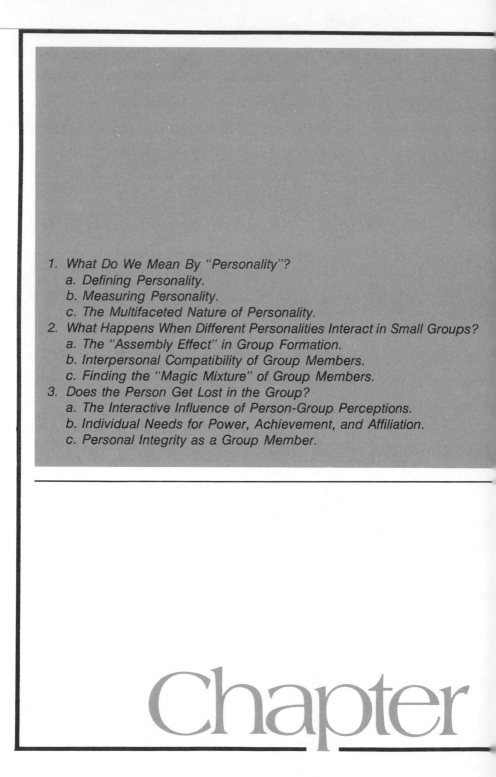

Chapter

The personality of human beings has been a favorite subject of social-psychological study for many years. Unfortunately, the intrapersonal dimensions of human thought and experience that add up to something called "personality" are not easily traced to communication behavior. Consequently, we will work from two different perspectives when discussing personality. First, we shall consider personality as it is inferred from tests and measures designed to construct a composite image of the individual. Second, we will also discuss personality as it is inferred from observed behavior. After looking at personality as an abstract property, the remainder of the chapter will delve into some of the ways that people with various personalities relate to each other and how much a person's personality is affected by group membership. Our thinking is focused on three important questions related to an individual's personality and group interaction. (1) What do we mean by the term *personality*? (2) What happens when different personalities interact in small groups? (3) What happens to individual personalities submerged in a small group?

2

personality and group membership

WHAT DO WE MEAN BY PERSONALITY?

Defining Personality

To define the concept of personality is really to specify a way of understanding (categorizing) how and why a person behaves in particular ways. The notion of personality itself alludes to the complex of drives, motives, thoughts, and experiences characteristic of an individual. This all-encompassing perspective is echoed in the following definition of personality used by McGrath:

> *Personality* (italics his) refers to the total organization of the individual's motives, attitudes, beliefs, ways of perceiving, and ways of behaving. Personality does not mean 'sociability,' not something individuals have more or less of. Nor is it a matter of good or bad. We can speak of well-adjusted or poorly adjusted individuals, but only meaningfully in the context of some social setting (McGrath, 1964, p. 42).

Using McGrath's definition, we can say that a person's personality is actually a number of clusters of behavior that are more than just overt social acts or general characteristics of social appearance. More important is McGrath's admonishment that an analysis of behavior must proceed in such a way that the *social context* of behavior, places where people act, is given appropriate weight as a producer of human activity; social context is not just a convenient stage where an individual behaves. Simply put, people will, to some extent, behave in ways consistent with how they believe others expect them to behave.

A key to this conceptualization is that people behave in a reasoned manner based upon their selective perceptions about a setting and others with whom they interact. Consider the following scenerio:

> Ruth is an executive secretary who is regarded as having a "cold" personality. She is unfriendly to sales representatives seeking appointments to see her boss, she eats lunch alone and even elects on her breaks not to drink coffee and socialize with other employees. Ruth is regarded by her boss as extremely efficient and dependable but he wishes she were much "nicer" to people she has contact with on the job. Consequently, he was on the verge of dismissing Ruth. After extended conversations with her, the following information emerged. She had recently experienced a divorce and her mother died shortly after the separation. These events were having a significant effect on her general disposition. However, Ruth also believed an important part of her job was to insulate her boss from undue interruptions. Therefore, she felt it was her responsibility to discourage eager sales representatives. Since she took memos and dictation from other company executives, she felt it imperative to maintain a "tight lip" about company policies and actions. She noticed that all other employees liked to visit on their lunch and coffee breaks, thus she avoided them as a means of not

being quizzed on confidential matters. Ruth's "unapproachable personality" was a source of pride to her, and she believed her boss viewed her as
a highly effective secretary. You might imagine Ruth's surprise when the
boss talked about dismissing her for having an "unpleasant" personality.

Similar to the definition offered by McGrath is Newcomb's (1950)
perspective that "personality" represents an individual's organization of
his or her predisposition to behave in certain ways. Newcomb stresses the
point that personal behavioral predispositions are organized as specific
sets of complex patterns which facilitate a person's adaptation to the
social world. These orientations are based on social experience and help
the person differentiate how she or he will behave with respect to other
people in social settings.

As an abstract entity, Newcomb views personality as being *unique, persistent, dynamic, social,* and *organized.* The uniqueness of personality stems
from our organization of experiences and response tendencies that is in
some way different from our neighbor's (although there are many
similarities across groups of people). Human personalities are persistent
in that they are resilient and resist substantial changes over a lifetime.
Changes do take place but they are accompanied or preceded by significant changes in our social environment. To say that personality is
dynamic relates to a field theory orientation of behavior which assumes
(quite appropriately) that personality dimensions are developed and
changed as a person adapts to the social environment. Since personalities
are dynamic, they are also social entities, for the formation and change
of behavioral dispositions happens as we interact with other people in
various social settings. The organization of an individual's personality is
what creates its uniqueness. The persistence of personalities results from
a general tendency for people to develop behavioral patterns they can
justify to themselves and resist changing once they are established.

We would add this qualifier to Newcomb's view. All people share the
same personality traits. Everyone is sincere, quiet, friendly, cheerful,
intelligent, and so on to some extent. What distinguishes one individual
from another is the predominance of certain traits. Giffin and Barnes
(1976) note that the success of charlatans and fortune tellers is often due
to our tendency to see positive characteristics within ourselves and to
believe that they are unique to ourselves, when in reality they are shared
by many.

The view of personality as reasoned behavior in a situational context
assumes a non-evaluative analysis. In a group setting, members act according to the facets of their personalities that determine what kind of
behavior is most appropriate for that setting. Domination of a group, for
example, is not necessarily "bad" if it fits the needs of other group
members and the task. We often naively assume that equal participation

is desirable in a group. Should some members have nothing worth contributing while others, with valuable information, are stifled due to a demand for an even spread of participation, the group may labor under a significant disadvantage. Personality characteristics are often drawn out of people by the needs of others. Extreme caution should be used in placing an evaluative label on a group member's personality. Such behavior may reflect the person's reasoned analysis of action appropriate for the situation or a habitual pattern of behavior that cuts across many different relationships. Moreover, the actions we observe for one person may have been precipitated by the personalities of others.

Measuring Personality

It is not our intent to go into a detailed explanation of how human personality has been studied by behavioral scientists. In fact, a now dated review conducted by Mann (1959) showed that small group researchers have used over five hundred different ways of measuring personality in studies related to small group behavior. Instead of reviewing specific methods of measurement, we will only deal with a categorization of various personality measures that examine similar behavioral traits. Using a classification similar to that developed by Mann, Shaw (1971) devised five categories for classifying personality variables studied in small groups. The categories are Interpersonal Orientation, Social Sensitivity, Ascendant Tendencies, Dependability, and Emotional Stability.

Interpersonal orientation. Whenever we interact with other people, each of us exhibits a certain style of behavior that is consistent with how we conceive of ourselves as social communicators. The particular style we exhibit is a product of our social experience and the ways we define appropriate social behavior for ourselves. This style of behavior is relatively constant and reflects both our needs for certain kinds of interpersonal transactions and the image we want others to see.

Probably the most commonly known personality trait is *authoritarianism*. Research into the trait of authoritarianism was initiated by Adorno, et. al. (1950) and was stimulated, in part, by an interest in the concomitants of fascism at the conclusion of World War II. The typical assessment of authoritarian personality traits is derived from the California F–scale developed by Adorno and his associates. While the F–scale has been criticized on a number of technical grounds (see Christie and Jahoda, 1956), persons scoring high on the instrument have been found to exhibit markedly different behaviors in small groups than low scoring, nonauthoritarian persons. Research by Haythorn, et al. (1956a, 1956b) demonstrated that people with high authoritarian scores, when assigned as group leaders, are rated by other group members as having less sensitivity, striving for less group approval, being less equalitarian and more autocratic, and having less "effective" intelligence. Moreover, high authoritarian group members led by less authoritarian group leaders rated their leaders as being more aggressive, autocratic, and achieving greater individual prominence in the group.

A second important attribute of Interpersonal Orientation is the extent to which a person needs to maintain close personal relationships with others, or needs *affection*. In an extensive review of the small group literature, Hare (1976) proposed that the affective dimension of behavior is crucial to small group behavior. Research on the effect of this dimension has been conducted by Schutz (1955, 1958, 1961). While Schutz's research was involved in developing a more comprehensive theory of interpersonal behavior, the most promising aspect of his research dealt with interpersonal needs for affection.

Schutz proposed that people have needs to give affection to others and to receive affection from others. An individual could have a high need to give affection, for example, but a low need to receive affection from others. The reverse is also possible or both dimensions could be high or low. A compatible group is one in which the needs of each member are satisfied by other members. Obviously, a person found to be low in need for receiving affection would be incompatible with someone who has a high need to give affection. The most consistent finding has been that groups composed of members with compatible needs for affection (either high or low) are more productive and harmonious than incompatible groups.

Social sensitivity. Intuitively, we are aware that some people seem to understand us better than others do. This adeptness at social insight, or social sensitivity, may be regarded as empathy, rapport, insight, or social judgment (Shaw, 1971). Research by Bell and Hall (1954), Haythorn (1953) and Cattell and Stice (1960) has shown that group members who achieve high scores on social sensitivity measures of personality are more likely to be accepted as group leaders, have greater participation and acceptance in the group, and are rated as friendlier by group members. Shaw's review of the research also indicates that persons who are more independent and resolute are usually viewed as less friendly and have less effective participation in small groups.

While the specific relationships between social sensitivity and group production are not clear, McGrath's discussion of the affect (friendship) structure in small groups suggests that negative affective relations tend to impede group progress. Therefore, we might conclude that having group members with high social sensitivity is not actually a necessary requirement for "good" group performance, but members with low Social Sensitivity reduce the effectiveness of groups.

Ascendant tendencies. When we are placed in a small group, or when a small group develops out of interpersonal contacts in a larger group context, some group members (aside from a formally designated leader) are more assertive than others. This assertiveness takes many forms in relation to what the group is doing, but the general characteristic of being assertive, aggressive, dominant, or trying to control group action is evident in the style of behavior exhibited by some members. Ascendant Tendencies are the attributes of personality that lead people to assert their individual prominence and control a group.

An early study of group productivity in communication networks conducted by Berkowitz (1953) found that high ascendant group members had higher initial rates of communication, transmitted less task relevant information, and showed higher rates of individual sub-task completion than persons rated low on ascendancy. Borg's (1960) research on ascendancy has shown that group members with high ascendant tendencies are more assertive, less likely to be good followers, and exhibit leadership qualities more than less ascendant members. A study by McDavid and Sistrunk (1964) also indicates that highly ascendant people are less likely to conform to group norms than others.

Dependability. Whatever our personal definitions of dependability or conventionality may be, all of us expect the people we interact with in groups to conform to some generally accepted definition of appropriate attention to their roles as group members. Shaw divides the notion of dependability into two subgroups of behavior: self-reliance and responsibility, and unconventionality. A "dependable" person is perceived as reliable and responsible. Similarly, someone who is unconventional in his or her responses to others or manner of doing things is less likely to be viewed positively. Thus, unconventional people will impede group progress when interacting with others who are more conventional in their behavior (or less able to adapt to unconventional people).

Emotional stability. There has been a considerable amount of research conducted on the effects of personal stability of group members on the functioning of small groups. The results of this research have demonstrated what most of us would assume: the more emotionally stable people are, the more they will positively affect group outcomes (Cervin, 1956; Haythorn, 1953; Stogdill, 1948). Shaw's review of the research literature led him to conclude that group members with high anxiety tend to reduce group progress, and group members that are well adjusted (as a general personality trait) tend to facilitate group effectiveness.

The Multifaceted Nature of Personality

As we have seen, personality is an extremely complex, multidimensional concept that influences small group achievement in a number of ways. No one dimension alone can explain why, or predict how, a person will behave in a group or how that behavior will affect the group as a whole. We may add to this confusion by saying that no matter what the *absolute* nature of a person's personality may be, the consequences of behavior in any situation are ultimately determined by how others perceive the behavior and its motivation. Heider's (1958) initial work on the dynamics of *interpersonal perception,* and subsequent research by a number of social psychologists, indicates that all of us create rather stable ways of perceiving other people and explaining their behavior to ourselves (Hastorf, Schneider, and Polefka, 1969). Our own personality based behavior, which is usually thought to be relatively unique, is actually highly dependent upon how others interpret it.

At this point we need to make the distinction between the nature of personality as a complex entity that is relatively stable and enduring, and those impressions that a person's behavior stimulates in the minds of others. A person's personality is salient in the study of communication only in relation to interaction with other personalities. Therefore, we will make the distinction between a person's *absolute personality* (those attributes that show up on measuring instruments) and *effective personality* (those behaviors we attribute to the personalities of others as we perceive them during social interaction).

Recent work by Bales (1970) has attempted to provide methods for structuring perceptions of interpersonal behavior in groups. He cautions that it is not possible to determine, given a limited amount of information about a person, whether behavior is grounded in the person's *group role* (caused by the person's reactions to the specific dynamics of a group) or in some more permanent cognitive structure, like individual personality. His theory pertains to a way of using our perceptions to make more reliable and valid inferences about personality and group role behaviors. Bales' theory uses a three-dimensional model for observing and explaining personality and role based behavior in groups. The three dimensions are described below in terms of "ideal types" of behavioral tendencies.

The first dimension is the *upward-downward* dimension and is similar to Ascendant Tendencies discussed in the previous section. An "upward" person is oriented toward material success and power. Bales (1970, p. 193) describes the upward group member as being perceived by others as, "active, talkative, and powerful, but not clearly either friendly or unfriendly." Nor does the upward member tend to be overly task oriented. In contrast to the upward group member, persons viewed by other members as downward are likely to devalue themselves as people. Bales describes the downward member as

> self-effacing and completely non-self-assertive, passive and powerless. He accepts others in the group and the nature of things as they are without requesting anything for himself, but also without any enthusiasm or desire. He is neither friendly nor unfriendly, neither dutiful nor resistant to . . . task demands (Bales, 1970. p. 377).

The second dimension is a *positive-negative* dimension. People that are perceived as positive appear to strive for equalitarianism for the group. Bales describes them as friendly and sociable, treating others as equals, being about average in ascendant tendencies (but not totally submissive), and being concerned with people as individuals, not because of their status or adeptness at task performance. The negative person in the typology is viewed as unfriendly, disagreeable and detached or "self-concerned." The negative person is neither highly ascendant nor particularly task oriented but is viewed as "defensively secluded and negativistic" (Bales, 1970, p. 289).

The final dimension of the model is a *forward-backward* dimension that relates, in part, to group achievement and definition of group goals and procedures. The group member perceived as forward is task oriented, analytical, and adapts easily to problem solving demands. The person has a conservative definition of group work and is relatively impersonal, though not unfriendly, toward others. Forward members are about average in ascendant tendencies and hold a tentative orientation toward opinions and interpretations of themselves and others. Group members viewed as backward tend to propose unconventional goals for the group and are generally at odds with the definition of group activity accepted by forward members. Backward members appear skeptical of established traditions and ways of proceeding but are not highly ascendant or unfriendly. The backward member appears to be lost in personal fantasy and unable to decide on or strive for anything in the future (Bales, 1970, p. 305).

The polar opposites of each dimension are "ideal types" and may never totally describe a particular individual. In fact, Bales has developed a twenty-seven category classification derived from various combinations of these three dimensions. Nor are the ways other people view a person always congruent with a person's self-definition. On the other hand, this classification scheme is valuable for its organization of interpersonal behavior and for its theoretical grounding as a means of differentiating and attributing effective personality in a logical, consistent, and potentially valid way. As competent communicators, we should remember that meanings attributed to the behaviors of others are filtered through our own perceptions and personalities and, consequently, are structured by our own mechanisms for handling interpersonal relationships.

WHAT HAPPENS WHEN DIFFERENT PERSONALITIES INTERACT IN SMALL GROUPS?

We now turn to a consideration of how people with different personalities and dispositions toward group behavior interact with each other in a small group setting. The amount of research literature on this subject is staggering and we will not attempt to review it here. Instead, we will select a few issues related to the personality compositions of most small groups and deal with them specifically.

The "Assembly Effect" in Group Formation

The reason we study personality, or any other intrapersonal variable, in relation to small group functioning is because there may be an appreciable difference in the outcomes of group interaction when people with certain personalities are placed together. Notice we are talking about something different than individual behavioral dispositions; instead, we are focusing upon what happens when particular combinations of certain personalities come face to face in a group. The end result of combining people with certain personalities is called the *assembly effect* (Shaw, 1971, p. 191). This process has been researched by varying the compositions of small groups on the basis of personality dimensions and other variables (abilities, beliefs, intelligence, and so on) and studying the effects.

The impact that people with various personalities have upon groups was, to some extent, reviewed in the previous section describing various dimensions of personality. We can summarize by saying that people rated (by themselves or others) high on attributes in the Interpersonal Orientation, Social Sensitivity, Dependability, and Emotional Stability areas, and low to moderate on Ascendant Tendencies will, when combined in groups with others of like personalities, produce group climates conducive to effective group action. It should be added that in some groups not all of these personality dimensions will be equally necessary or desirable. Ascendant Tendencies, for example, may be important insofar as one or two members with high ascendancy needs are necessary for group performance, but the nature of a group's work might not require members to be high on Social Sensitivity.

The primary impact of various compositions of group members is usually assessed in terms of group *cohesiveness*. Cartwright and Zander (1968) identify five different ways in which cohesiveness has been measured. These are: (1) interpersonal attraction between members; (2) evaluation of a group as a whole; (3) closeness or "identification" with the group; (4) expressed desire to remain in the group; and (5) composite indices (comprised of a variety of measures like those in numbers 1 through 4).

While many possible approaches can be used to understand cohesiveness in groups, as is seen above, the amount of interpersonal attraction between members is one of the most frequently used methods of inference. Turning to Cartwright's (1968) analysis, attraction is determined by four sets of factors that combine to influence a person's attraction to a group, which are

> (a) his *motive base for attraction* consisting of his needs for affiliation, recognition, security, money, or other values that can be mediated by groups; (b) *the incentive properties of the group,* consisting of its goals, programs, characteristics of its members, style of operation, prestige, or other properties of significance for his motive base; (c) his *expectancy,* the subjective probability, that membership will actually have beneficial or detrimental consequences for him; and (d) his *comparison level*—his conception of the level of outcomes that group membership should provide (Cartwright, 1961, p. 98).

While attraction to a group, and therefore the primary element of cohesion itself, is a complex intrapersonal and interpersonal process, we can generalize to say that attraction and cohesiveness are determined by the following factors: personalities of group members (motivational bases); psychological or material reasons (incentives) for membership; prediction (expectancy) that some positive or negative consequences will follow from group membership; and how a person evaluates rewards and costs of group membership compared to other potential channels for personal activity. At least these factors are salient considerations when people with different personality complexes interact in a group setting. We should note that people's motives for membership and their prediction of expected consequences of group membership are directly related to individual personality factors and the interpersonal perceptual filters that are used to evaluate social settings and interaction.

Interpersonal Compatibility of Group Members

From our discussion of the assembly effect there is good reason to believe that some combinations of personalities are more effective in groups than others. A question to consider is whether the critical factor in the personality composition of groups is having the right *number* of different people (heterogeneity) or if some more overriding judgment should be made. Hare (1976), for example, believes that in groups where close interpersonal relations are necessary for the completion of group work, "compatibility" of group members is necessary. Compatibility refers to a meshing together of people with particular interpersonal orientations; it is a mixing of people who complement one another.

An elaborate series of studies investigating the nature of interpersonal compatibility was conducted by Schutz (1958). He theorized that human beings have three fundamental interpersonal "needs" which must be met in social settings to facilitate psychological health—*inclusion, control,* and *affection*. Inclusion is the need to establish satisfying (personally rewarding) social relationships with others (discussed previously under the Interpersonal Orientation dimension). Control is the need to maintain satisfying power relations with others, by either dominating (having power) over others or being satisfied with assuming a submissive position. Affection is a special type of interpersonal orientation relating to needs for establishing strong emotional ties with others or, conversely, to act out dislikes of others.

A unique feature of the Schutz theory is that he believed these needs can operate in two different directions. Therefore, the needs of inclusion, control, and affection function both in terms of the amount we wish to express toward others and the amount of each need that we want others to express toward us. The idea of "need compatibility" focuses upon how much of the three interpersonal needs we wish to express toward others and how much we need others to express toward us. Actually, the notion of compatibility is not quite that simple because it depends upon ways in which people can satisfy each other's needs through interpersonal communication. It is possible for two or more people to have similar needs, or requirements that each communicator could satisfy, but be incompatible due to their inability to effectively satisfy each other's needs.

Schutz outlines three possible sources of compatibility: *interchange compatibility, originator compatibility* and *reciprocal compatibility*. We will briefly discuss each one of these in the context of a two-person (dyadic) situation. Where two people are high on inclusion, their relationship will be compatible to the extent that both are able to give and receive messages that indicate inclusion. We must be careful to note that the *amount* of need to be expressed, rather than whether it is given or received, is important for understanding interchange compatibility. To the extent that one person cannot satisfy the amount of inclusion needed by another, the relationship is incompatible. Similarly, to the extent that one person feels unable to express enough inclusion toward another, the relationship is incompatible.

Reciprocal compatibility functions in a somewhat different way. It is based on the correspondence between expressed and wanted satisfaction of a particular need. In the hypothetical situation above, for example, if one person had a high need to receive (wanted) inclusion but had a low need to express inclusion, and the other person had a high need to express inclusion toward others but a low need to receive signals of inclusion, the relationship (although a somewhat unlikely one) would be considered compatible because of the reciprocity (a balanced exchange) of needs between the two people.

Originator compatibility is an outgrowth of reciprocal compatibility. Using the need for control as an example, if one member of our improbable pair from above had a high need to control people, and the other had a high need to be the object of control by others, they would be compatible on the basis of reciprocity of control needs. But, if the person with a high need to control could not display controlling behavior, and if the person with a high need to be dominated could not effectively show a need for domination, they would be incompatible on the basis of originator compatibility. Neither person would be effective in communicating needs, and the pair would find it difficult to remain in close contact or to work productively together.

Finding the "Magic Mixture" of Group Members

Research conducted by Schutz is impressive but not totally conclusive, as has been demonstrated by Rosenfeld and Frandsen (1973), and by Shaw (1971), who reviewed the work done on exploring compatibility of group membership. At this point then, we must ask whether there is some "magic mixture" of personality dimensions that compliment or facilitate group functioning. Moreover, when we are not in control of the way a group is formed, how do we go about dealing with the situation as it exists? Both questions are not easily answered and, in fact, they may be unanswerable to some degree. We will, however, venture a few reasoned guesses about compatibility and how to cope with incompatible group compositions.

Shaw's review of available information points toward two tentative generalizations. First, groups with a primary goal of producing or performing some given task or work activity tend to function more effectively (productively) with compatible members than groups with incompatible members; second, groups with compatible members tend to be more satisfied with their work together than groups with incompatible members. These generalizations seem to hold for groups composed of members selected for their personality compatibility as well as other properties (sex or skills, for example).

An important limitation of the compatibility-productivity principle is referred to by Bennis (1973) as the "doppelganger" effect. Bennis notes that top executives generally tend to surround themselves with key assistants who look and think like themselves (dopplingers). In order to insure that people whom they must rely on will make decisions similar to their own, executives look for those with similar views and compatible personalities. This means of course, that contrary opinions and information are rarely heard. An executive level committee which places a high priority on compatibility and cohesiveness may develop a fatal flaw because of its single-minded orientation.

The problem of what can be done in groups with incompatible members requires a combination of personal introspection and effective communication skills. If any of us is to deal effectively with those attributes of others that impede interpersonal relationships, we need to take stock of our own ways of reacting to others. Rather than focusing on what we want to be (some ideal personal notions of ourselves), we must first consider how we actually project to others (our effective personality). We might even attempt to gain some personal feedback about ourselves from others, being careful not to solicit feedback we want to hear.

After we have a pretty good understanding how we stand personally, we should try an *adapt, disclose,* and *monitor* cycle of communication. We adapt by working on certain things we can immediately change, in terms of our behavior and expectations for others, that will bring us into closer harmony with group members. Once we are sure we have implemented some personal changes, we disclose to other members how we see the group and things we believe the group should do to help us adapt better. These disclosures must correspond to periods when the group will be receptive to such information, possibly when it has already begun considering some interpersonal strains, and must be presented in language that is not demanding or likely to produce defensive reactions. Monitoring takes place after the other two steps have been completed. It is a time when we assess how effectively the preceding steps have produced desired changes within the group. If no change has taken place, or things have become worse, we begin the cycle again.

If there has been a noticeable change for the better, we continue monitoring so that we do not mentally "let down" and find the same problems occurring again. Remember that personality characteristics are strong internal motivators of individual behavior. Interpersonal problems caused by initially incompatible mixtures of people are not easily solved. A group may make serious attempts at changing some of the effective personality dimensions of its members, with some initial success, only to find that members have "regressed" to old behavior patterns. Continuous monitoring of a group's interpersonal behavior is an important part of each group member's responsibilities. Awareness of the personal behaviors that detract from group performance is needed to detect potential interpersonal strains in the group.

DOES THE PERSON GET LOST IN THE GROUP?

You may be wondering what happened to the *person* in all of the foregoing discussion about personality dimensions, assembly effects, and group compatibility. Groups do exert a great amount of influence over their individual members. On the other hand, each member also exerts a tremendous influence on the group. Let's consider for a moment where the individual, as an individual, fits into the scheme of group processes.

The Interactive Influence of Person-Group Perceptions

No one leaves a group in exactly the same psychological condition that they were in originally. What we gain or lose from group membership is directly related to our view of the group and other members' view(s) of us. These perceptions are partially based on how members assess rewards and costs of interacting with each other. Should group members perceive your behavior as too costly to them, and below their Comparison Levels for group satisfaction, they will probably find ways of behaving to reduce your rewards below your Comparison Level for Alternatives and pressure you out of the group.

The *person-group* relationship is really an artificial kind of distinction. People who compose groups interact and draw upon each other in their efforts to work together. How any person views other group members is a result of her or his personality and its unique relationship with the personalities of others. The "uniqueness" of a group really results from the ways each person interacts with other members. How each person perceives other members will affect personal behavior and the group as a whole.

Individual Needs for Power, Achievement, and Affiliation

Behavioral studies of small groups indicate that a person's view of other group members or the actions of a group is related to the individual's needs for power, achievement, and affiliation. These needs are strong motivators of behavior and can be seen in terms of an individual's effective personality. As personality-based behaviors, the relative importance of one or more of these needs will affect relationships between individual and group and the process of group performance.

Some group members will be satisfied with what a group does as long as they are able to find a comfortable way to fulfill their personal needs. Therefore, they will not be highly motivated to see that the group "makes a decision" or "solves a problem" if they are more interested in satisfying affiliation needs. Likewise, some people may not be effective in helping the group reach a particular goal unless they are responsible for directing the group and its activities (need for power). Such a person may even block group progress in quest of satisfying personal needs.

These are some examples of how effective personality influences group movement. We should emphasize that effective personality really accounts for a person's behavior as an individual. Group behavior is more difficult to assess because we cannot conclusively determine how individual behaviors will interact to produce the new dimension of group behavior. We do know that groups develop a "personality" which reflects the personalities of all group members. By observing the three major dimensions of personal behavior it is easier to infer how each person influences a group. Certain combinations of personal attributes are more effective than others for maximizing group performance. Moreover, individual motivations to exhibit certain behaviors are often stronger than group abilities to change or suppress those behaviors.

Personal Integrity as a Group Member

Whenever a person enters a small group there is an *exchange* that takes place between that person and other group members. Each member gives up some initial freedom and control over his or her personal behavior in return for rewards that the group can provide. To obtain these rewards it may be necessary for members to change certain personally valued behaviors. Many times an individual may not be able to accept the demands of group membership. This often happens in juvenile peer groups that turn to antisocial activities. Some group members will find it easy to conform to group expectations; other members will not be able to personally justify changes in group-sanctioned activity and are "pressured out" by members that demand strict conformity to group expectations.

The central values, attitudes, and personality dimensions of a person's effective personality mediate behavior and structure perceptions a person forms as a group member. The attributes of a person are not easily changed by his or her presence in a group. Obviously, a person's attraction to a group and ability to change and adapt to the personal demands of membership will affect the person's behavior as a group member. These effects may be short term or long term, depending upon the specific group and the person's desire for membership.

REFERENCES

Adorno, T.W., Frenkel-Brunswick, E., Levinson, D.J. and Sanford, R.N. 1950. *The authoritarian personality.* New York: Harper & Row, Pub.

Bales, R.F. 1970. *Personality and interpersonal behavior.* New York: Holt, Rinehart & Winston.

Bell, G.D. and Hall, H.E., Jr. 1954. The relationship between leadership and empathy. *Journal of Abnormal and Social Psychology 49,* 156–157.

Bennis, W. 1973. The doppelganger effect. *Newsweek,* 17 September 1973, p. 13.

Berkowitz, L. 1953. Personality and group position. *Sociometry 19,* 210–222.

Borg, W.R. 1960. Prediction of small group role behavior from personality variables. *Journal of Abnormal and Social Psychology 60,* 112–116.

Cartwright, D. 1968. The nature of group cohesiveness. In *Group dynamics: Research and theory,* 3rd ed., eds. D. Cartright and A. Zander, pp. 91–109. New York: Harper & Row, Pub.

Cattell, R.B. and Stice, G.F. 1960. The dimensions of groups and their relations to the behavior of members. Champaign, Ill.: Institute for Personality and Ability Testing.

Cervin, V. 1956. Individual behavior in social situations: Its relation to anxiety, neuroticism, and group solidarity. *Journal of Experimental Psychology 60,* 175–181.

Christie, R. and Jahoda, M., eds. 1956. *Studies in scope and method of "Authoritarian Personality."* New York: Free Press.

Giffin, K. and Barnes, R. 1976. *Trusting me, trusting you.* Columbus, Ohio: Chas. E. Merrill.

Hare, A.P. 1976. *Handbook of small group research.* 2nd ed. New York: Free Press.

Hastorf, A.H., Schneider, D.J. and Polefka, J. 1969. *Person perception.* Reading, Mass.: Addison-Wesley.

Haythorn, W. 1953. The influence of individual members on the characteristics of small groups. *Journal of Abnormal and Social Psychology 48,* 276–284.

Haythorn, W., Couch, A., Haefner, D., Langham, P. and Carter, L. 1956a. The behavior of authoritarian and equalitarian personalities in group. *Human Relations 9,* 57–74.

Haythorn, W., Couch, A., Haefner, D., Langham, P. and Carter, L. 1956b. The effects of varying combinations of authoritarian and equalitarian leaders and followers. *Journal of Abnormal and Social Psychology 53,* 210–219.

Heider, F. 1958. *The psychology of interpersonal relations.* New York: John Wiley.

McDavid, J.W. and Sistrunk, E. 1964. Personality correlates of two kinds of conforming behavior. *Journal of Personality 32,* 420–435.

McGrath, J.E. 1964. *Social psychology: A brief introduction.* New York: Holt, Rinehart & Winston.

Mann, R.D. 1959. A review of the relationships between personality and performance in small groups. *Psychological Bulletin 56,* 241–270.

Newcomb, T.M. 1950. *Social psychology.* New York: Holt, Rinehart & Winston.

Rosenfeld, L.B. and Frandsen, K.D. 1973. Fundamental interpersonal relations orientations in dyads: An empirical analysis of Schutz's FIRO-B as an index of compatibility. *Speech Monographs 40,* 113–122.

Schutz, W.C. 1955. What makes groups productive. *Human Relations 8,* 429–465.

Schutz, W.C. 1958. *FIRO: A three-dimensional theory of interpersonal behavior.* New York: Holt, Rinehart & Winston.

Schutz, W.C. 1961. On group composition. *Journal of Abnormal and Social Psychology 62,* 275–281.

Shaw, M.E. 1971. *Group dynamics: The psychology of small group behavior.* New York: McGraw-Hill.

Stogdill, R.M. 1948. Personal factors associated with leadership: A survey of the literature. *Journal of Psychology 25,* 35–71.

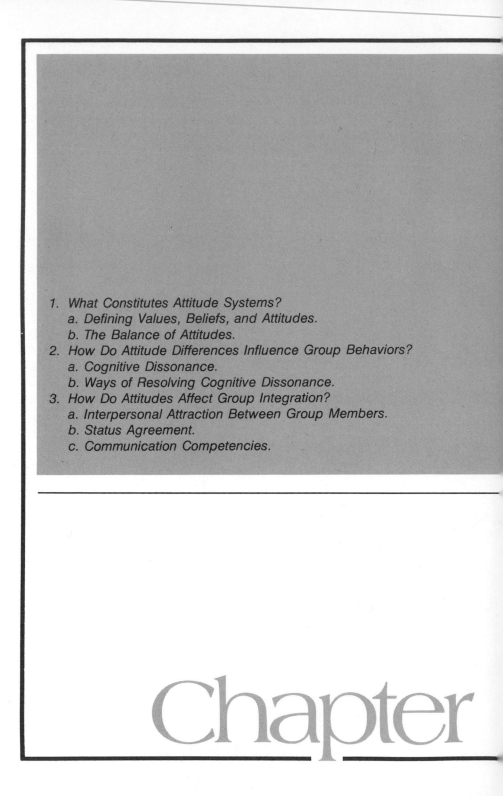

Chapter

In Chapter 2 we examined some personality characteristics that people may bring to a group. To the degree personalities of group members are compatible, a group may be effective in task accomplishment and satisfying to its members. When personalities clash, the results may be uncomfortable for everyone and can have a detrimental effect on efficient, effective task accomplishment. Generally speaking, personality characteristics are viewed as stable elements which motivate individual behavior irrespective of a setting or task. Except under special circumstances, typical of those generated in psychotherapy or behavior modification groups, we would not expect to find significant changes in someone's personality as a consequence of group membership. In terms of the system's model, member personalities are input variables which will remain relatively unaltered during interaction. Under most circumstances we can expect member personalities to emerge relatively unaltered at the end of group life.

While closely related to personality, an individual's system of attitudes is much more amenable to change. For example,

3 attitudinal orientations and group behavior

Sue might have a "friendly personality" but could attend a sorority meeting with a hostile *attitude* toward the sorority president. Sue's hostility may be based on her current feelings about the president's attitude on study hours in the sorority house. During the meeting, members may try to change Sue's attitude. The distinction between attitude and personality, as demonstrated in this example, is that attitudes are limited to particular subjects or categories of topics while personality refers to more generalized response tendencies. Group members may have difficulty, however, making this distinction since both psychological concepts remain somewhat in the "eye of the beholder." If you meet someone for the first time and she or he grumbles a greeting before wandering off, you would probably wonder why that person had such an unpleasant attitude toward you. You might be comforted to hear a friend explain " . . . the person is just that way" (in other words, this person has a negative orientation to interpersonal relations with others). Should you value the person's esteem, you might seek to change his or her attitude toward you; however, should you believe the behavior was a function of personality you may simply take the person's gruff manner in stride. Similarly, a group will seek to alter, or at least influence, attitudes of its members and will try to adapt to member personalities.

Member attitudes are open to change, so any given attitude may be a product of member feelings and perceptions generated by group interaction. In many cases, previously held attitudes become solidified, intensified, or more clearly articulated as a result of group interaction. Individuals often leave a group with attitudes which are a combination of previously held convictions and newly shared group perspectives. Therefore, we should keep in mind that while we are examining attitudes from an input perspective in this chapter, these same attitudes are a source of interaction and member change (outputs).

WHAT CONSTITUTES ATTITUDE SYSTEMS?

We now turn our attention to the issue of what constitutes a *system of attitudes*. The underlying assumption is that each individual has a system of attitudes that makes sense to that person. Most people believe their values, beliefs, and attitudes are balanced, consistent, or complementary (this does not mean they are "balanced" from anyone else's perspective). After discussing the make-up of a balanced attitude system, we will discuss what happens when imbalances or inconsistencies occur within and between attitude systems. We maintain that tensions, strains, and anxieties develop within and among group members until the inconsistencies are resolved. The final issue we will examine is the effect of attitudes on group *integration* (how the group operates as a total unit). Given the assumption that people need consistent systems of attitudes, and that tensions result from inconsistencies, we should be able to predict certain attitudinal effects on group integration. As with compatible personalities, we conclude that groups with compatible attitude systems will be more effective and efficient in task completion and more satisfying to group members than incompatible groups.

Defining Values, Beliefs, and Attitudes

Most theorists agree that our cognitive (mental) system is made up of values, beliefs, and attitudes. While all of us have literally thousands of attitudes and beliefs, we have relatively few values. *Values* can be regarded as enduring, cultural and social conceptions of desirable states (situations) used as criteria for developing belief preferences and justifications for behaviors. They are central to our lives and, unlike beliefs and attitudes, are unlikely to change except over prolonged time periods and in conjunction with competing sets of social values. When group members disagree over value issues, resolution of the differences will be difficult. In recent years the debate over the right to an abortion has centered on the values of "a right to life" versus "a right to free choice." Resolution of the issue has been virtually impossible due to the sharply contrasting sets of values involved.

Attitudes are made up of elements regarded as beliefs. A *belief* is a personal proposition describing the way one views some facet of *reality*. The content of a belief may *describe* an object, person, or idea ("I believe that the earth is round"), *evaluate* an object, person, or idea ("I believe that chocolate cake is good to eat"), or be *prescriptive* about an object, person, or idea ("I believe that meetings should start on time"). In each case, beliefs represent a predisposition to respond in a preferential way to the object, person, or idea focus of the belief.

An *attitude* is simply an organization of interrelated beliefs centered on a common subject. Most theorists maintain that attitudes are learned predispositions to behave in a favorable or unfavorable manner towards a person, object, or idea (Katz, 1960). These predispositions are learned from past experience and are in a constant state of development and change.

Acquisition of attitudes. Most social psychologists explain attitude formation (or beliefs and values, for that matter) in ways that parallel socialization into society. As we grow and mature, parents, relatives, friends, and others constantly teach and reinforce certain kinds of behaviors and discourage others. As a college student, for example, you

probably come from a home that has instilled a positive value for education and knowledge. You probably believe that college is a good source
of education and knowledge. Therefore, you may have a positive attitude toward college attendance.

Many attitudes we hold as adults are products of values, beliefs, and
attitudes implicit in social training received as children. In fact, *socialization* can be viewed as the transmission of parental attitudes and values to
the child (Lindesmith and Strauss, 1969). As we grow older and expand
our associations (through school, jobs, recreational activities) our attitudes are influenced by these new contacts. It is not uncommon to find
adolescents and young adults with attitude systems dissimilar to those of
their parents but similar to those of peers.

Attitudes are also based on personal experiences and ways we learn to
perceive the world. A brother and sister, for example, may come from
the same home environment with similar values but may have vastly
different attitudes due to different friends, experiences, and perceptions. This is not to suggest that all, or even most, of our attitudes
undergo radical change as we mature. Many attitudes directly related to
central values remain rather stable throughout our lifetime.

Social attitudes, then, are learned response dispositions toward objects, people, and ideas. Some of these responses are learned on our
own, but many emerge from interaction with others and depend upon
positive or negative reinforcements attached to our behaviors. Each
group member has had a variety of experiences which play a role in
shaping attitudes toward group behavior. Current behaviors in a group
are a product of past group experiences, current feelings and perceptions about the task, situation, fellow group members, and expectations
for the group. All of these attitudes affect how behavior in a group can
ultimately affect group development and achievement.

Attitudes towards people create motivations to behave in particular
ways and strongly influence expectations about the behavior of others. A
case in point is the behavior of female and male group members. It has
been long been known that men and women hold somewhat differing
sets of expectations for themselves and members of the opposite sex
when participating in various social settings (see, for example, Maccoby
and Jacklin, 1974). Evidence also exists from early research on jury
deliberation outcomes that men and women have differing kinds of
participation. Male jurors were found to have high rates of task oriented
statements while female jurors tended toward more positive social-
emotional activity such as agreement or promoting cohesiveness
(Strodtbeck and Mann, 1956).

It would be dangerous to assume, however, that men and women *should* differ in their expectations of one another. Moreover, there is some reason to question whether the manner in which men and women behaved in decision making jury groups twenty years ago accurately reflects group behavior today. In a more recent investigation using human relations training groups, Mabry (1976) found that female group members had proportionately higher amounts of both task oriented and social-emotional statements. Hence, there is some reason to believe that women may be just as likely as men to assume responsibility for task or goal direction. More important, however, is the necessity for both sexes to recognize attitudes they hold and guard against behaving in ways that might reflect inaccurate or repressive sex role stereotypes.

Reinforcement is a critical consideration in the development of attitudes. Groups can be used effectively to influence and modify attitudes as long as the influence of a group is stronger than external forces. Parental admonitions may be the most significant influence on attitudes until the need for independence from parental constraints and the desire for peer group acceptance swings the pendulum in favor of peer group associations. The peer group eventually loses its influence as the youth finds a spouse or a college roommate to serve as a dominant influence. At each stage, lack of reinforcement to meet the changing needs of the individual results in a declining influence on attitude formation.

The same condition occurs when individuals are taken out of their normal environments and placed in a group for purposes of attitude change. Encounter or T-groups were once considered a cure-all for company misfits until follow-up studies determined that trainees often "regressed" back to their original attitudes (*Sales Management*, 1966). A group can be a powerful influence; however, without regular reinforcement and without constant modification to meet members' changing needs, a group can lose its impact.

No single source will have an enduring influence on all individuals. As a person's needs, aspirations, experiences, and outside influences change over time, the strength of a source will change. The longer individuals are group members and are shielded from significant external influences, the more likely thay are to retain socialized attitudes. Long term membership in a group not only has the advantage of consistent reinforcement of attitudes but also provides members with common experiences which can enhance interpersonal attraction. Over time, diverse group members find commonalities of interests and attitudes. Even those members who initially believe they have little in common find topics of mutual concern within a group. As members orient themselves to one another, the strength of their similarities serves as a motivator to resolve differences.

Attitude components. Attitudes are composed of multiple bits of information and are believed to have three interrelated components: cognitive, affective, and behavioral. The *cognitive component* represents a person's knowledge and "rational" thinking process about the object of an attitude. It does not matter whether this knowledge is accurate or whether the thinking would appear to be rational to anyone else. If men are viewed as leaders and women are viewed as secretaries in a group, then they will probably perform those duties regardless of whether they are capable of other roles or not.

The *affective component* refers to feelings of arousal about the object of an attitude. These feelings may be positive or negative and will vary in intensity. Arousal will generally be higher when group members speak against an attitude than when they agree with it. For example, if John proposes that a group approve a new auditing system, he will accept approval as a matter of fact. Arguments against the system, however, will probably stimulate John's thoughts and feelings about the topic and those who oppose it.

The *behavioral component* represents actual behavior that a person uses in regard to the object of an attitude. Observable behavior most directly affects evaluations and reactions by others. However, there is ample evidence to suggest observed behavior is not always a valid reflection of our cognitive and affective evaluations of others (Kiesler, Collins and Miller, 1969). Many times our behavior may contradict the other components, especially if there are external situational demands placed on us. If a member anticipates a group is about to approve a course of action, the member may publicly vote in favor of the action, while privately disapproving of it.

It is difficult to isolate the three components or to point with any degree of confidence to the sources of information that are most important in attitude formation and change. For example, few, if any, of us rely upon a single source of information to determine whom we will vote for in an election. We may carefully read each candidate's position in the local newspaper, evaluate appearances on television, note the number of campaign buttons and fliers around public places for a particular candidate, talk to friends and co-workers about their preferences, and, possibly, meet one of the candidates at a campaign appearance. By the time we make our choice, so many bits of information have influenced us that it may be impossible to isolate precisely what motivated our decision.

Attitude dimensions. Attitudes vary according to *direction, intensity,* and *saliency.* Each of these dimensions should be viewed as a continuum. Direction refers to the favorable or unfavorable evaluation of a subject or person. The middle point on this continuum reflects neutrality. As direction moves away from neutral, intensity often increases. However, direction and intensity cannot be placed on the same continuum since a moderate position could then be upheld tenaciously. Intensity might be thought of as a scale ranging from 0 to 100; the stronger one's senti-ment, the higher one's attitude would appear on the intensity scale. The third dimension, saliency, can also be thought of as *centrality.* Saliency is determined by the degree to which a subject or person is important to an individual. Picture yourself in the center of a series of concentric circles with attitudes falling within various rings. Attitudes in rings nearest you fall in a region of commitment, farther away, a region of interest and, finally, the most distant rings represent spheres of transient attention. As life experiences change, attitudes once given only slight attention may shift to a more central region (Pilisuk, 1968). Attitudes toward hiring females in traditionally male positions may not concern some men, for example, until they feel their jobs or promotions are in jeopardy.

Applying these dimensions specifically to group settings, we might begin with an assumption that each member enters a group with certain attitudinal biases toward the group as an entity, toward the group's task(s), and toward other members. These predispositions may range from hostility to affection (direction) with varying degrees of affect (in-tensity). At the same time, each member's view of the relevance (salience) of task issues or group goals may differ. To get a better idea of how these dimensions could affect group action, consider the following situation:

> A manager calls a meeting of three engineers to discuss a policy decision he is contemplating. One engineer arrives in a huff while thinking, "Why doesn't he do his job and let me do mine. Every minute I'm in this meeting I will be taking time away from my own work. The best thing for me to do is keep quiet and get this meeting over." The second engineer arrives in a different frame of mind and wonders, "What is this all about? I sure have a lot of work to do at the desk but, then, the boss wouldn't have called this meeting if it wasn't important." The third engineer fills his cup of coffee and enters with a smile thinking, "Hey, the boss is finally giving us an opportunity to participate in some of the decisions around here! I'm look-ing forward to sharing my views with the others since we seldom have a chance to get away from the desk."

Each person brings to the group an attitudinal bias that will directly influence that person's own behavior and the behaviors of others at the meeting.

In summary, attitudes are learned predispositions to behave in a favorable or unfavorable manner toward a person, object, or idea. They are based upon underlying beliefs and values. A belief is a perspective about the nature of objects, people, and ideas and the types of actions that should be taken toward them. Any given attitude is based on a number of interrelated beliefs. Beliefs that are relatively enduring are regarded as values. Values, beliefs, and attitudes combine to form a *cognitive* system. Structurally, we may think of several beliefs contained in an attitude, several attitudes within an attitude system, and all beliefs, attitudes and values within a cognitive system. Each attitude system needs to make sense to an individual. Balancing of attitudes in order to make sense of one's reality will be the next area of discussion.

The Balance of Attitudes

Attitude systems involve a group of interrelated attitudes, beliefs, and values about an object, person, or idea. A common assumption about attitudes, beliefs, and behaviors is that they are organized in consistent ways. Heider (1958) was one of the first theorists to discuss the organizational properties of attitude systems. He referred to a need to maintain *balance* among cognitive components of attitudes.

Heider speculated about the ways attitudinal balances affect interpersonal relationships. He theorized that the two types of relations between people are sentiment relations and unit relations. *Sentiment relations* deal with how one person feels about another person and how this feeling is influenced by objects or other persons to which the two people are in some way associated. Positive sentiments are signified by liking and negative sentiments by disliking. *Unit relations* are composed of separate entities which are perceived to belong together, such as separate members belonging to a group or individual attitudes joining in a common system.

According to Heider, sentiment and unit relationships tend toward a *balanced state*. A balanced state is one in which everything fits together harmoniously. For example, if a group likes a member, that member will tend to like the group. Furthermore, if a group likes a member and the group is positively oriented to a particular task, a member will like the group and the task. In this case, the relationships are said to be harmonious or *in balance*. Harmonious situations are generally preferred over those that are unbalanced or unharmonious.

Sentiments toward an object, person, or idea tend to be homogeneous. In other words, there is a tendency to make all individual attitudes toward a subject agree. If a group leader is personally liked, members will tend to accept the leader's opinions on task related issues. In other words, positively valued people develop "halos" (referred to as a *halo effect*) around all areas of their behavior. If the well-liked leader behaves in a disliked manner, group members may rationalize the incongruent behavior. Of course, no one is totally good or bad, nor is any issue totally right or wrong. People vary in their ability to mentally balance those differences.

It is important to realize that the principles of balance theory are open to exception. One can easily think of cases where an individual likes a group but the group dislikes the individual. However, balance theory provides a point of departure for analyzing unbalanced situations. Research conducted by Tagiuri (1958), for example, found that in an unbalanced dyad in which person *P* liked person *O* but *O* disliked *P*, person *P* perceived *O* as *liking* him while, conversely, person *O* perceived *P* as *disliking* him. Such results should be a vivid reminder that it is what we *think* we see that counts. Only in cases where the relationship is perceived to be unbalanced by one or both parties will an attempt be made to balance the relationship.

People we interact with frequently will be positively related to us unless there is a great dissimilarity of attitudes. The fact that we talk with friends frequently and avoid interacting with people we dislike supports the association between interaction and liking. Not as easily supported by experience is Heider's idea that we tend to interact with someone we come into close contact with repeatedly. The limit of the interaction and closeness (or proximity) principle was demonstrated by Schachter (1951). Small groups were devised with a confederate who opposed an already accepted group opinion. Communication was directed toward the deviant until it was determined that the person would not endorse the group's opinion. Balance was restored when the positive sentiment for the deviant was changed to a negative sentiment, and further interactions with the deviant were avoided. Figure 3.1 diagrammatically represents the unbalanced relationship and the eventual balancing.

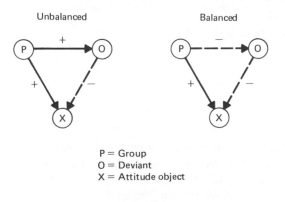

P = Group
O = Deviant
X = Attitude object

Figure 3.1

Heider proposed eight possible unit or sentiment relationships. Four are balanced and three are unbalanced (see Figure 3.2). The eighth relationship occurs when a person negatively perceives another person (or group) and both people hold negative attitudes toward a common

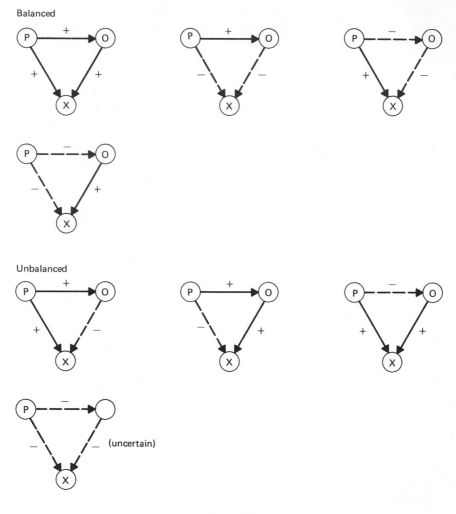

Figure 3.2

subject. Assume, for example, that you are a Democrat who dislikes the Republican party but you also dislike the Democratic nominee for governor. Does your dislike of the nominee result in liking the Republican party more, or does dislike of the Republican party convince you to vote for the Democratic nominee, or, perhaps, do you simply dislike both without a need to restore balance? The answer is ambiguous. With this one exception, balanced and unbalanced states can be easily determined by calculating the algebraic product of the three elements in the relationship. The relationship is unbalanced if the product is negative and balanced if it is positive.

Heider looked at the organization of beliefs and attitudes from the perspective of one person. Newcomb (1968) took Heider's idea about balanced states and applied it to communication between two or more people. According to Newcomb, there is a *strain toward symmetry* which leads to a commonality of attitudes between two people (A and B) oriented toward an object (X). He suggests that when two people are mutually attracted to one another because of proximity, mutual experiences, and friendship, they will try to search for commonality on issues where they differ. Newcomb's theory predicts that the stronger the forces toward person A's *coorientation* (interpersonal relatedness) with person B in regard to issue X, (a) the greater will be A's strain toward symmetry with B in regard to their mutual perception of X, and (b) the greater the likelihood increased symmetry will occur between A and B as a consequence of one or more communicative acts.

In order to test some of his assumptions, Newcomb (1956) established a house at the University of Michigan which offered free rent for one semester to seventeen students. Residents of the house were observed, questioned, and rated each week during the semester. His findings revealed a tendency for those who were attracted to one another to agree on many issues (X's) including how they perceived themselves and their attractions for other group members. Moreover, these similarities, real as well as perceived, increased over time.

Newcomb makes an assumption that person A not only is aware of an attitude toward person B and issue X but also is aware of B's attitude toward A and X. Generally, if A likes B, A is relatively confident that B's feelings are similar and feels confident in "knowing" B's attitude toward X. If A dislikes B, A may be much less certain of B's attitudes toward A or X. A further complication in group settings is that members may be limited to behavioral representations of attitudes that provide little concrete information from which to draw conclusions.

Changes in attitudes have also been studied by Osgood and Tannenbaum (1955). Their *principle of congruity* proposes that when a change in attitude occurs, it generally will occur in the direction of increased congruity with a prevailing frame of reference. In other words, judgments move toward maximal simplicity, such as all-or-nothing or black-and-white, with a continuing pressure toward polarization. A common example of this idea is that after a person buys a car she or he tends to read as many advertisements and articles supporting that decision as possible. Similarly, Democrats and Republicans attend speeches and programs by fellow party supporters who provide reinforcement for their original views.

Balance theories, including strain toward symmetry and congruity theories, are supported with research data indicating that dissonance, unbalanced situations, and incongruencies arouse anxiety and result in a drive towards re-establishing balance and stability (Smith, 1968). The initial development of attitudes and the eventual resolution of inconsistencies are largely unique to each individual's *perceptual system*. A perceptual system is the total integration of physical abilities to obtain social stimuli (sight, sound, and so on); the accumulated set of neurophysiological mechanisms for processing stimuli; and the learned symbolic structures (attitudes, values, etc.) used to interpret processed stimuli. Therefore, even commonly shared group experiences may result in differing attitudes, and subsequent resolution of differences may vary from individual to individual.

HOW DO ATTITUDE DIFFERENCES INFLUENCE GROUP BEHAVIORS?

Given a group of three or more people with differing backgrounds, experiences, psychological make-ups, and expectations, we should not be surprised to learn that each member often upholds attitudes and beliefs differing from those of other members. When differing attitudes are expressed, there are many ways other members can react, which can either facilitate or hamper task accomplishment. Before exploring this issue further, note that perception of conflicting attitudes is unique to each individual and that each person will respond to his or her perception in a unique way.

Cognitive Dissonance

A theory of cognitive dissonance was developed by Leon Festinger (1957, 1964) to explain what motivates one to change nonfitting relations among one's knowledge, beliefs, and attitudes about the environment and oneself. *Cognitive dissonance* is the antecedent condition leading to activities stimulated to reduce imbalance. Festinger's basic thesis is that when two attitudes or beliefs are perceived to be incompatible, the result is mentally unpleasant. An individual will attempt to reduce or eliminate the unpleasantness and will avoid situations that might increase it. The severity or intensity of dissonance varies with the number and importance of the attitudes and beliefs involved in a nonfitting relationship. The drive to reduce, eliminate, and avoid dissonance is a result of its severity.

Dissonance can be reduced by (1) adding new cognitions (attitudes, beliefs, and knowledge) to one side of the unbalanced relationship, or (2) changing existing cognitions in such a way as to make the relationship less contradictory or the contradiction less important. The process of *dissonance reduction* usually results in a passive mental exercise like *rationalizing*. However, if dissonance cannot be reduced through rationalization, an individual may actively seek additional information or opinions to assist in dissonance reduction. Let us assume that you do not believe in "unidentified flying objects" (U.F.O.s). One evening you observe a bright light shooting across the sky. In all probability you will dismiss it as a comet, satellite, or figment of your imagination. Researchers of U.F.O.s indicate that most people don't report sightings until at least a year later or until other people make similar reports. If the experience is so vivid that it cannot be dismissed, you may change your attitude in favor of U.F.O.s and seek additional support for your newly formed attitude.

Festinger's dissonance theory has generated extensive research and can be credited with moving us much closer to a link between behavior and cognitive and affective attitudes. A major difficulty in applying the research findings to group behavior is that people differ in their capacity to cope with or accept dissonant information. Some dissonant information may be perceived and acted upon while other dissonant cognitions may be ignored. Contradictory attitudes may be tied to different belief systems. When a contradiction is perceived, the mental gymnastics may be so quick and easy that discomfort is never experienced. Furthermore, attitudes often involve complex relationships between attitude objects and an individual's needs and fears—which may be stronger forces than needs to maintain balance. Some children, no matter how much they like Popeye, cannot be persuaded to "like" spinach. According to balance theory, however, the more a child likes Popeye, the more the child should like those cans of power.

It is also true that we often enjoy clashes of opinions and the sharing of differences in a group. All of us enjoy the magician whose task is to create dissonance—how can a rabbit be drawn out of an empty hat? The magician performs an event which is impossible on the basis of previous knowledge (Zajonc, 1960). Similarly, if we dislike and avoid dissonance, why do we make so many decisions? In many decisions, the unchosen alternatives contain positive features and the chosen alternative contains some negative features. The answer to this problem is that a set of cognitions are dissonant only to the extent they motivate a person to modify one or more relationships within a set of attitudes.

Ways of Resolving Cognitive Dissonance

When people perceive dissonance, they can resolve it through various methods. The chosen method may depend upon their "mental development" Kaplan and Crockett, 1968). It is useful to distinguish between three levels of development, the primitive, intermediate, and advanced. Those at a *primitive level* permit only one-sided perspectives and make no attempt to combine discrepant attitudes. Some group members are unable or unwilling to listen to differing views, and may not even recognize that they voice attitudes that are viewed as contradictory by other group members. Those at the *intermediate level* attempt to resolve inconsistencies by using: (1) *linguistic reinterpretations*—they reinterpret words used to express inconsistency towards consistency, (2) *contextual variability*—they assume that people behave differently in different situations, (3) *pseudopersonality traits*—they explain incompatibility on the basis of personality splits or variations, and (4) *gross differentiation of sources*— they view a member with incompatible information as unlike others who uphold the view. At the most *advanced stage* of mental development, explicit and highly articulated consideration of many factors other than immediate information may be used to explain discrepancies. In general, individuals at an advanced stage may use more inferences to integrate information and may, in fact, seek out and integrate inconsistent information.

While people may be quite rational in their striving to make sense out of their environment, some of the means used to achieve cognitive balance might seem quite irrational to observers. For example, when a group member is confronted with an inconsistency in an expressed attitude, the response may be to not believe the person who made the assertion (a primitive level response style of denial). As a means of avoiding confronting unbalanced attitudes, a person may adopt dysfunctional behaviors such as verbally attacking other members and their ideas. *Defensiveness* is adopted as a response to a perceived threat to one's self, ideas, or attitudes. A person's defensive responses to others may be to become rigid *(certain)* in an attitude, to adopt an air of *superiority* over other members, and to attempt to take *control* of the group's discussion. A defensive person may simply withdraw from further patricipation (or act neutrally) in a group or adopt a variety of strategies to manipulate group members (Gibb, 1961).

Unfortunately, other group members may not understand the motives behind an individual's defensiveness. Assume that Mike perceives himself in a power struggle with Sue over group control. When Sue offers a rather innocuous suggestion about when the group should meet again, Sam adds his agreement. Mike curtly responds to Sam by asking, "Don't you think others ought to have a chance to decide?" Surprised and hurt by the challenge, Sam tells Mike to "Sit on it, wise guy!" Sam's defensive response is unfortunately a typical response to defensive behavior. Instead of analyzing possible reasons for Mike's behavior, the group may adopt a generalized climate of defensiveness. If we could step inside of Mike's head, we might find his perception of Sue's suggestion to be a threat to his own control of the group. Rather than confront the source of his tension (Sue), Mike becomes aggressive toward a less powerful person who is not central to the source of conflict. As seen in this example, a member who snaps a curt response or seems hostile to group operations may be harboring an internal conflict not easily recognized by other members.

Another defense mechanism in response to dissonance is to *project* one's own discomfort onto others. Assume in the above example that Mike has a strong positive self-image but also perceives himself as being relegated to a minor role in the group. In order to cope with the discomfort of his role failing to fit his self-image, Mike may conclude that he isn't performing well due to other group members not working up to their capabilities. In other words, he attributes his lack of status to the failures of other group members but not to his own actions. Another form of projection Mike could use would involve showing how his faults and weaknesses are similar to those of a high status group member. In this way he can conclude that his behavior isn't so bad since the higher status person also shares the weakness. In general, the greater the dissonance experienced, the more a person is likely to use projection as a method of reduction. For people who perceive themselves to have both good and bad qualities, recognition of a bad trait may not be as dissonant as it would be for a person with a strongly positive self-image.

In most cases defensive communication works against healthy group behavior. However, the concept of dissonance can be used to a group's advantage. Let us assume that most voluntary group members choose to join a group after weighing other courses of action (such as staying home to watch television). Quite often people do not have a strong positive attitude about joining a group. What would happen if membership was difficult to obtain? According to a classic study of individual responses to "severity of initiation" into a group, membership appeal may be enhanced by increasing admission requirements. Aronson and Mills (1959) studied female college students that were invited to join a group involved in discussing the psychology of sex. As a prerequisite to membership, they were asked to listen to a segment of the group's discussion. The taped discussion was designed to be as dull as possible. Each woman was then asked to read a series of obscene words to a male confederate as a test of willingness to participate. Severity of initiation into the group varied by the degree of obscenity to be read. In the severe condition, the females read twelve obscene words and two vivid descriptions of sexual activity. In the mild condition, they read five sexually related but nonobscene words. Results indicated that females who underwent a severe initiation perceived the group as being significantly more attractive than did those who received only mild initiation or none at all. A replication of the study by Gerard and Mathewson (1966) that used electric shocks as an initiation procedure produced similar results.

The Marine Corps and fraternities have virtually created a legend around their use of initiations. In essence, the theory holds that the more difficult it is to get into a group, the more appealing the group becomes. Approached from a slightly different perspective, the lower the reward for doing something undesirable, the more a person will rationalize the desirability of the act. Conversely, the higher the reward for engaging in undesirable behavior, the less attitude change can be expected (Cohen, 1960; Aronson, 1968). High reward, by adding compelling reasons for compliance, makes the act of compliance less a matter of one's own choice and reduces the need for attitude change.

Ideally, leaders and group organizers should create conditions in which members volunteer participation and involvement. Under those conditions, individuals will need to mentally justify their own actions. In contrast, if members perceive their actions as merely forced compliance, there may be less dissonance and subsequent attitude change. Aronson (1968) created a dull task and asked participants to tell others that the task was interesting. Part of the participants were paid for lying while the remainder were asked to merely comply. Those who were not paid to lie changed their attitudes in favor of the task's attractiveness while those who were paid did not alter their initial negative attitudes toward the task.

In answer to the original question of how attitude differences will affect group behavior, we may conclude that, to varying degrees, clashes will create a strain or need for resolution. How people respond to that need depends on their personal response styles and developmental differences. In general, when dissonance is experienced people will avoid or reduce the stress by: (1) seeking additional support for their own attitudes, (2) changing the attitude of others upholding opposing views,

(3) avoiding thinking about the dissonant relationship, (4) changing their own attitudes, (5) changing their attitude toward the source of a contrasting view (for instance, ceasing to like the individual or group), or (6) reducing the importance of the subject. If the imbalance cannot be reduced, removed, or in some way altered to the satisfaction of the individual, the strain or tension may hamper group integration.

HOW DO ATTITUDES AFFECT GROUP INTEGRATION?

The reason for devoting so much attention to explaining attitude development and change is that attitudes toward people with whom we work and socialize are powerful predictors of member and group behavior. Attitudes we hold toward group members, toward the group as an entity, and toward tasks on which a group is working may promote a sense of cohesion. Group cohesiveness is reflected in verbal and nonverbal messages by members. In the remainder of this chapter we will explore some of the ways group integration is facilitated or impeded through the attitude sets of group members.

Interpersonal Attraction Between Group Members

Recall from our discussion of personality and group membership that attraction between group members is usually thought of as a strong predictor of cohesiveness in a group. The basic elements of group cohesion viewed as attraction to a group were motivation, incentive, prediction of certain consequences, and comparison levels for group involvement. Not surprisingly, these elements were also found to be basic elements in the attraction of one person to another (Berscheid and Walster, 1969). Whether we are attracted to someone or not is determined by the attitude we develop toward that person. Berscheid and Walster observed that a current running through all of the research on attraction involves an attitudinal, positive or negative, reaction toward another person or persons. Interpersonal attractions are affective (emotional) attitudes we form about people; they are a consequence of our own attitudes and personalities and the behavior of others toward us.

These affective evaluations are also extended to a group after we become members. Davis (1969) notes that group attraction can be increased by a group's successful attainment of member goals. An interesting by-product of this is that, in groups with high member cohesiveness, group production can actually be diminished by a desire to maintain good interpersonal relationships. Expectations for cohesiveness between members can produce incorrect group decisions and interpersonally expedient, but low quality, products because of conflict avoidance.

The nature of interpersonal attraction between members can vary depending on the primary reasons for those affective evaluations. A well documented proposition about interpersonal attraction is that people are attracted to others with attitudes and beliefs perceived to be similar to their own. The "similarity breeds attraction" proposition has received much support from a variety of laboratory experiments and field studies (Newcomb, 1961; Byrne and Nelson, 1965; Byrne and Griffitt, 1966). Berscheid and Walster point out this may be a "cyclical" process. People tend to associate with others who reinforce their self-esteem, or sense of self-worth. Initial interactions allow people to determine whether they have similar attitudes and beliefs over and above those that brought them together.

In its most general form, attraction can be viewed as an exchange, or reciprocation, of liking or rewards between people. This is the essense of the exchange theory thesis presented by Homans (1961) and Thibaut and Kelley (1959). Although there may be some exceptions to this position, interpersonal attraction appears to depend on a similarity of attitudes and beliefs sufficient to make the attracted parties interested in maintaining a relationship.

Recall from our previous discussion of exchange theory that people have *Comparison Levels* against which they implicitly measure the extent of rewards and costs of interacting with others. Our attraction to someone will depend on how we assess the rewards and costs of interacting. An example of this could be found in a group of neighbors planning a joint effort to beautify their neighborhood. Mr. Richards may not have much in common with Mrs. Roberts, but they both find their common attitude toward the neighborhood program is sufficient to reward them for their interaction. Should they find their initial attitude toward the program helps them discover other commonalities, both Mr. Richards and Mrs. Roberts may develop a lasting friendship. While this example is oversimplified, there is evidence to suggest that most friendships start out this way. If you can remember a time when you moved into a new neighborhood and began to make friends, you may recall that a similar sequence of events took place between you and your new friends.

Status Agreement

The direction and strength of attitudes we hold toward other group members, and they toward us, form the basis of many important facets of group functioning. One of these facets involves how we perceive a member's *status* (influence or power) when compared to other members. *Status agreement,* or *status consensus*, reflects the extent of group agreement on the status of its members. It is a composite of how members rank each others' impact on the group.

These rankings evolve from perceptions and attitudes linked to each member's group behavior. They are seldom overt but are seen in the ways members respond differently to each other. A member who irregularly attends meetings and doesn't say much when present will not usually be accorded high status by other members. Someone who attends regularly, maintains a high level of participation, volunteers for projects, and generally encourages others to participate will usually be perceived as an influential force and accorded a higher status than some other members.

Making clearcut judgments about status is difficult. In fact, we are seldom aware of such judgments. Moreover, reasons for ranking a person lower or higher than someone else can be diverse and vary considerably from one group member to the next. Our judgments are often based on whether people agree with us on certain issues. Also, a clash of personal styles may lead to unfavorable evaluations.

The status a person attains as a group member is related to the person's *role* (sets of group responsibilities and individual social performances). Obviously, a person's status and group role(s) are highly related. They tend to evolve and stabilize together and, for many group settings, personal status and group roles are indistinguishable. Shepherd (1964) nicely summarizes the process of role development in the following way:

> Given similarity, high interaction, a cooperative atmosphere, and active communication, members of a group seek actively to influence each other. As their interaction increases, gradations of influence begin to emerge which, over time, lead to the development of agreement and to *role differentiation* [italics ours]. In such a group, influence attempts are high—the perception of similarity is tested and, when disagreement exists, a determinded effort to resolve it takes place (Shepherd, 1964, p. 65).

Slater (1955) conducted an interesting study on the effects of status consensus (agreement) and role development on group interaction. His investigation showed that small task oriented groups usually have three distinct types of roles performed by one or more group members, namely, a *task specialist,* a *social-emotional specialist* and a *participation*, or *ideational, specialist*. The social-emotional specialist is not frequently identified as having good ideas or high participation; this person expresses the most reactions, both positive and negative, to ideas. Task specialists, those people usually responsible for directing a group toward a decision, are seldom chosen as the most liked group member. Participation specialists are idea people. They maintain a relatively high and constant rate of giving opinions, suggestions or information. Quite often participation and task specialists are one in the same.

Status consensus has other consequences for behavior in a group. Slater's results indicate that in groups with high consensus (high agreement between group members on their ratings of each other), members with high ratings on task ability tend to be high on overall participation. The task specialist and ideational specialist is often the same person. Conversely, in groups with low consensus (low agreement between member ratings of each other) task ability and participation are not related and more than one person emerges to play each role. Moreover, in groups with high consensus, specialists tend to interact with each other more than in groups with low consensus.

Status agreement is a way of understanding collective attitudes of group members toward each other. This agreement is, to some extent, determined by the status members have in other groups. The *conferred* status a member receives because of other group memberships can influence attitudes members develop toward that person. These attitudes affect interpersonal attractions between group members and may distort the rankings members assign to each other. This could happen either by increasing or decreasing the status of a member, or affecting status agreements between members.

Communication Competencies

Social attitudes we bring to a group and those we develop about other members and group operations ultimately influence our communicative behavior. They affect our ability to function as competent social communicators. Bochner and Kelly (1974) list five skills associated with our competencies to engage in effective interpersonal communication: empathy, descriptiveness, owning feelings and thoughts, self-disclosure, and behavioral flexibility. Our ability to use these skills, assuming we have developed them to some degree, will depend upon our attitudes toward other members and the group as a social unit.

Empathic communication involves the ability to perceive how other people react to our communicative messages. Effectively employing our empathic skills requires that we accurately process feedback information others give us and, just as important, that we accurately predict how others might react to our messages. *Descriptiveness* relates to the clarity and concreteness of feedback responses we give others. Feedback messages obtain a high degree of descriptiveness when we focus on behaviors that are observable and verifiable (that is, behaviors that we can see and describe to others in ways that could be confirmed or denied). *Owning feelings and thoughts* means forming messages in ways that show we are responsible for our reactions. It means avoiding messages that accuse or blame others for our reactions. Expressions of feelings that are not "owned" are vague and indirect messages that shift the burden of responsibility for how we feel to the person or persons who elicited those feelings in us. *Self-disclosure* is the voluntary giving of personal information about oneself to another that the other person might not otherwise learn. Research by Jourard (1964, 1971) and Pearce and Sharp (1973) has shown that self-disclosing communication, as opposed to emotional detachment and an unwillingness to discuss feelings, can facilitate interpersonal relations between people. *Behavioral flexibility* is an individual's ability to adopt new ways of behaving in order to obtain desired goals. As our discussion of personality indicated, a person's behavioral tendencies may inhibit the capability to formulate new, adaptive behaviors. Attitudinal factors that positively value behavioral flexibility can be effective mechanisms for extending personality boundaries and assimilating new behaviors. This can be accomplished while maintaining integrity with conceptions of ourselves and behavioral tendencies we've built up over years of social experience.

REFERENCES

Aronson, E. 1968. Dissonance theory: Progress and problems. In *Theories of cognitive consistency*, eds. A. Abelson, et al., pp. 5–27. Skokie, Ill.: Rand McNally.

Aronson, E. and Mills, J. 1959. The effect of severity of initiation on liking for a group. *Journal of Abnormal and Social Psychology 59*, 177–181.

Berscheid, E. and Walster, E. 1969. *Interpersonal attraction*. Reading, Mass.: Addison-Wesley.

Bochner, A. and Kelly, C.W. 1974. Interpersonal competence: Rationale, philosophy, and implementation of a conceptual framework. *Speech Teacher 23*, 279–301.

Byrne, D. and Griffitt, W. 1966. A developmental investigation of the law of attraction. *Journal of Personality and Social Psychology 4*, 699–703.

Byrne, D. and Nelson, D. 1965. Attraction as a linear function of proportion of positive reinforcements. *Journal of Personality and Social Psychology 1*, 659–663.

Cohen, A.R. 1960. Attitudinal consequences of induced descrepancies between cognitions and behavior. *Public Opinion Quarterly 24*, 297–318.

Davis, J.H. 1969. *Group performance*. Reading, Mass.: Addison-Wesley.

Festinger, L. 1957. *A theory of cognitive dissonance*. Evanston, Ill.: Row-Peterson.

Festinger, L. 1964. *Conflict, decision and dissonance.* Palo Alto, Calif.: Stanford University Press.

Gerard, H.B. and Mathewson, G.D. 1966. The effects of severity of initiation on liking for a group: A replication. *Journal of Experimental and Social Psychology 2,* 278–289.

Gibb, J.R. 1961. Defensive communication. *Journal of Communication 11,* 141–148.

Heider, F. 1958. *The psychology of interpersonal relations.* New York: John Wiley.

Homans, G.C. 1961. *Social behavior: Its elementary forms.* New York: Harcourt Brace Jovanovich.

Jourard, S. 1964. *The transparent self.* New York: Van Nostrand Rinehold.

Jourard, S. 1971. *Self-disclosure: An experimental analysis of the transparent self.* New York: John Wiley.

Kaplan, B. and Crockett, W. Developmental analyses of modes of resolution. In *Theories of cognitive consistency,* eds. A. Abelson, et al., pp. 661–669. Skokie, Ill.: Rand McNally, 1968.

Katz, D. 1960. The functional approach to the study of attitudes. *Public Opinion Quarterly 24,* 163–204.

Kiesler, C., Collins, B. and Miller, N. 1969. *Attitude change.* New York: John Wiley.

Lindesmith, A.P. and Strauss, A.L. 1969. *Social psychology.* 3rd ed. New York: Holt, Rinehart, & Winston.

Mabry, E.A. 1976. Female/male interaction in unstructured small group settings. Unpublished paper presented at the Speech Communication Association Convention, Interpersonal and Small Group Interaction Division, San Francisco, Calif., December, 1976.

Maccoby, E. and Jacklin, C. 1974. *The psychology of sex differences.* Palo Alto, Calif.: Stanford University Press.

Newcomb, T.M. 1956. The prediction of interpersonal attraction. *American Psychologist 11,* 575–586.

Newcomb, T.M. 1961. *The acquaintance process.* New York: Holt, Rinehart & Winston.

Newcomb, T.M. 1968. Interpersonal balance. In *Theories of cognitive consistency,* eds. A. Abelson, et al., pp. 28–51. Skokie, Ill.: Rand McNally.

Osgood, C.E. and Tannenbaum, P.H. 1955. The principle of congruity in the prediction of attitude change. *Psychological Review 62,* 42–55.

Pearce, W.B. and Sharp, S.M. 1973. Self-disclosing communication. *Journal of Communication 23,* 409–425.

Pilisuk, M. 1968. Depth, Centrality, and tolerance in cognitive consistency. In *Theories of cognitive consistency,* eds. A. Abelson, et al., pp. 693–699. Skokie, Ill.: Rand McNally.

Sales Management. 1966. The pursuit of excellence. 18, March, 81–98.

Schachter, S. 1951. Deviation, rejection and communication. *Journal of Abnormal and Social Psychology 46,* 190–207.

Shepherd, C. 1964. *Small groups: Some sociological perspectives.* San Francisco: Chandler.

Previous chapters have dealt specifically with the influence of personal characteristics on interaction between group members. The *person* in a group setting is a known factor influencing what a group does in relation to its goals. The job, or *task,* a group works on is both a source of group goals and a stimulus for individual participation. Groups do perform tasks—though members may not view group activities as "tasks" *per se.* For example, a group of friends trying to decide whether to go dancing or to a movie have a distinct task that structures their interaction for a period of time. A group of managers that must decide how to implement a new accounting procedure in their offices is not significantly different from the group of friends attempting to decide on a recreational activity. Both groups are *decision making* groups in terms of their task demands at that point in time. The groups' goals, although dissimilar in specific content, are quite similar in other respects. This chapter will explore some of the properties of group tasks and the social settings where they exist. Some of the issues we will address include the kinds of tasks groups work on, environmental

4 group tasks and the work environment

effects on group task completion, and how group members can be matched to group tasks.

WHAT IS THE TASK A GROUP MUST COMPLETE?

As our examples above demonstrate, groups exist for different reasons but often engage in similar kinds of activities. It is important to understand that group goals and group tasks are related. By this we mean the objectives for group membership that keep a group together (maintain cohesiveness between members) help the group define relevant tasks and, conversely, the tasks a group works on help to reinforce and fulfill group goals. In this section we will describe some relevant dimensions of group tasks, constraints placed on task completion by a group, and methods for group organization that provide systematic means of completing certain types of group tasks.

Task Dimensions Relevant to Group Work

Quite often texts such as this one will discuss group tasks in terms of the outcomes which follow task completion. A task might be viewed as a "problem solving task" which assumes that the objective of the group is to "solve a problem." Other tasks may be labeled "decision making tasks" and imply a group must select one course of action from a set of alternatives. Some groups are involved in "production tasks" such as those of factory assembly lines. Finally, we might consider a "therapeutic task" which could be found in a psychotherapy group.

The difficulty with this method of task identification is it says more about group goals than it does about the properties of a task. A second problem is the danger of confusing various interactive processes in a group with the supposed nature of its task. A practicing group psychotherapist, for example, would readily agree that "problem solving" and "decision making" are integral parts of group psychotherapy. For these reasons, we will discuss group tasks in terms of specific evaluative properties without reference to what a group is supposed to be doing. As we proceed, we will point out how some of these *task qua task* properties relate to group goals and are affected by them.

Shaw (1963) has analyzed the properties of over one hundred group tasks used in laboratory experiments to simulate group work. Through a review of research and theory, Shaw arrived at a set of dimensions which he believed to represent the range of characteristics of these tasks. Using some rather sophisticated statistical analyses, Shaw derived four "factors" or dimensions to evaluate the tasks reviewed. These dimensions are *difficulty, solution multiplicity, cooperative requirements,* and *population familiarity.* Let's consider each of these dimensions separately.

Difficulty. Task difficulty relates to the amount of difficulty a group encounters while trying to complete a task. This is probably the most straightforward of the four dimensions. We should keep in mind that "difficulty" rests in the eye of the beholder. Solving a problem related to the information routing of a large corporation might appear to be unmanageable to some people while to others it would be routine. The fact that some people perceive a task as "too difficult for me to handle" and others view it as "too simple for someone of my talents" will affect motivation to participate in task completion. Some people may not be adequately prepared to deal with certain tasks (thereby viewing them as too difficult) and will be ineffective participants for that reason.

Solution multiplicity. A second facet of group tasks is the number of possible alternatives open to the group for reaching a solution, and the extent to which a solution can be tested for correctness or appropriateness. Another way of saying this is to ask how "complex" the solution to the task will be. The complexity or *solution multiplicity* of a task may determine such things as: (1) how long a group takes to complete a task, (2) prerequisites for skills or abilities group members must possess (for example, creativity or intelligence), and (3) necessary member attributes (such as tolerance for ambiguity).

As opposed to the difficulty dimension, solution multiplicity is somewhat less in the eye of the beholder. Consider, for example, the differences between a task that requires a rational process of decision making for selecting between alternative actions (terminating an employee on the basis of performance records), versus a task that requires a group to make a decision based upon criteria that it is also required to generate and to defend (developing and applying a workable definition of something called "adequate performance" for an occupational position). Both tasks require the groups to make a decision, but the task assigned to the former group is clearly spelled out and more easily testable than the task assigned to the latter group.

Cooperative requirements. There is an old saying that observes, "a camel is a horse put together by a committee." There may be some truth to this observation; the requirements of cooperative interaction for effective task completion may have a lot to do with such an outcome (in other words, maybe the assembly of a horse is better left to one person). The issue of individual versus group effectiveness has been summarized by Shaw, who states:

Groups are more effective than individuals on tasks which require a variety of information, which can be solved by adding individual contributions, and which require a number of steps that must be correctly completed in a definite order; individuals are better on tasks that call for centralized organization of parts. Groups perform better than individuals when the process is learning or problem solving, but not necessarily when the process investigated is judgment (Shaw, 1971, p. 71).

Beyond this consideration is the fact that some tasks assigned to groups in larger organizational settings require members to share task responsibilities equally and to reach a group consensus (unanimous decision). More importantly, such tasks may bind group members because they represent different units of an organization that will have to join together and "live" with the group's task outcomes.

Population familiarity. Similar to the dimension of difficulty, population familiarity represents a simple aspect of group tasks—the extent to which group members have worked upon similar types of tasks before or possess information essential for task completion. Both common sense and systematic investigation show that group members with some experience at working upon certain tasks will perform more effectively than inexperienced members. We can extend this information to groups as a whole and generalize that groups with experienced members, other things held constant, will perform more effectively as groups than groups composed of inexperienced members (Davis, 1969; Shaw, 1971).

Group Constraints on Task Completion

Not only do tasks place restrictions on the behavior of group members, but group members place restrictions on themselves. Constraints are formed by the ways members view a task and view each other. A group might, for example, work on a task with high population familiarity like those found in weekly management staff meetings or even assembly line factory work. Such a group will, over a period of time, develop *norms* that regulate how group members should act in relation to its tasks. Norms are not explicit written codes of behavior; instead, norms develop over time as group members accumulate experience working with each other. This "collective experience" leads to mutually shared perceptions about group members and tasks. In a management group, for example, a norm might stipulate that members will treat group sessions as "bull sessions" where stated objectives for the group are not fulfilled. This might occur because some members do not like the idea of the sessions in the first place, no effective leadership is imposed on or emerges from group interaction, or the group has experienced failures in the outcomes of previous meetings, which have decreased member interest.

Prevailing norms adopted by group members exert great control over individual activity. In early experiments on the impact of group norms, Sherif (1936) demonstrated that a group of people will use some type of reference point, or standard, to make decisions. Without any direct communication between group members, these individual reference points for making a decision converge, become similar, for group members. A later experiment by Asch (1956), designed to better understand how and why people conform or deviate from group norms, demonstrated that most people will accept the inaccurate judgment of other group members and will change their own judgments when they perceive other members' judgments as representing a group norm. A field study of adolescent peer groups by Sherif and Sherif (1964) also showed that group members adopt a set of perspectives about appropriate group behavior and enforce the demands implicit in these perspectives to control each member's personal behavior.

Group norms come about as the result of interaction between members. Norms form constraints on each person's behavior while in the group and prescribe attitudes or actions considered appropriate as a group member even when the member is not with other members. Norms can motivate members to achieve group goals for task productivity or other forms of social behavior (how members will act to gain approval from peers, for example).

The ways a group controls the behavior of its members can be found in the exchange of positive or negative feedback. Negative feedback can appear in a variety of forms. Verbal messages with subtle innuendos may spell out the displeasure of others toward a deviant member (making a person the brunt of jokes or labeling the person with an undesirable nickname). Nonverbal messages may include such behaviors as negative facial expressions, stares, and "silencing strategies" (Zuk, 1965) designed to pressure a deviant member into changing inappropriate behavior (for example, not talking to the person or excluding the person from conversations on topics of obvious interest).

The evidence on group norms is convincing and has been documented with respect to their influence on group productivity in factory work groups. In a classic study of productivity at a Western Electric plant, researchers tried to determine whether monetary rewards could be used to induce faster work on an electrical piecework assembly task. Despite an apparent ability to work faster and the promise of increased pay, workers maintained the same general level of output. Close investigation of workers' interactions determined that those workers who deviated from group defined acceptable levels of output were labeled "chislers" (cheating the company) or "rate busters" (pressuring other workers to produce more). The Employees willing to accept the embarrassment associated with such labels were also punished for defiance by a practice called "binging," an occasional sharp blow to the shoulder given by a co-worker. Not only did the blow physically punish the person, but it also served as a sign for other workers to aid in bringing the deviant into conformity with norms for the work group (Roethlisberger and Dickson, 1939).

How group members perceive norms will determine how they behave in a group and, in turn, how they will be viewed by other members, and what kind of feedback their behavior will generate. Groups that develop nonproductive norms are not easily changed, especially by the actions of individual members. Norm changes, or group behavioral changes, are brought about gradually. They require a long process of small sequential changes of reference points (assumed standards for group behavior) used in the process of building conformity to a group. A norm is changed through a series of persuasive attempts to shift the ways members evaluate other members and the group as a social entity.

Organizing the Group for Work

One of the most frequent questions that arises among members is, "How do we get this group to accomplish something?" There are many ways to start a group on a course of action that will help it become effective and productive. We will consider four methods of approaching group tasks. These are the "reflective thinking" method, the Program Evaluation and Review Technique (PERT), the Nominal Group Technique, and the "behavioral contract" approach. Each method is useful in some group settings and has both advantages and disadvantages associated with its use.

An underlying assumption about many systematic methods of organizing group activities is that there is an analogy between human thought processes and efficient group work. The earliest of the popular approaches was originated by Dewey (1933) and is called "reflective thinking." The reflective thinking method assumes that human thought on intellectual problems begins with some perceived ambiguity, proceeds to clarification and definition stages, is followed by generating probable resolutions to the ambiguity, moves to a choice of alternatives stage, and ends with a testing stage, which determines whether the chosen alternative indeed resolves the ambiguity.

Dewey assumed this process to be the logical sequence of human thought. Whether this process accurately models the process of human thought is not too important. It is important that the basic elements of this model have been incorporated into a number of methods for organizing group activities which are assumed to be "rational" methods of work organization for abstract tasks. Bormann (1969) has labeled this orientation to rational thinking in groups as the "assumption of rationality." He is quick to point out there is no particular reason to believe that effective group work is "rational" nor that a particular model of human thinking can presume rationality.

A more concise representation of human thought based on scientific finding has been constructed by Bourne and Battig (1966). They propose human thinking is a multistage process which includes: (1) *conceptualization* of an issue; the reception and organization of necessary information from within the individual or from outside sources, (2) a process of *problem solving* that consists of using conceptualizations to form alternative courses of action (or answers), and (3) a final *decision making* phase where an alternative from the problem solving stage is selected and used. The three-stage sequence proposed by Bourne and Battig is not a statement of assumed rational behavior. It is an assessment of research information about learning and decision making which points to these stages as important connecting links in a chain of complex cognitive (thought) processes associated with human reasoning.

Reflective thinking pattern. The most well-known methods of rational organization of group work on abstract tasks (usually called problem solving or decision making tasks) are adaptations of the Dewey model (Gulley, 1968; Harnack and Fest, 1964). In the case of a "problem solving" discussion, the following organizational pattern is usually suggested: (1) defining key terms on issues and narrowing the problem to a manageable scope, (2) analyzing the major aspects of the problem, including collecting relevant information, (3) generating a list of possible solutions, subject to the constraint that each solution conform to certain predetermined standards of appropriateness and practicality, (4) selecting the most desirable solution, and (5) assessing a selected alternative's validity.

The advantages of using a reflective thinking pattern, or some variation thereof, in group discussions are not totally clear. Brilhart and Jochem (1964) demonstrated that groups trained in using a problem solving pattern produce higher quality solutions than groups without such training. However, there is information to suggest that knowledge of a rational discussion organization format does not guarantee its use. Fisher (1970) has shown, using groups familiar with the methods of rationality in discussions, that the sequential process of decision emergence greatly differs from reflective thinking patterns. Disconfirming evidence of another sort was presented in a study by Bayless (1967) that compared different types of rational models. On the other hand, Maier (1953) found that discussion leaders trained in conducting group meetings (including organizational methods like reflective thinking) had more productive groups and were usually rated superior to nontrained leaders. Hence, research does not produce unequivocal evidence supporting or disconfirming the utility of reflective thinking models in groups. But it does unequivocally support the advantage of some sort of rational decision making agenda.

Program evaluation and review technique. A second, more recently developed, type of rational method has gained support. The Program Evaluation and Review Technique (PERT) was designed from computer based models for conducting evaluations of existing or proposed action programs. In contrast to the process of reflective thinking methods, PERT begins with the established goal of a group and successively works backward to determine the various activities, resources and activity/resource allocations necessary for reaching the goal.

Operational procedures for PERT are as follows: (1) state desired outcomes (goals, actions, and so on) for the group, (2) specify the group operations necessary to reach the goal(s), (3) assign an operating sequence to each operation, noting where each fits in relation to the final outcome, (4) estimate the amount of time for each ranked operation, (5) separate each operation into a distinct "subsystem" and operationalize it using procedures 1 to 4 above, (6) assign action priorities to the sequentially ordered operations, and (7) allocate available resources, by priority, to each operation.

The usefulness of a PERT-type method has been investigated by Bayless (1967). He compared groups using traditional reflective thinking methods, modified PERT methods, and a method of solution generating called "brainstorming." Brainstorming is a technique designed to promote creativity in groups. It is most commonly used as a method of generating ideas. The group allots a certain amount of time during which members are able to spontaneously give as many ideas as possible. All ideas are recorded for subsequent review. The only rule for conducting brainstorming activities is that ideas cannot be criticized when they are given. This, it is assumed, will provide a freer climate for creative action. Bayless' results tended to favor the PERT method for quality of group solutions but not on other factors, such as speed of solutions.

We should point out that PERT methods may have limited applicability depending on the nature of a task. In tasks where solution multiplicity is high (that is, where there is a variety of possible goals or solutions and a group has not settled on one), a PERT method will not function well until *after* a goal is specified. If the primary goal of a group is to make a decision based upon a number of possible alternatives, a PERT method will not be adequate for decision making about the selection of an alternative. Should the goal of the task group be to evaluate a decision (such as the impact of a planned freeway) then a PERT method would be very useful.

Nominal group technique. In contrast to the two methods already reviewed, the Nominal Group Technique (Van deVen and Delbecq, 1971, 1974) is designed to structure interaction in a group *and* to produce group solutions to abstract problems. Initially, participation is structured by having each member write down as many problems or solutions as possible. In a round-robin, nonevaluative session, each member contributes one idea to a list posted for all group members to view. It is important that each member contribute only one idea on each round. Whenever all of an individual's ideas have been presented the person can "pass" but is permitted to re-enter on subsequent rounds if another member's contribution triggers a new idea. This particular phase is similar to brainstorming because the purpose is to generate as many ideas as possible without evaluation. Unlike brainstorming, the amount of participation is controlled to assure input from all members.

The next phase is discussion and clarification of contributions. A predetermined time limit is established for discussing each item in order to avoid the common tendency to spend too much time on initial items and too little time on later items. The discussion leader makes an effort to separate items from their original contributors so that they can be evaluated objectively and not according to their contributors' status.

A third phase involves rank ordering the three to five best items. Each group member writes on slips of paper the item number and rank of the most significant contributions. All slips are collected and rankings for each item are posted beside the list appearing on the board. The most frequently identified items become agenda items for subsequent discussion. A final vote is taken with each member writing the top choice on a slip of paper which is collected and tallied. Written votes are solicited rather than the usual voice or hand vote as a means of controlling, once again, the influence of high status and/or dominant members.

Nominal Group Technique is based upon the Delphi system developed by the Rand Corporation (Dalkey, 1968). While a relatively new problem solving technique, it has been shown to enhance the productivity of groups (Penley, 1975). By controlling for personality and status differences, a nominal group format somewhat assures that the group's best ideas will emerge. This point is predicated upon the assumption that all group members have similar input potential. Substantial consideration must be devoted to selecting group members. Another assumption is that a chosen task actually warrants the amount of time expended on the process. The quickest problem solving technique is for one person to make a decision. As additional input is added, the decision making process slows down. A third limitation could be based upon a consideration of personality needs such as those discussed in the previous chapter. Members with high needs to control and influence others will inevitably be less satisfied with a technique that assures greater spread of participation and lessens opportunities for dominance. Nevertheless, nominal group technique can be particularly useful for certain tasks in some settings.

Behavioral contract approach. The use of behavioral contracts in group work developed in human relations groups using encounter or sensitivity training models of personal learning and self-awareness. Unlike many other types of small groups, human relations groups usually combine individual and group goals into a reciprocal, even symbiotic, relationship. The success of these groups is usually determined by how well all individual goals are satisfied. Given the immense complexity and potential ambiguity surrounding such groups, one method for providing initial group structure and a starting point for stimulating work on personal objectives is to establish "contract" groups (Egan, 1970).

Contract groups aim to develop personal insight into interpersonal behavior and interpersonal relationships for individual members. Insights are stimulated through the use of an ongoing group culture that reinforces exchanges of valid feedback between members. Individual contracts are established between group members and the group regarding learning oriented objectives each member values relevant and desires group membership to help accomplish. Contracts specify facets of interpersonal relations an individual wants to deal with as a group member and the method(s) to be used. Inherent within each contract is an understanding that the individual will work to achieve personal goals and facilitate achievement of other group members' goals. Sometimes contracts are made with the group leader, or facilitator, in advance as a condition of entrance into the group.

Behavioral contracts such as those described in the encounter context are useful in that they help orient the individual to personal learning objectives. Goldstein and Sies (1974) have suggested the use of communication contracts in a wide range of interpersonal relationships. Some couples have even elected to write a contract for their marriage relationship in which the rights and responsibilities of each partner are clearly specified and contractually agreed upon. Therefore, an additional advantage of a behavioral contract is that it can make group role relationships explicit rather than ambiguously implied. By their very nature, behavioral contracts have limited application to most group settings. However, behavioral contracts may be useful in specific situations where group task performance is subdivided into a division of labor. In that context, behavioral contracts would delineate expected role behaviors and the rewards or punishments associated with role performance.

Our discussion of group methods for organizing task performance has shown relationships between task elements and methods for coping with task demands. We have not mentioned methodologies relating to tasks that are highly structured (that is, those with low solution multiplicity and few cooperative requirements). Additionally, the methods discussed incorporate the three sequential phases of human thought that were discussed earlier—conceptualization, problem solving and decision making. This is not accidental. It illustrates how this process occurs in a variety of methods purporting to represent efficient group action.

DOES THE ENVIRONMENT HAVE AN EFFECT ON GROUP WORK?

In the previous section, we discussed relevant dimensions of group tasks, limitations to task completion, and methods by which groups can organize their task work. We now move to an examination of task *environments*, human and physical, that can influence the outcomes of task activities in small groups. The discussion will examine the productivity of groups (the intended outcomes of group task involvement) as it is influenced by environmental factors. The three major areas to be covered are (1) group productivity as it relates to task settings, (2) how larger systems of which groups are a part influence group productivity, and (3) effects of environmental changes on group output.

Task Settings and Group Production

Historically, the study of individual productivity in various social contexts was the springboard for the study of group productivity. These investigations took one of three forms: *nominal interaction, participatory noninteraction* and *participatory cointeraction*. Studies of nominal interaction examined the influence of individual productivity when a person was subject to observation (but not evaluation). Typical of this research about "audience" effects on individual productivity was an early study by Travis (1925). He demonstrated that performance on a manual dexterity task increased when individuals familiar with the task performed in front of a group of observers as opposed to only the investigator.

Investigation of *participatory noninteraction*, often labeled "coaction," involved assessing how a person's individual performance was influenced by working with a group of people who were also working on the task. This line of investigation resulted in the "social facilitation" theory, developed by Zajonc (1965). Research on social facilitation processes has demcnstrated that working on tasks that require previously learned behaviors in the presence of others tends to increase productivity. On the other hand, when a task requires learning new behaviors, or working with behavior that is newly acquired or in the process of being acquired, productivity tends to decrease when working in the presence of others engaged in the same task.

A *participatory cointeraction* setting is the one we ordinarily associate with everyday group activities. The work of groups ranging from legislative committees to church social committees involves participation between members (cointeraction) to arrive at group decisions and solutions to problems. In this social context we can more realistically examine the effects of human and physical factors on small groups. Probably the most influential human element involved in small group productivity is the collective orientation toward a task that develops among group members. These collective orientations are translated into group norms that act as behavioral standards.

Group norms have two central implications for a group. First, they present a collective image of optimal behavior for group members. Second, they implicitly specify the limits of permissible deviations from optimal group behavior. Group norms perform both *integrative* and *informational* functions for an individual. Kiesler and Kiesler (1969, p. 33) provide a brief summary of the motivational responses to group norms:

Integrative Functions

1. The other group members will accept and like him, or will not reject him.

2. The group goal will be successfully attained.

3. The continuation of the group will be ensured.

Informational Functions

1. Gaining "correct" information about reality.

2. Validating one's own opinions and making sure they are consistent with the opinions of others.

3. Evaluating oneself and others.

Not only do group norms prescribe appropriate behavior for group members but they also are attached to specific group roles that members fulfill. Role behaviors are governed by the expectations that the group sets for each member's task performance and social-emotional participation.

Norms influence both the method and outcome of task related and social-emotional interaction. A summary of research results on group risk taking given by Davis (1969) suggests that group choices of "risky" or "cautious" decisions are influenced by (1) a combination of individual perceptions of group expectations, and (2) the values individual members hold toward risk or caution. Reviewing investigations of industrial productivity, Olmstead (1959) noted that social norms in work groups (both noninteractive and cointeractive) can have greater salience than direct monetary rewards.

Although social-psychological factors like norms and defined social roles have a great impact on groups, the "social ecology" of a group is also quite important. Social-ecological features of groups relate to group size, distance and space available for group use, and sources of contact bewteen group members.

The size of a small group may have a variety of effects on group members. In an early study of verbal participation in small groups, Bales, et al. (1951) found that interaction rates decreased as group size increased when frequencies of interaction were averaged across all participants. Moreover, as group size increases so do the chances that a group will be dominated by the participation of only a few members. A study of decision making accuracy and group size indicated decision making accuracy increases as groups get larger, but the *rate* of increased accuracy *diminishes* as size increases (Lorge and Soloman, 1955). A study by Gibb (1951) relating problem solving to group size found a negative relationship between increases in problem solving ability and group size; the number of solutions provided increased, but at a slower rate, as group size increased. Gibb also observed that group members felt more inhibited as the size of the group increased.

Given that larger groups result in increased inhibitions and decreased participation, it is not surprising researchers have found member satisfaction in churches, industry, schools, and other organizational groups decreases as group size increases. Research reviewed by Porter and Lawler (1965) showed that as organizational size increased there was a decrease in job satisfaction reflected in increased absenteeism, employee turnover, and labor disputes. Students almost inevitably report liking small seminar classes better than large lecture classes.

One limitation to the size-satisfaction relationship is that if power increases with increased size then members of larger groups may experience greater satisfaction. In the League of Women Voters, for example, larger local chapters are given greater voice in the national organization. Typically, increased power and influence compensates for lower individual member participation. This is particularly true if a large group can subdivide into smaller groups to facilitate increased individual involvement.

Organizations trying to compensate for their size by forming smaller task groups have experienced at least two problems. Members of sub-groups may perceive their group as too small to achieve assigned tasks or may feel the smallness of a group gives them too much exposure. Reticent communicators may decrease interaction in large groups but may also reduce contributions in groups of two or three members because they perceive too much attention being directed to their behavior. A second limitation emerges when members perceive a group will have little or no impact upon a larger organization. Such groups regard their tasks as "busy work" or resent what they interpret to be an obvious attempt to manipulate their involvement in the organization.

Another factor associated with increased group size is decreased cohesion (Gouran, 1969). The rationale behind this idea is that too many *individuals* can get "lost in the crowd." Because of decreased attention to individual behaviors, normative reinforcement is weakened and members are able to significantly deviate from group expectations. As individuals find deviance is not punished or recognized by the group, they may conclude the group no longer holds an appeal or interest. When several members perceive their impact holds no significance for a group, the overall group system may be less cohesive. Following this line of reasoning, larger groups may also be more conservative on issues and less prone to task accomplishment due to a splintering of member opinions (Cartwright and Zander, 1968). Small groups run the risk of developing "group think" behaviors because of strict normative enforcement of deviant actions or thoughts and high cohesion. By contrast, larger groups may also permit so much independent thinking that only the most compromised positions can gain final approval from all members.

Closely related to the size of a group is the amount of available distance and space a group can use. According to Hall (1959), human beings are culturally accustomed to a minimum amount of distance in their day-to-day routines and ordinarily need from two-and-a-half to four feet of available space to call their own. A group setting may not afford the minimum space but there is insufficient evidence to suggest just exactly what effects reduced space has on a group. To a great extent, spatial effects may depend upon prevailing interpersonal or task climates (competitive, cooperative or coactive, for example) that a group develops. Sommer (1967) has shown that relationships between dyad partners and role-status relations (leader-member for example) create different spatial use patterns. There is a tendency for dyad partners working on a cooperative task to choose closer distances for interaction than partners working on a competitive task, although research by Mabry and Kaufman (1973) has shown this behavior is strongly influenced by sex and attractiveness of the dyadic partner. As for leadership and spatial behavior, Sommer's research indicates group members take their cues for seating distance from group leaders. Members project where a leader may sit and then choose seating positions consistent with their desires for group domination. Generally, group leaders are accorded more distance than other group members—either in terms of open seats between leader and members or seat adjustments for distance—and are generally expected to take prominent or visible seats (such as head of table or center seats).

The size of a group and distance between group members is also related to modes of interpersonal contact between group members. The most frequent form of behavior associated with gaining and maintaining interpersonal contact is *eye contact*. Extensive research on "visual interaction" by Argyle (1969) and eye behavior in relation to facial expression by Ekman, Freisen, and Ellsworth (1972) indicates that: (1) eye contact is the principle behavior referred to when determining who will talk in a group, (2) *duration* of direct eye contact is used in understanding the nature of interpersonal relations between group members, such that the shorter the duration the more task oriented group members are likely to be, (3) eye contact is also influenced by distance in that strangers are less likely to maintain visual interaction for more than a brief time when sitting close together, (4) eyes provide considerable information at times of extreme emotional displays like anger or happiness, and (5) visual interaction is more likely to be maintained in situations where people are attracted to each other, even though the normal visual interaction distance is decreased.

The direction of visual contact is itself an influential factor. Steinzor (1950) found that in groups of nine to twelve members, verbal participation usually involves members farther away from, and in more direct eye contact with each other. Picture a group of people seated in a circle; members separated by the greatest distance are also in the most direct visual contact. This phenomenon, called the "Steinzor effect," has been found to vary with the type of group leadership. Domineering or autocratic leaders produce more "side conversations" because their behavior discourages cross-group interaction. More democratic leaders, who encourage group discussion, increase the probability that a Steinzor effect will surface (Hearn, 1957).

Organizational Climate and Group Productivity

Understanding the role of small groups in large social organizations is not easy unless you have a method for visualizing relationships between groups in larger social contexts. The systems theory orientation of our discussion of group-systems provides a useful perspective for understanding large social organizations composed of many small groups. Vardaman and Halterman (1968) argue, for example, that organizational management is most appropriately viewed as a problem of information control and decision making which simultaneously influences the various unit-groups of an organization. Units in an organization depend upon the flow of information between them; in other words, each unit-group depends upon other groups for information.

Information channels link groups together and form task-related bonds between them. They are equally necessary for transmission of information about how groups perceive each other's influence and usefulness. Therefore, communication channels between groups form a kind of *structure* that evolves from functional requirements for interaction between unit-groups (called the *formal structure*). Such networks are equally involved in the creation of alternative structures based upon perceptions each unit holds for other units. These kinds of networks are referred to as *informal structures*.

The intragroup processes we are studying are also applicable for understanding intergroup relationships. The formal structure of a group defines at a public level how sub-unit-groups in the larger organization are supposed to interact with each other. By contrast, the informal structure of an organizational system emerges as norms and roles develop through interaction between sub-unit-groups (or people within each unit-group) or are created by social-psychological pressures to comply with demands for interacting within the formal structure. Communication along informal networks helps relieve the tension of playing a rigidly prescribed "occupational role." Thus, while all members of an organization are part of the "team," one frequently hears about the no good so-and-so's in other departments that are always responsible for "our" department having problems.

The nature of communication along information channels may be measured to assess the *climate* of an organization. By "nature" of communication we mean the ways people react to their communicative contacts with others, or the interpersonal relationships which develop from daily contact. The idea of a *communication climate* actually encompasses a number of complex processes related to human interaction. The communication climate of an organization is best understood by assessing the satisfaction individuals, sub-unit-groups, and unit-groups gain from their interaction in the organization. This satisfaction, in turn, results in the amount of motivational energy available to the organization.

Weick (1969) proposed a model of human organizing processes that helps to define the elements of communication climates. His model is based upon a systems theory perspective of how information is simultaneously created and used in large groups. Weick begins with the premise that all groups face some amount of *equivocality* (or uncertainty) in relation to their existence as groups or organizational units. Groups develop "collective structures" from their interaction experiences which help them resolve equivocality. Stated another way, groups develop norms and roles that define group behavior. The collective structure of a group is constantly changing (small increments at a time) as the experience of past interactions is processed, evaluated, and applied to group projections of new uncertainties that might have to be faced.

The basic sequence of activity Weick proposes is *enactment-selection-retention*. These three phases of group or member actions are related to reducing uncertainty within a system. The enactment phase refers to those instances where people, whether in groups or as individuals, attach meaning to the things they do.

According to Alfred Schutz (1967), behaviors (acts) can only be interpreted in *retrospect*—in the past tense, so to speak. Hence, assigning meanings to behaviors is a retrospective process. In fact, Schutz asserts that how we will behave tomorrow, in some instances, is merely a *projection* based on our retrospective accounts of how and why we think we behaved already. You might, for example, have supported an idea your supervisor had about changing some work procedures. Later, you asked for an opportunity to leave work early and received approval for the request. Your account of these happenings might go like this: "I agreed with Grindstone about something and later got off work early because I was agreeable." Now, if someone were to ask whether you could get off from work early tomorrow, you might say: "I'll look for some way to make Grindstone's dumb ideas look good and then ask to get off early." The first account is based on assembling observations of acts which led to other acts. The second (projected) account, what you will do in a future interaction (tomorrow), is based on the proposition that what worked before will work again. This is precisely how we set about assessing the relative amount of certainty (or uncertainty) present in a given situation. At any point in time behavior has meaning only to the extent that it can be reaccounted and interpreted in light of present circumstances.

As used in Weick's model, the enactment phase is a point where sequences of *acts* are reaccounted (meaningfully interpreted) to yield some tentative statement about the amount of equivocality (informational uncertainty) which exists in the organizational system at that time. The *selection phase* applies a set of rules for processing equivocality that was interpreted in the enactment phase. Note, the enactment phase eliminates a certain amount of equivocality by the very nature of putting prior acts into an interpretive perspective. The set of rules for processing equivocal information varies in relation to the amount of equivocality that exists. In general, effective information processing requires that an organization have sufficient rules to cover potential equivocality (that is, to sort out ambiguous messages) and be able to successfully apply those rules enough times to eliminate the equivocality. The final activity is a *retention phase* which stores the resultant *unequivocal* information derived from enactment and selection phases. This retained information is then retrievable for use in constructing new rules for resolving other equivocal units of information.

The communication climate of an organization may, therefore, be assessed in terms of its information processing capabilities. Since organizational climate and communication climate are, for all practical purposes, the same thing, productivity relies upon the ways information is processed at all levels in the organization: individual, group, multigroup unit, and in the organization as a whole. Weick proposes that individual productivity is tied to the ability of a worker to reduce equivocality in the environment (as that environment is uniquely defined by the person). He speculates that productivity, and therefore satisfaction, is directly related to the amount of equivocal information a person can reduce in relation to the instrumental task(s) performed. Simply stated productivity and satisfaction should increase as equivocality decreases. Although group task accomplishment is considerably more complex than that of an individual, the same generalization should hold true for groups.

Productivity and Changes in the Work Environment

The foregoing discussion of organizations as information processing systems has implications for approaching the difficult question of how productivity can be affected by changes in the work environment. The most difficult problem to overcome in this "environment-productivity differential" is that an "environment" is in the eye of the beholder. Environmental changes must, in effect, come from those people who *enact* the environment—from the workers themselves. Where work is accomplished by task groups or teams, problems of effective change are even more complex. At a minimum, environmental changes require a convergence of attention from all social strata of the organization (high level executives, managers, foremen, and so on).

Certain aspects of physical environments can be easily adapted to more comfortable working conditions. Greater space can be allocated in some instances or space can be arranged so that visual interaction is increased or decreased to facilitate definitions of suitable surroundings. Better meeting rooms can be found or built, noise or safety features changed. The human elements of the environment resulting from information processing requirements of tasks to be performed cannot be engineered so easily. Often strong resentments emerge from imposed changes intended to influence social-psychological elements of an environment. As Berger (1963) points out, the ability to manipulate one's role in avoidance or contradiction of prescribed role expectations (to get away with deviant acts) is substantially ego gratifying, and, we might add, one method of reducing equivocality within a particular task environment.

The Participatory Decision Making (PDM) model has been shown to increase productivity through environmental changes involving human relationships. Used most frequently with middle management personnel, a PDM model has also been tried with some success in industrial assembly jobs. Bjork (1975) reported on a cooperative research project between labor unions, manufacturing companies, and behavioral scientists in Sweden. His extensive study of one plant showed that semiskilled workers within a production department could be highly productive (above company standards) when left to organize their production-assembly tasks as a group. With continuous counselling in human relations skills and problem solving procedures, production groups revised pay scales for piecework production, redesigned production areas, acquired a knowledge of other workers' skills not known before (so that a "rotation" method of work could be used to help overcome boredom) and became involved in their work in emotionally ego gratifying ways.

While PDM techniques do not always produce outcomes of the sort described above, the "industrial democracy" experiment conducted by Bjork and his team is encouraging in light of the type of worker that was involved. The PDM model does provide one essential ingredient for a systems approach to organizations: the individual, group, or larger unit must be able to enact a role to account for equivocality and interpret the meaning of the enactments. Furthermore, they must have some *creative control* over those enactments. Creative control emerges from a cooperative effort to provide additional freedom in defining and normatively maintaining the legitimacy of role behaviors. On the other hand, a person may create illegitimate behaviors to gain such freedom. The latter activity leads to a reduction in productive outcomes for the organization while the former holds some promise of increasing productivity.

HOW DO WE MATCH GROUP MEMBERS AND GROUP TASKS?

The last section of this chapter will deal with another aspect of group dynamics related to task completion: matching people to groups. We will confine our discussion to (1) the relationships between group goals and individual goals, (2) organization constraints and incentives for productivity, and (3) retraining persons and groups for effective action.

Group Goals and Individual Goals

The goals of an organization are not always clearly defined for groups that constitute its network of communication channels. Weick (1969) argues that the goals of an organization are less important than its execution of its information processing as a behavioral system. One might quickly agree that the goal of a large corporation like General Motors or Exxon is to increase profits. One might also readily concede that an assembly line worker or pipe fitter is far removed from the profit motives of a corporate employer. Moreover, Weick would contend the acquisition of corporate profits depends much more on the abilities of work groups to deal with their information environment than to work toward a goal of increased corporate profits.

You might wonder where something called "goals" fits in the scheme of things. Obviously, there is a difference between publicly stated goals of a service bureaucracy like the Social Security Administration and the interconnected patterns of people which constitute such an agency. The difference is that goals are artifacts used in the retrospective interpretation of enactments; their scope correlates with the abilities of people to *control* their environments. Goals have meaning only in the social context from which they emerge as interpretive tools for understanding behavior. Therefore, goals are relevant insofar as they reduce equivocality for a person, group, or organization.

Using this perspective, it is easy to understand why an assembly line worker would be amused if someone said that the motivation to work should be to increase company profits. A line worker has little or no control over profit structures of a large corporation and such an explanation does not provide that person with an adequate interpretation of reality. By contrast, to tell that worker the motivation for working is to provide food and clothing for self and family comes closer to a kind of explanation which realistically interprets the person's behavior within a controllable social context.

Individual and group goals are useful in that they provide a means for interpreting personal and group behavior. A group member's personal goals promote interdependency between self and others if they can be attained as the group also attains its goals. Conversely, personal goals that detract from interdependency between group members are those which cannot be fulfilled as the group strives for goal achievement. These relationships between goal states are illustrated in the following example:

> Joe is not happy in his job as a photographic layout person in the advertising department. His formal training is in graphic design but there are no openings in the graphics department and his experience with photography landed him in advertising. Joe is creative with photographic equipment

and could be a great asset to the team working on advertising but he does not want to look "too good" for fear that he will never be able to shift over to graphics when a position is available. Hence, Joe acts as a technician in staff meetings and usually contributes little to the creative substance of those meetings. In turn, other members of the group do not like him because he doesn't seem motivated and is not very helpful. The staff meetings are dampened by Joe's attitude and the reactions of other group members toward him. Moreover, Joe's lack of participation and the group tension created by it makes it difficult for the group to manage task demands.

This example demonstrates a common group task performance problem resulting from a clash between personal and group goals. Joe's reluctance to effectively participate at an expected level has a number of consequences. First, the group is operating below its potential as an information processing unit. Second, Joe is a source of equivocality for the group and drains off energy that would otherwise be devoted to task demands. Third, Joe's behavior challenges group norms vis-a-vis his role expectations which are both a source of equivocality and interpersonal tension with respect to relationships outside group meetings. The latter problem has considerable impact on other group members, particularly if Joe is perceived as a "likeable guy" in casual social contexts, because they must deal with their contradictory perceptions of Joe from different interaction contexts. This equivocality is twofold because it derives from a clash of perceptions that must be resolved in a consistent way that will cover all social contexts.

Organizational Constraints and Incentives for Productivity

Consistent with our perspective for assessing group work within an organizational system is the relationship between information processing demands and reasons for group (or individual) productivity. Production of anything by a group or individual, be it advertising campaigns or steering assembly parts for a Ford, is socially prescribed behavior within the organization. There is good reason to believe the very nature of control mechanisms produce worker alienation and a kind of social sterility within work environments (Bjork, 1975).

The constraint-incentive relationship within an organization may be approached from two directions. The reward-cost properties for a task group are both *instrumental* (material) and *psychological* (emotionally gratifying or aversive). Moreover, these two types of rewards and costs operate simultaneously and the correspondence of each to the other is essential for group functioning. Figure 4.1 shows the four ways congruent and incongruent rewards match.

Table 4.1 Instrumental and Psychological Reward Matrix

		PSYCHOLOGICAL REWARDS	
		High	*Low*
INSTRUMENTAL REWARDS	*High*	Positive Congruity	Psychological Incongruity
	Low	Instrumental Incongruity	Negative Congruity

A group may view its prescribed outputs as adequately rewarded from a material standpoint (for example, increased earnings for members or letters of recognition) but find that it is not adequately rewarded in a psychological sense (the work is boring, the members have little creative input, and so on). Positive congruent rewards come about when both instrumental and psychological rewards are perceived as satisfactory by the group. The three other possible reward-cost contingencies, besides positive congruence, in Figure 4.1 produce negative reactions and can lead to a reduction in productivity.

The nature of organizational systems is such that many tasks which groups and individuals in groups must perform are redundant. Therefore, the task itself can be a constraint that is not easily overcome. Even if an organization recognizes a necessity for providing alternative methods of participation in structuring task environments, there is no guarantee that organization members will accept the additional responsibilities associated with such freedom. As Bjork pointed out about the company he studied, workers were reticent to participate fully during various stages of work reorganization planning for fear of losing income, misunderstanding the consequences of human aspects related to group work, not being motivated to maintain psychological involvement necessary for the experiment, and a host of other reasons.

The above considerations notwithstanding, organizations place constraints on groups and individuals because methods for completing many tasks are evaluated on the basis of cost efficiency. Human elements of tasks, especially those related to the production of "things" as opposed to ideas, are usually not high priorities to production planners. Moreover, moving many jobs from "piecework" to "salary" pay rates tends to eliminate the effectiveness of monetary incentives and individual initiative. There are, however, examples of group pressures overcoming the effects of monetary incentives.

Bureaucratic organizations, where the emphasis is on a service rather than producing a product, are considerably more complex in the ways groups can be motivated. The rigid nature of occupational roles that groups and individuals occupy is the greatest constraint to productivity. There is no less rigidity in the role of an Internal Revenue Service Claims Analyst than there is in the role of an assembly line welder. The primary difference is that a tax analyst has considerable flexibility in task execution compared to a welder. Until organizational systems are able to provide role flexibility for individuals or groups that perform productive activity, or until a greater amount of role diversity (performing additional roles) can be found within the tight constraints of a system, humanistic incentives to improve people's impressions of organizational systems are not likely to materialize. Unfortunately, the impact of monetary incentives on role performances does not appear to effectively generate positive regard for the tasks of large organizational systems.

Retraining Persons and Groups for Effective Action

Fitting the right person or group to the proper task within the organizational system is a complex job of social engineering. If we take the admonition by Weick (1969) that organizational systems must supply work that provides for removal of equivocality from the occupational roles of workers to increase their productivity and satisfaction, we must also consider the abilities of people to deal with information that has differential properties of clarity and complexity. Kelly (1955) has proposed that people can be differentiated on the basis of their ability to perceive their social, symbolic world. Work by Schroder, Driver, and Streufert (1967) has shown that information processing demands of a task have a considerable impact on a person's task performance. People not psychologically equipped to process information that is too ambiguously stated will have difficulty completing tasks where information is presented in that way. Moreover, the amount of information a task requires persons or groups to process is also important. Too much information at one time creates equivocality that cannot be met unless there are sufficient rules to reduce equivocality.

The most important aspect of the information processing dilemma is that decision rules for resolving information equivocality must either be stated prior to its introduction or evolve out of individual or group interaction. Therefore, it is not likely that people can be trained to personally deal with modes of information inputs they can not psychologically accommodate. On the other hand, it is possible to train people to use or create rules for processing information within familiar occupational roles. Tasks can be introduced into organizational environments in ways that better suit the needs of people who must work on them. Typically, prescribed behavior for occupational tasks is not part of an interactive process of system adaptation; people adapt to systems as a precondition for organizational membership. Therefore, information processing rules and demands are already prescribed. Increasing the flexibility of information inputs could alleviate many of the problems we have mentioned.

REFERENCES

Argyle, M. 1969. *Social interaction.* New York: Leiber-Atherton, Inc.

Asch, S.R. 1956. Studies of independence and conformity: A minority of one against a unanimous majority. *Psychological Monographs 9* (whole issue).

Bales, R.F., Strodtbeck, F.L., Mills, T.M. and Roseborough, M.E. 1951. Channels of communication in small groups. *American Sociological Review 16,* 461–468.

Bayless, O. 1967. An alternative pattern for problem-solving discussion. *Journal of Communication 17,* 188–197.

Berger, P. 1963. *Invitation to sociology: A humanist perspective.* New York: Doubleday.

Bjork, L.E. 1975. An experiment in work satisfaction. *Scientific American 232,* 17–23.

Bormann, E.G. 1969. *Discussion and group methods: Theory and practice.* New York: Harper & Row, Pub.

Bourne, L.E. and Battig, W.F. 1966. Complex processes. In *Experimental methods and instrumentation in psychology,* ed. J.B. Sidowski, pp. 541–576. New York: McGraw-Hill.

Brilhart, J. and Jochem, L. 1964. Effects of different patterns on outcomes of problem-solving discussions. *Journal of Applied Psychology 48,* 175–179.

Cartwright, D. and Zander, A. 1968. The structural properties of groups: Introduction. In *Group dynamics: Research and theory,* eds. D. Cartwright and A. Zander, pp. 485–502. New York: Harper Row, Pub.

Dalkey, N.C. 1968. *Experiment in group prediction.* Rand Corporation.

Davis, J.H. 1969. *Group performance.* Reading, Mass.: Addison-Wesley.

Dewey, J. 1933. *How we think.* Lexington, Mass.: Heath.

Ekman, P., Freisen, W. and Ellsworth, P. 1972. *Emotions in the human face: Guidelines for research and an integration of findings.* Elmsford, N.Y.: Pergamon Press.

Egan, G. 1970. *Encounter: Group processes for interpersonal growth.* Monterey, Calif.: Brooks/Cole.

Fisher, B.A. 1970. Decision emergence: Phases in group decision-making. *Speech Monographs 37,* 53–66.

Gibb, J.R. 1951. The effects of group size and of threat reduction upon creativity in a problem-solving situation. *American Psychologist 6,* 324.

Gouran, D.S. 1969. Variables related to concensus in group discussions of questions of policy. *Speech Monographs 30,* 387–391.

Gulley, H. 1968. *Discussion, conference and group process.* New York: Holt, Rinehart & Winston.

Hall, E. 1959. *The silent language.* New York: Doubleday.

Harnack, R.V. and Fest, T. 1964. *Group discussion: Theory and technique.* New York: Appleton-Century-Crofts.

Hearn, G. 1957. Leadership and the spacial factor in small groups. *Journal of Abnormal and Social Psychology 54,* 269–272.

Kelly, G. 1955. *A theory of personality: The psychology of personal constructs.* New York: W. W. Norton Co., Inc.

Kiesler, C.A. and Kiesler, S.B. 1969. *Conformity.* Reading, Mass.: Addison-Wesley.

Lorge, I. and Soloman, H. 1955. Two models of group behavior in the solution of eureka-type problems. *Psychometrica 20,* 139–148.

Mabry, E.A. and Kaufman, S. 1973. The influence of sex and attraction on seating positions in dyads. Paper contributed to the Interpersonal Division, International Communication Association Convention, Montreal, Canada, 1973.

Maier, N.R.F. 1953. An experimental test of the effect of training on discussion leadership. *Human Relations 6,* 161–171.

Olmstead, M.S. 1959. *The small group.* New York: Random House.

Penley, L.E. 1975. An empirical evaluation of the qualities of the *nominal* group. Paper contributed to the International Communication Association Convention, Chicago, Ill., 1975.

Porter, L.W. and Lawler, E.E. 1965. Properties of organization structures in relation to job attitudes and job behavior. *Psychological Bulletin 64,* 32–51.

Roethlisberger, F.J. and Dickson, W.J. 1939. *Management and the worker.* Cambridge, Mass.: Harvard University Press.

Schroder, H., Driver, M. and Streufert, S. 1967. *Human information processing.* New York: Holt, Rinehart & Winston.

Schutz, A. 1967. *The phenomenology of the social world.* Evanston, Ill.: Northwestern University Press.

Shaw, M.E. 1963. Scaling group tasks: A method for dimensional analysis. Technical Report No. 1, ONR Contract NR 170–266, nonr-580(11), University of Florida.

Shaw, M.E. 1971. *Group dynamics: The psychology of small group behavior.* New York: McGraw-Hill.

Sherif, M. 1936. *The psychology of social norms.* New York: Harper & Row, Pub.

Sherif, M. and Sherif, C. 1964. *Reference groups.* New York: Harper & Row, Pub.

Sommer, R. 1967. *Personal space: The behavioral basis of design.* Englewood Cliffs, N.J.: Prentice-Hall, Inc.

Steinzor, B. 1950. The spacial factor in face-to-face discussion groups. *Journal of Abnormal and Social Psychology 45,* 552–555.

Travis, L.E. 1925. The effect of a small audience upon eye-hand coordination. *Journal of Abnormal and Social Psychology 20,* 142–146.

Van de Ven, A. and Delbecq, A.L. 1971. Nominal versus interacting group processes for committee decision-making effectiveness. *Academy of Management Journal 14,* 203–212.

Van de Ven, A. and Delbecq, A.L. 1974. The effectiveness of nominal, delphi and interacting group decision-making processes. *Academy of Management Journal 17,* 605–621.

Vardaman, G.T. and Halterman, C.C. 1968. *Managerial control through communication: Systems for organizational diagnosis and design.* New York: John Wiley.

Weick, K. 1969. *The social psychology of organizing.* Reading, Mass.: Addison-Wesley.

Zajonc, R.B. 1965. Social facilitation. *Science 149,* 269–274.

Zuk, B. 1965. On the pathology of silencing strategies. *Family Process 4,* 32–49.

If groups are composed of human and environmental inputs, what happens to the input variables? How are they melded together? What happens when individuals attempt joint action? These and other issues are discussed in the chapters of this section. Human groups do not act without communication. Hence, we begin this section by dedicating Chapter 5 to the assessment of verbal and nonverbal messages. Remaining chapters discuss relationships between communicative behavior and other social processes that regulate how members behave: norms, roles, interaction networks, leadership and personal influence (Chapters 6 and 7).

INTEGRATIVE PROCESSES

Part

Three

Chapter

Being the member of a group is not as simple as one might imagine. How, for example, can you make "sense" of multiple messages simultaneously exchanged between group members. Remember, four or five people may be sharing reactions on how they view a number of issues. That means a lot of verbal and nonverbal message cues are emitted within a short period of time. Each person is expected to keep up with the content of conversation; to keep up with the *sense* of conversational behavior. This consciousness, or sense of awareness, we acquire as group participants is directly tied to our understanding of communicative messages transmitted between members. This chapter will review (1) the problems and responsibilities of group participation, (2) how communicative messages (verbal and nonverbal) can be classified and (3) the importance of understanding and interpreting regularities which emerge in group interaction.

5 assessing interaction between group members

HOW CAN MEMBERS OF SMALL GROUPS
ASSESS THEIR RESPONSIBILITIES?

No one can attend to all of the verbal and nonverbal messages exchanged by group members during the life of a group or even within a
single meeting. Most of us can recall an uncomfortable feeling of being
so involved in group participation that the sense of what was happening
began to uncontrollably slip from our mental grasp. Scenes like the
following can easily occur: Without apparent explanation, Roger was
behaving as though no one liked him, Sharon was pushing a viewpoint
one would never expect her to endorse, and Mary was making snide side
remarks about group "accomplishment." All of this happened as a result
of previously unnoticed events. Often we become so involved in our
personal roles as participants that we forget to critically analyze group
behavior as an integrated system.

Just as it is difficult to appreciate the forest because all those trees get
in the way, so it is that understanding a group becomes complicated by
being a member and trying to deal with other members. Possessing a
means of sorting out interaction between members requires having some
conceptualization of that interaction. A conceptual scheme is merely a way
of sorting, grouping, and labeling some set of stimuli. In the case of
communicative message cues, a conceptual scheme becomes the method
by which messages are sorted, grouped together, and labeled. Therefore, rather than attend to a specific message like, "I think that is a very
good idea, Mike!" we can speak in terms of underlying concepts, such as
agreement. This section focuses on how group participants can maintain
some control over the volumes of messages (and their implications) exchanged between members.

A Participant-Observer Orientation
Toward Group Membership

Attending to all of the messages emitted in a group is difficult. The
difficulty is greater than one might realize because these messages are
related to two distinct levels of behavioral interpretation—one more
complicated than the other. The less abstract level encompasses verbal
and nonverbal message *content*. The more abstract level is the *process*
level. It involves the interpretation of relationships between group
members. These interpretations depend upon an awareness of the content, frequencies, flow (between members), and sequences of messages
over time.

Only by close attention to both content and process levels of group
functioning can members fully understand the dynamics of their group.
Furthermore, this attentiveness forms what we call a *participant-observer*

orientation toward group membership. Effective participation as a group member depends on one's ability to be simultaneously involved in participatory task responsibilities and engage in ongoing observation and analysis of the behavioral elements that constitute a group's communication system. Participant-observation is somewhat like being "rationally schizophrenic" because you must act both as an involved group member and semi-detached observer. No one can be totally successful at simultaneously practicing this dual role. Instead, this orientation represents an ideal toward which to work. Accepting such responsibility should positively influence your perceptions and behaviors as a group member. If this sounds prespective to you, you're right! The basic assumption is that understanding interaction dynamics is one way of obtaining information potentially helpful to a group's goal attainment.

Information gained as an observer can be used as *feedback* about how a group functions. Feedback can address four different levels of group functioning: *personal, goal definition, structural* and *identification.* Personal feedback is directed toward other group members about their personal style of behavior and expressed attitudes or opinions. It is intended to let other people know how you *feel* about some aspect(s) of them as individuals. This level of feedback can be contrasted with goal definition feedback. Reactions about goal definition *may* be made to an individual but are more likely to be made to the group as a whole. Goal definition feedback focuses attention on the relationship between what a group is doing and its stated objectives. Structural feedback pertains to how responsibility, authority, and power are allocated among group members. For example, someone might challenge the way another member performs a role such as "leader." Such feedback has implications for the division of power and status among all members (the *social structure* of the group). Identification feedback is typified by comments which relate to the development of group identity or a sense of *groupness.* Often group members are moved to comments like, "I think we are closer to each other now than we have been in weeks." or "I think we have lost our enthusiasm for working together."

Interjecting feedback during group interaction is not always an easy task. First, we may lose sight of our own motivation for providing feedback. Second, some groups appear insensitive or antagonistic to feedback and seem to be formidable opponents to messages which take issue with some aspect of group operations. Third, most of us are not really experienced in providing feedback—postive or negative—in a straightforward manner. A simple model of the action sequences necessary for using feedback is the *observe-intervene-assess* cycle. The sequence begins with (1) observation (conceptualization) of some aspects of group behavior, proceeds to (2) intervention in the group with feedback messages aimed at one or more levels of functioning, and concludes by returning to (3) observation assessment focusing on the effects of feedback.

Levels of Group Involvement

Content level behavior in a group is concerned with the reception and perception of messages. Message reception, because of its dependence on perceptual mechanisms, is influenced by such things as visual and auditory acuity, environmental constraints on accurate perception, and attitudes. Message reception is also influenced by other social-psychological factors. Semantic aspects of language—ways we understand the meaning of words or symbols—have substantial impact on message reception. Likewise, attitudes toward a message sender have substantial effects on both perception and reception (Heider, 1958; Hastorf, Schneider and Polefka, 1969), as does the recognition of similarities and differences between sender and receiver (Berschied and Walster, 1969; McCroskey and Wheeless, 1976).

The content level. How group members overtly act toward one another constitutes what we label the *content* level of a group. By content, we mean the verbal and nonverbal messages which are emitted by group members. Consider the dialogue of group members provided in Example 5.1. It may be evident that Mike and Tom are operating on one set of assumptions about what the group should be doing while Dick, Joyce, and Sharon have considerably different impressions. At this point in the dialogue we can note the following: (1) Mike and Tom agree with each other, (2) Dick, Joyce, and Sharon disagree with Mike and Tom, and (3) Mike and Sharon are beginning to exhibit some antagonism toward other members.

Many aspects of content level behavior cannot be found in the transcript of Example 5.1. These are the *nonverbal* cues members may have emitted. Notice that exclamation marks are used with Mike and Sharon's transcribed comments. What do you usually assume is happening when reading passages containing exclamation marks? Obviously, there can be a number of interpretations. However, if you thought about increases in *intensity, emphasis,* and/or *vocal volume* associated with those comments, you're on the right track.

The process level. That we can infer such things as agreement, disagreement, and intensity attests to the fact that we are focusing on message content. Quite often content level behavior is not sufficient for understanding what goes on in a group. Consider Dick's comments for a moment. We know he disagrees with Mike and Tom. But *how* does he disagree? His reactions are not punctuated by exclamation marks. Notice

Example 5.1   Content Level Behaviors

Joyce: I really don't think we have a good idea of where this group is going.

Tom: I thought we did! We were about to act on Mike's suggestion to divide the research work among us.

Mike: Yeah! That's what I thought we were heading towards; some kind of division of labor, I think it's called. Why do you always bring these things up anyway, Joyce!

Sharon: Wait a minute! Dividing up the research work doesn't help us a bit! I don't have the foggiest idea about what things we should be researching or why! It's not Joyce's fault your idea is no good!

Dick: I'm afraid I have to disagree with you, Tom. Joyce and Sharon put their collective fingers on the problem. Mike's suggestion is fine except that it seems premature. At least three of us are not sure how to define this problem to research it. How do you view that issue Tom?

---

how Dick breaks up his thoughts. He disagrees with Tom, indicates his perspective is similar to that held by both women, gives his opinion about Mike's suggestion, gives information about what the source of conflict in the group seems to be, and brings Tom back into participation by asking for his opinion. These behaviors have implications which are better discussed as *process level* elements of group interaction.

We can say with reasonable assurance that our hypothetical group was experiencing a conflict. How did we arrive at that inference? Was it because some members raised their voice or openly disagreed? While these are certainly important factors, there were other things happening as well. Mike didn't just think Joyce was wrong; he implied she had on other occasions engaged in behavior he thought was less than useful ("Why do you always bring these things up anyway, Joyce?"). Sharon's immediate response to Mike was hostile. It also bore the implication that Sharon was defending Joyce from Mike's remarks (It's not Joyce's fault your idea's no good!").

Now let's analyze Dick's behavior. First, he avoided a direct clash with Mike by addressing his comments to Tom. Second, he voiced a position similar to that of Joyce and Sharon's without directly supporting Sharon's heated defense of Joyce (note his comments about Mike's suggestion). Third, Dick summarized the primary blocking points of the group's progress—the group is divided on how it understands what it should be researching. Last, Dick turned consideration of the problem back toward Tom by asking for his opinion. What has Dick's behavior accomplished for the group? If you said he helped the group focus specifically on something it had not considered up to that point, you're right. If you said he shifted the group from personal to goal definition feedback levels, you're also right. If you thought Dick was instrumental in "resolving" a conflict between Joyce, Mike, and Sharon, you are mistaken. That course of action will have to wait for another opportunity.

Dick's action also contains considerable information about the group's process level behavior. Notice he did not call direct attention to the defensiveness and hostility of Mike towards Joyce, and Sharon towards Mike. His comments only shifted attention away from the conflict to a group level concern—goal definition. Dick provided no feedback about the conflict. Why? Here we can only speculate, but at least four possibilities exist. First, Dick may not have perceived the conflict. Second, he might have thought focusing on goal oriented behavior was more important than dealing with personal feelings. Third, he could be a close friend of Mike's and not want to strain their friendship. Fourth, he might dislike Joyce and/or Sharon but share their concern about goal definition. Therefore, Dick might let them "fend for themselves" with Mike and specifically focus on one narrow aspect of the group's process. In any event, Dick's decision to intervene and change the group's conversational focus interrupted, but did not resolve, a significant facet of process level behavior that could again emerge to block task progress.

HOW CAN WE CLASSIFY GROUP COMMUNICATION?

Thus far we have restricted our discussion of group interaction to relatively abstract concerns. Attending to rather small, precise units of behavior is crucial to maintaining a clear understanding of what happens in a group. In this section we will review various methods of classifying communication in small groups.

Classifying Verbal Content and Feelings

The most difficult aspect of participant-observation entails accounting for messages that flow between group members. Unless you possess exceedingly good recall abilities, keeping track of what members say or how they behave is an impossible task. Researchers investigating group behavior have developed several methods for coding (classifying) verbal acts and feelings. These methods focus on coding message *themes ideas,* or *acts.*

Thematic methods attempt to identify underlying themes of interaction between one or more group members. Mabry (1975), for example, devised a thematic coding method by which observers classified time

units of interaction according to whether the units reflected such themes as focusing on group members' personal attributes (or "qualities") versus members' task achievements (or "performance").

Assessing ideational content in small group interaction is similar to classifying thematic content. A major difference is that content labels usually refer to types of ideas related to task completion. The approach was first proposed by Crowell and Scheidel (1961). They devised it as a means of tracking the progress and modification of "reasoning" used by group members during problem solving. Each *ideational unit* (defined as any coherent word sequence which could logically be classified) was coded on any one or more of five dimensions. For example, an assertion versus a question, information versus inference, volunteered versus requested statements, and so on.

Methods focusing on specific acts (such as agreement or opinion) are by far the most common. Due to the relative simplicity of coding message acts we will study this method more closely. The most widely used method of analyzing verbal acts in small groups is Interaction Process Analysis—IPA (Bales, 1950; 1970; Bales and Hare, 1965). After much experimentation, Bales has developed a reliable system for measuring interaction in small groups. The basic unit of measurement is an *act* which consists of the "smallest discriminable segment of verbal or nonverbal behavior to which the observer . . . can assign a classification" (Bales, 1950, p. 37). Acts include verbal messages of one word (such as Wow! Me?, and Ugh.), sentence fragments, and phrases. The only limitation is that the meaning must be understood by an observer. Complex sentences almost always include multiple acts that can be scored separately. In addition to verbal exchanges, meaningful facial expressions, gestures, and nonverbal acts of various kinds are recorded (Bales, 1950, p. 38).

A twelve-category scheme is used to classify *task* and *social-emotional* behaviors. Task behaviors consist of questions and attempted answers. Three types of messages forming the questions and answers are giving (or asking for) *information, opinions,* and *suggestions.* Social-emotional behaviors are positive and negative acts. Positive acts are *friendliness* (positive personal level feedback), *dramatization* (supportiveness or assertiveness through analogy or metaphor), and *agreement.* Negative acts are *unfriendliness* (negative personal level feedback), *showing tension* (nonfluent acts, joking) and *disagreement.* Keep in mind the word "negative" does not imply an act is wrong or bad. Negative behaviors are as natural as positive behaviors in a group. Why? No one should seriously expect to be totally comfortable or satisfied with a group. Clashes of opinions, suggestions, personal styles, and a host of other psychological, sociological, and environmental factors which affect group behavior come into play. Many times we have positive feelings about a group and/or specific members while other times we have negative feelings.

The twelve categories are somewhat self-explanatory. The difficulty is in trying to determine a category for a specific act that could be viewed from more than one perspective. Four general rules are offered by Bales (1970, pp. 134–135) when an observer is undecided where an act should be recorded:

1. When there is a question about whether to categorize an act in "Dramatizes" and "Shows Tension," give priority to "Dramatizes."
2. When any interpersonal feeling is shown, give priority to "Seems Friendly" or "Seems Unfriendly."
3. "Gives Suggestions" or "Asks for Suggestions" should have priority over "Gives Opinions."
4. After an act of disagreement or agreement, scoring reverts to appropriate impersonal categories (Information, Opinion, Suggestion), as the basis for disagreement is explained.

Recording Observations

Example 5.2 contains a transcript of dialogue from a hypothetical group session. Each sentence or thought unit is classified into one of the twelve IPA categories. Seeing "coded" group interaction in this form makes recording observed behavior appear rather easy. Unfortunately, such appearances can be misleading. Keeping track of rapidly occurring and sometimes overlapping interaction sequences is not easy. Observation data about group communication processes are valuable only if obtained in a reliable and valid manner.

Example 5.2   Interaction Transcript for Members of a Hypothetical Five-Person Group

Mike: This is really going to be a tough job (*Gives Opinion*). I've never had to put together a campaign for a product like this before (*Gives Information*).

Sharon: I think it will be particularly hard because we aren't real sure of our primary goal (*Gives Opinion*). I guess it's up to us whether this campaign will focus on exposure or motivation (*Gives Suggestion*).

Tom: We can get to that issue in time (*Gives Suggestion*). What I wanted to know was who has experience with this type of product (*Asks For Information*)?

Joyce: This is all a little new to me (*Shows Tension*). I've had experience in media campaigns before but not with a product like this one (*Gives Information*).

Dick: Well Tom, you and I have both seen tougher assignments (*Seems Friendly*). Personally, I would like to find out where everyone thinks we should go from here (*Asks For Suggestion*).

Mike: The first thing we should do is find out which part of this problem each of us will be responsible for completing (*Gives Suggestion*).

Joyce: It seems as if we need to decide what approach we will take (*Gives Suggestion*). What are we going to use as a slant—exposure or motivation (*Asks for Opinion*)?

Sharon: I think you're right, Joyce (*Agrees*). I've been on several projects in the past few months and know what can happen when a team doesn't begin with a clear idea of what it wants (*Gives Opinion*).

Tom: Mike's suggestion was a good one (*Gives Opinion*). We need to do a lot of background research before we can put this thing to bed (*Gives Suggestion*). This is an experienced team and all of us know what a good campaign looks like (*Gives Opinion*). So, we better get organized and off the ground before we fall behind schedule (*Gives Suggestion*). What do you think, Dick (*Asks For Opinion*)?

Dick: That's true, Tom, sometimes, jumping right into the work is like diving off a pier—you don't always know whether the water is twenty feet or two hundred feet deep (*Dramatizes*).

Tom: But you don't know until you take the plunge, right (*Disagrees*)? Anyway, I'm more concerned about keeping on schedule (*Gives Information*).

Joyce: I really don't think we have a good idea of where this group is going (*Gives Opinion*).

Tom: I thought we did (*Disagrees*)! We were about to get on with using Mike's suggestion to divide up the research work (*Gives Opinion*).

Mike: Yeah (*Agrees*)! That's what I thought we were heading towards; some kind of a "division of labor" I think it's called (*Gives Opinion*). Why do you always bring these things up anyway, Joyce (*Seems Unfriendly*)? If you knew more . . . (*Shows Tension*), I mean, you don't have quite as much experience as the rest of us (*Gives Opinion*). Maybe you should just *Listen* more (*Seems Unfriendly*).

Sharon: Wait a minute (*Shows Tension*)! Dividing up the research work doesn't help us one bit (*Disagrees*)! I, for one, don't have the foggiest idea about what things we should start researching or why (*Gives Information*). Anyway, it's not Joyce's fault your idea's no good (*Seems Unfriendly*).

Dick: I'm afraid I have to disagree with you, Tom (*Disagrees*). Joyce and Sharon put their collective fingers on the problem (*Seems Friendly*). Mike's suggestion was O.K. but it also seemed premature (*Gives Opinion*). At least three of us are not sure how we could begin to divide up research responsibilities until we make a decision about direction (*Gives Information*). How do you think we should handle this issue (*Asks For Suggestion*)?

Tom: I guess if a majority of the group want to begin a different way, it's O.K. with me (*Agrees*). What do you think, Mike (*Asks For Opinion*)?

Mike: Sure, that's allright with me (*Agrees*).

Joyce: Now we're getting someplace (*Gives Opinion*). I think we can make a decision about campaign focus pretty quick (*Gives Opinion*). It is important to keep on schedule like you pointed out, Tom (*Seems Friendly*).

Sharon: I think you're right Joyce (*Agrees*). Tom was pretty astute when he said we had a lot of work to accomplish (*Agrees*). I think we should be able to get back to your idea pretty soon, Mike (*Seems Friendly*).

Reliability and validity of observed behavior is quite important. Both factors relate to ways we can assess the overall accuracy of the behavioral measurements. Observation methods like Interaction Process Analysis do represent rudimentary *measurement* techniques. We perform these measurements by translating naturally occurring verbal and nonverbal behaviors into discrete *bits* of information according to the defining characteristics of each IPA category. In other words, we count the number of information bits placed in each category. The twelve IPA categories can be labeled *variables*. They are variables because each distinguishes different kinds of behaviors and the frequency of information bits coded into each can fluctuate over time and across groups. Hence, using IPA helps us account for twelve communication *content* variables.

These measurements are not very useful if they lack reliability and validity. *Validity*, in this case, means category definitions and observation procedures permit the bits to be placed in the "right" or "true" categories. *Reliability* means that two or more observers will classify the same bits into the same categories with very little margin of error. Consider the following example:

Ed: I think you're mad at me, Ann. Have I done something to upset you?

Ann: Yes!

Ed: Would you rather have me leave now?

Ann: Yes!

Would you classify Ann's "Yes" comments into an Agreement category? Probably not. How about a Seems Unfriendly category? That makes a lot of sense. If the IPA method required all "Yes" statements to be coded as agreement, the results would not always be valid. However, preceding statements or thought units can be employed to make sense out of other statements and many problems like this one are alleviated.

Picture yourself and another person observing the interaction in the above example. Suppose you coded "yes" responses into the Seems Un-

friendly category while your partner coded them as Agreement. A reliability problem has now occurred. Quite often these problems arise because people have evolved slightly different category definitions. The
problem can usually be resolved by reviewing the definitions. The best
approach we have found for those just learning the system is to pair two
observers together and have them observe two group members. Both
observers should not have too much difficulty keeping pace, and they
can check with each other to determine similarities and differences in
recording acts.

Additional data can be obtained by recording "who talks to whom"
along with simple content classifications. Coding this kind of information is more complicated. It requires using some method of identifying
group members other than by name. Each member might be assigned a
code letter or number (for example, Joe is 1, Sue is 2, and so on); the
entire group is also identified (for instance, "G") since members often
address comments to everyone rather than another single member. Noting who speaks to whom can be a useful technique for identifying high
and low status members, sources of interpersonal conflict, and emerging
subgroups. In our sample dialogue, for instance, coalitions obviously
exist between Sharon and Joyce and between Tom and Mike. But, what
is Dick's role? Observation of who-to whom patterns might clarify
whether he is an ally of the women, men, or simply a moderator of
differences. Our experience indicates neophyte observers do not find it
difficult to reliably identify who speaks to whom in small groups.

Interpreting Observations

Once observations of group sessions have been made, the "raw
data" must then be summarized and interpreted. It is seldom necessary
to go beyond simple addition and division when summarizing observation data. Many insights can be gained by adding up frequencies of
interaction for each group member and each IPA category; percentages
are sometimes useful for comparative purposes. Earlier we spoke of
content and process levels of communicative behavior. Using the transcript in Example 5.2 to provide our data, we can explore some interesting and useful interpretations for observed interaction on both levels.

Content level interpretations. At least four kinds of content level
analyses, summaries, and interpretations are possible (Patton and Giffin, 1973). The first involves summing each participant's acts and calculating percentages of total group interaction for each member.
Member and group totals are located at the bottom of Table 5.1. Note
that the number of group acts totalled fifty. Therefore, Dick's eight acts
represent approximately 16% of the group total. Since these totals do

not reflect quality or type of interaction, relatively little information can be generated from these analyses. There is, however, some evidence to suggest those who interact more frequently attain higher status, achieve greater influence, and are assigned leadership roles by other members (Bavelas, et al., 1965; Bales, 1970, p. 478). In our hypothetical group, Tom contributed the most and Joyce the least with participation fairly even among all group members.

Table 5.1   Summary Classification of Verbal Behavior Recorded in Example 5.2

		GROUP MEMBERS				
CONTEXT CATEGORIES	*Dick* *(1)*	*Joyce* *(2)*	*Mike* *(3)*	*Sharon* *(4)*	*Tom* *(5)*	CATEGORY TOTALS
1. Seems Friendly	II	I		I		4 = 8%
2. Dramatizes	I					1 = 2%
3. Agrees			II	III	I	6 = 12%
4. Gives Suggestion		I	I	I	III	6 = 12%
5. Gives Opinion	I	III	III	II	III	12 = 24%
6. Gives Information	I	I	I	I	I	5 = 10%
7. Asks for Information					I	1 = 2%
8. Asks for Opinion		I			II	3 = 6%
9. Asks for Suggestion	II					2 = 4%
10. Disagrees	I			I	II	4 = 8%
11. Shows Tension		I	I	I		3 = 6%
12. Seems Unfriendly			II	I		3 = 6%
Member Totals	8 = 16%	8 = 16%	10 = 20%	11 = 22%	13 = 26%	50 = 100%

The second kind of analysis involves summing and finding percentages of acts which appear in each category. These calculations are found in the right hand column of Table 5.1. With these data, interaction by the group can be compared with estimated norms (Bales, 1970, p. 92). Table 5.2 contains ranges of group acts for each category. The ranges provide a general guideline for high and low cut-off points. The type of task, history of the group, and length of observation will affect the data for individual groups. However, when these boundaries are exceeded some consideration should be given to why the norms were not reflected by the observed interaction.

While reading the transcript, you may have sensed a higher than normal amount of negative social-emotional behavior. If this is true, it should be reflected in the data. Categories can be grouped into a task area and positive and negative social-emotional behavior areas. The percentage of task related acts was roughly 58% of the total. Approximately 22% of all acts fell in the area of positive social-emotional behavior. Both of these percentage figures fall within the range of estimated norms.

The negative social-emotional area reflects 20% of total group interaction and that exceeds the upper normative level. Thus, the data do indicate a possible problem area for the group.

Table 5.2   Percentage of Group Participation in IPA Categories Compared with Estimated Norms

CONTENT CATEGORY	PERCENT	ESTIMATED NORMS*
1. Seems Friendly	8	2.6 – 4.8
2. Dramatizes	2	5.7 – 7.4
3. Agrees	12	8.0 – 13.6
4. Gives Suggestions	12	3.0 – 7.0
5. Gives Opinions	24	15.0 – 22.7
6. Gives Information	10	20.7 – 31.2
7. Asks for Information	2	4.0 – 7.2
8. Asks for Opinions	6	2.0 – 3.9
9. Asks for Suggestions	4	0.6 – 1.4
10. Disagrees	8	3.1 – 5.3
11. Shows Tension	6	3.4 – 6.0
12. Seems Unfriendly	6	2.4 – 4.4
Total	100%	

*R.F. Bales, Personality and Interpersonal Behavior *New York: Holt, Rinehart and Winston, 1970)*, p. 96.

Useful information can also be obtained by looking at individual categories. However, percentages can sometimes be misleading. For example, Seems Friendly contains 8% of group interaction, well above the norm of 4.8% but only four acts fell in this category—with Dick generating half the total. The group percentages also reflect a small amount of Gives Information in contrast to a high percentage of Gives Suggestions. A possible "solution" to some of the social-emotional problems may be to provide additional information with less advice-giving. Actually, the group could benefit from additional input in the areas of Gives Suggestions, Opinions and Information. According to Bales and Hare (1965, pp. 239–258), the area of giving answers should exceed the area of asking questions by a ratio of 5:1 or 6:1. The ratio of our group is roughly 4:1 with a specific deficiency in the Gives Information category.

A third level of analysis involves calculating individual member participation by category as a percentage of total group acts. Table 5.3 contains those calculations for each group member. Once again, the small sample of group interaction observed makes inferences and conclusions tenuous. This level of analysis can be useful for determining specific feedback to individual members. We have found greater success with encouraging increased contributions in category *areas* than in trying to discourage contributions by members.

Table 5.3 Individual Member Percentage of Total Group Acts According to IPA Category

CONTENT CATEGORY	GROUP MEMBERS				
	Dick	Joyce	Mike	Sharon	Tom
1. Seems Friendly	4	2	—	2	—
2. Dramatizes	2	—	—	—	
3. Agrees	—	—	4	6	2
4. Gives Suggestion	—	2	2	2	6
5. Gives Opinion	2	6	6	4	6
6. Gives Information	2	2	2	2	2
7. Asks for Information	—	—	—	—	2
8. Asks for Opinion	—	2	—	—	4
9. Asks for Suggestion	4	—	—	—	—
10. Disagrees	2	—	—	2	4
11. Shows Tension	—	2	2	2	—
12. Seems Unfriendly	—	—	4	2	—
Total	16%	16%	20%	22%	26%

The fourth type of analysis involves calculating a member's category acts as a percentage of the member's total interaction. Bales (1970) suggests that member roles can be analyzed according to how a person interacts. Comparing predetermined ranges and interpretations of behaviors (see Table 5.2) to each member's percentage of acts per category permits us to assess group role behavior. This data can be viewed as behavioral indices of effective personality and interpretated using Bales' (1970) three-dimensional model previously discussed in Chapter 2. Group behavior is labeled "up (U)—down (D)," "positive (P)—negative (N)" and "forward (F)—backward (B)." with twenty-six possible role type combinations.

Briefly, *upward* group members, are those people who are perceived to be *ascendent.* Their actions are interpreted as attempts to influence group movement in the direction of some goal. *Downward* members are perceived as submissive and desire to be directed or controlled by other members. Those persons identified as *positive* are viewed as needing and promoting among other members interpersonal warmth, solidarity, and friendship. *Negative* members, by contrast, are seen as avoiding friendship, cold or neutral, and insensitive to the needs or desires of other members for developing harmonious interpersonal relationships. Members who hold attitudes and values about how the group should accomplish task objectives, which are viewed by other members as appropriate and acceptable (that is, normal or within the majority), are labeled *forward.* Conversely, those members who possess attitudes and values about task accomplishment which are perceived as unacceptably deviant from those of most other members are labeled *backward.* The implication is that forward members will help advance the group's progress toward a goal while backward members impede progress. Table 5.4 contains Dick's percentages and ranges for each category and role type. As an exercise, the reader can do similar calculations and comparisons for other members.

Table 5.4   Percentage of Individual Member Acts in IPA Categories Compared with Group Norms

CONTENT CATEGORIES	DICK'S PERCENT OF HIS TOTAL	IF* LOW	MEDIUM* RANGE	IF* HIGH
1. Seems Friendly	25%	N	2.6 – 4.8	P
2. Dramatizes	12.5%	DF	5.4 – 7.4	UB
3. Agrees	—	NB	8.0 – 13.6	PF
4. Gives Suggestions	—	DB	3.0 – 7.0	UF
5. Gives Opinions	12.5%	B	15.0 – 22.7	F
6. Gives Information	12.5%	U	20.7 – 31.2	D
7. Asks for Information	—	DN	4.0 – 7.2	UP
8. Asks for Opinions	—	N	2.0 – 3.9	P
9. Asks for Suggestions	25%	UB	0.6 – 1.4	DF
10. Disagrees	12.5%	P	3.1 – 5.3	N
11. Shows Tension	—	UP	3.4 – 6.0	DB
12. Seems Unfriendly	—	P	2.4 – 4.4	N
	100%			

Adapted from Personality and Interpersonal Behavior by Robert Freed Bales. Copyright © 1970 by Holt, Rinehart and Winston, Inc. Reprinted by permission of Holt, Rinehart & Winston.

Process level interpretations.   Besides accounting for various verbal and nonverbal acts, we can obtain information about process level actions by assessing the flow of interaction among members. Aspects of a group's process level can be constructed using frequency and flow, or who-to-whom, data. Figures 5.1 and 5.2 show the distribution of task and social-emotional verbal acts, respectively, that members directed toward each other (connecting lines with arrows) and toward the group (blunted half-lines).

Inspecting Figure 5.1 we note that task behaviors were most often directed toward the group. There is nothing particularly unusual about that result. Task behaviors in the IPA scheme represent questions and attempted answers. It is reasonable to expect many questions will be directed to all group members. The responses, in turn, are likely to be focused on the group rather than the questioner. Note that every member except Sharon was connected to another member through messages either sent or received. In that regard, Dick stands out as the person who received the most messages. This is an indication that Dick

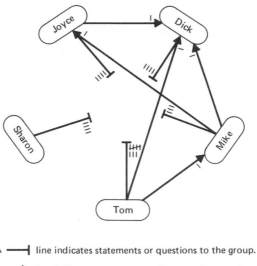

A ———| line indicates statements or questions to the group.

A ——▶ line indicates statements made to another member.

Figure 5.1

might have been performing a leadership role, at least in the area of task related work (Bales, 1965).

Figure 5.2 shows the distribution of social-emotional acts linking group members. One immediately notices how much more direct activity linked members together compared to that found in Figure 5.1. The logic of this behavioral dynamic is simple. Task related behavior is less oriented toward a specific person; it focuses on ideas, opinions, and information. Task behaviors may be directed toward certain group members more often than others (leaders or other high status members). Emotional behavior is quite often *reactive* behavior in that we respond to a person or, possibly, to one climate in a group; most often we respond directly to another's action—either positively or negatively. For these reasons we are more likely to find direct channels linking group members.

We will, in a subsequent chapter, explore in greater depth the significance of communication channels. For the moment, it is sufficient to point out how these *networks*, or participation linkages, add to our understanding of observed group action. Notice that Dick has similar participation links in both Figure 5.1 and Figure 5.2. He and Tom talked directly to one another more than the other group members. We might note Dick and Tom appeared to have the most control over the group. Tom seemed responsible for moving the group in a particular direction; he might have been the designated group leader. Dick appeared to

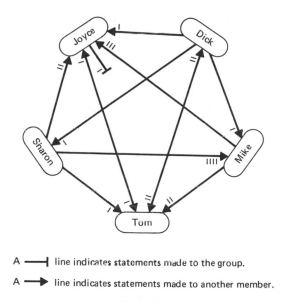

A ⊢ line indicates statements made to the group.

A → line indicates statements made to another member.

Figure 5.2

emerge and challenge Tom's position. He also helped alleviate the conflict between Joyce and Sharon versus Mike and Tom. Also notice that Joyce and Sharon were usually linked to other members through their social-emotional contributions (compare the two diagrams). Finally, we see how much more direct participation between members exists in social-emotional versus task activity diagrams. Members talked directly to one another more when making affective (emotional) statements than when making task statements. This upholds our previous observation that a substantive conflict existed.

A Point of Clarification

Before we end this section there is one issue that deserves special attention. Quite often we use the terms *communication* and *interaction* interchangeably. For our purposes here we have not always made a distinction between the two. There is, however, an important difference, and many scholars would argue that interaction is the most basic of all group activity. Our definitional perspective on communication in Chapter 1 underscored the significance of *exchanging* meaningful cues between people which add up to some sort of messages or symbolic framework which they share. In theory, the idea of "exchange" presumes that people continuously act and react to one another. Technically, an act-react message sequence correctly describes an instance of interaction between two people. However, it should be apparent that group members do engage in "communication" with one another even if they are not constantly and specifically talking to one another.

Some researchers (Fisher, 1971; Fisher and Hawes, 1971; Weick, 1969) argue that sequences of message units called *interacts* should be the focus of study for understanding group interaction. An interact occurs when person A emits a behavior followed by person B emitting another behavior. In other words, interacts are two-message sequences of verbal acts. The assumption is that any act is a motivation for any subsequent act. Therefore, whether group members specifically talk to one another is less important than the sequential nature of message acts. There is considerable merit to this assumption when communication is viewed as a symbolic exchange. In the context of a small group, it makes little sense to assume that members "communicate" only through direct dialogue uttered on a one-to-one basis.

HOW CAN WE CLASSIFY NONVERBAL
GROUP COMMUNICATION

The final section in this chapter deals with nonverbal message cues generically referred to as *nonverbal communication*. Virtually any human action, from involuntary muscular activity to the way we dress, can qualify as nonverbal communication. Due to the breadth of the subject matter related to this area it is impossible to provide a comprehensive treatment of nonverbal communication. Our primary intent in this section is to provide a convenient method for identifying and understanding the participation of group members. Thus, we limit our discussion of nonverbal behavior to its importance in augmenting verbal codes or as a *meta-communicating* (Leathers, 1976) function of communicative expression.

Types of Nonverbal Behavior

Three of the most frequently studied classes of nonverbal messages are called *proxemics, kinesics,* and *paralanguage.* Proxemics is the study of how people use space. Communication scholars usually focus on the way distances affect interaction with others and how we use distances during conversations and discussions. Kinesics is the study of body movement. Probably the broadest of the three classes, it covers behavioral cues as minute as eye blinks and as global as our posture or the way we walk. Paralanguage is the term used to represent nonlanguage vocal expression. It is the study of how meanings are inferred from auditory attributes of the voice (pitch, tone, intensity, inflection, and so on). The amount of behavioral cues covered by the three classes is immense! For this reason, we choose to consider nonverbal communicative behaviors in terms of how they *function* to affect perceptions of others in interpersonal relationships.

Functions of Nonverbal Communication

Mehrabian (1972) proposes that nonverbal behaviors function to signal expressions of *status, attraction,* and *intensity* in our relationships. Unhappily, it is not possible to say that certain kinesic, proxemic, or paralinguistic cues are more or less associated with those functions. Instead, cues must be interpreted within the context of interaction between group members. Thus, nonverbal cues may only be informative to the extent we understand other aspects of a group's communication behavior.

Status. Consider the following brief description of one person's experience in a group:

> Karen: The seven of us were seated around the circular conference table. Paul, our study group's leader, was leaning back in his seat and staring at the ceiling while I was giving my oral report to the group. Everyone else seemed to keep eye contact with me, lean forward in their chairs and looked interested. I wonder what Paul thought was so *wrong* about my report.

Was the disgruntled group member correct in being worried about Paul's nonverbal cues? Was he really disapproving of the report? Was he showing his dislike for Karen? Probably not. Most researchers agree that persons with higher status (such as Paul since he was the group's leader) have more options for their behavior. For example, Mehrabian (1972) points out that higher status persons are more likely to appear physically relaxed when interacting with persons having lower status. Higher status members are also more likely to control such variables as conversational distance and touching.

Social status dictates who controls the emotional tone and interpersonal relations between group members. Group leaders, for example, are known to affect the way other group members interact. Hearn (1957) has shown that highly directive, autocratic group leaders decrease the use of cross-group communication by other members, while less directive, democratic leaders seem to promote such interaction. Moreover, status seems to be related to the use of eye contact (Lott and Sommer, 1967; Efran, 1968; Efran and Broughton, 1966). Leaders or higher status persons are somewhat less likely to maintain eye contact with a subordinate while listening to them. Yet subordinates appear more conscious of maintaining eye contact even though the general tendency for any speaker is to reduce direct eye contact and eye-face gazing while talking.

Status in small group interaction is often difficult to determine. For example, "leaders" don't always appear as leaders should. Other members rise to prominence in groups due to a number of factors. Many times our impressions of others are determined by how they socially "present" themselves. We tend to assume that men with lower voices are acting in a more reasoned and deliberate manner than men with higher voices or that someone who is agitated will have a higher vocal pitch. Our perceptions of emotional states are effected by paralanguage cues used in the process of self-presentation.

Attraction. The term attraction does not necessarily mean romantic attachment. It does, however, imply liking and a desire to associate with those toward whom we feel attraction. Just as the amount of status or power someone has is a varying commodity, so is the attractiveness of members to each other. The more attractive other people are to us, the more we increase our tendency to seek out, maintain, or increase contact with them. Conversely, the less attractive they are, the less we will attempt to be near them or interact with them. Mehrabian (1972) talks about this as an "approach—avoidance" tendency.

In any group we will react more favorably to some members than to others. We show amounts of positive regard for others through both verbal and nonverbal messages. When we are attracted to someone, we are more likely to: (1) show support for their ideas and seek out their ideas and support (Berscheid and Walster, 1969), (2) decrease the amount of distance (space) we use during interaction (Mehrabian, 1972; Sommer, 1967), (3) assume physical posture orientations that favor a person either by showing attentiveness to or exclusion of others (such as turning more toward an attractive other), (4) use vocal qualities likely to show acceptance, and (5) attempt to increase frequency of interaction and contact.

Intensity. The emotional intensity a person uses in reactions toward group members (or the entire group) is an important way of determining that person's emotional state. The way we respond to others is also an important source of information in deciding whether verbal or nonverbal channels are more reliable message sources. As message receivers, we need as much help as possible when perceptions of verbal and nonverbal acts do not appear congruent. Mehrabian's (1972) research has indicated that ninety percent of the *meaning* in an emotional message is found in paralinguistic and kinesic cues—the rest is found in verbal codes.

Obviously, our attitudes toward others, as well as personal desires, play a great part in our individualized response styles. We are all familiar with the person who is *always* intense, the person who never seems to have a care in the world, or the person who always seems "ready to please others." Thus, intensity can be a relatively enduring facet of personal behavior. However, particular situations may also effect personal intensity. Recall in Figure 5.2 that some group members increased their intensity as they become more ego-involved in the discussion. Likewise, we can attempt to mask our feelings by "underplaying" self-presentations of how we "really" feel. We are seldom successful at such charades because our words, paralanguage cues, and kinesic behaviors (particularly facial cues) tend to contradict each other. The intensity of personal responses to group action is both perceptible and necessary for understanding how people are reacting as group participants.

REFERENCES

Bales, R.F. 1950. *Interaction process analysis.* Reading, Mass.: Addison-Wesley.

Bales, R.F. 1966. The equilibrium problem in small groups. In *Small groups: Studies in Social interaction,* eds. A.P. Hare, E.F. Borgatta, and R.F. Bales, pp. 444–476. New York: Knopf.

Bales, R.F. 1970. *Personality and interpersonal behavior.* New York: Holt, Rinehart & Winston.

Bales, R.F. and Hare, A.P. 1965. Diagnostic use of the interaction profile. *Journal of Social Psychology 67,* 239–258.

Bavelas, A., Hastorf, A.H., Gross, E.E. and Kite, W.P. 1965. Experiments on the alteration of group structure. *Journal of Experimental Social Psychology 1,* 55–70.

Berscheid, E. and Walster, E. 1969. *Interpersonal attraction.* Reading, Mass.: Addison- Wesley.

Crowell, L. and Scheidel, T.M. 1961. Categories for analysis of idea development in discussion groups. *Journal of Social Psychology 54,* 155–168.

Efran, J.S. 1968. Looking for approval: Effects on visual behavior of approbation from persons differing in importance. *Journal of Personality and Social Psychology 10,* 21–25.

Efran, J.S. and Broughton, A. 1966. Effect of expectancies for social approval on visual behavior. *Journal of Personality and Social Psychology 4,* 103–107.

Fisher, B.A. 1971. Communication research and the task-oriented group. *Journal of Communication 21,* 136–149.

Fisher, B.A. and Hawes, L.C. 1971. An interact system model: Generating a grounded theory of small groups. *Quarterly Journal of Speech 57,* 444–453.

Hastorf, A., Schneider, D.J. and Polefka, J. 1969. *Person Perception.* Reading, Mass.: Addison-Wesley.

Hearn, G. 1957. Leadership and the spatial factor in small groups. *Journal of Abnormal and Social Psychology 54,* 269–272.

Heider, F. 1958. *The psychology of interpersonal relations.* New York: John Wiley.

Leathers, D.G. 1976. *Nonverbal communication systems.* Boston: Allyn and Bacon.

Lott, D.F. and Sommer, R. 1967. Seating arrangements and status. *Journal of Personality and Social Psychology 7,* 90–95.

Mabry, E.A. 1975. An instrument for assessing content themes in group interaction. *Speech Monographs 42,* 291–297.

McCroskey, J.C. and Wheeless, L.R. 1976. *Introduction to human communication.* Boston: Allyn & Bacon.

Mehrabian, A. 1969. The significance of posture and position in the communication of attitude and status relationships. *Psychological Bulletin 71,* 359–372.

Mehrabian, A. 1972. *Nonverbal communication.* Chicago: Aldine.

Patton, B.R. and Giffin, K. 1973. *Problem-solving group interaction.* New York: Harper & Row, Pub.

Sommer, R. 1967. Small group ecology. *Psychological Bulletin 67,* 145–151.

Weick, K.E. 1969. *The social psychology of organizing.* Reading, Mass.: Addison-Wesley.

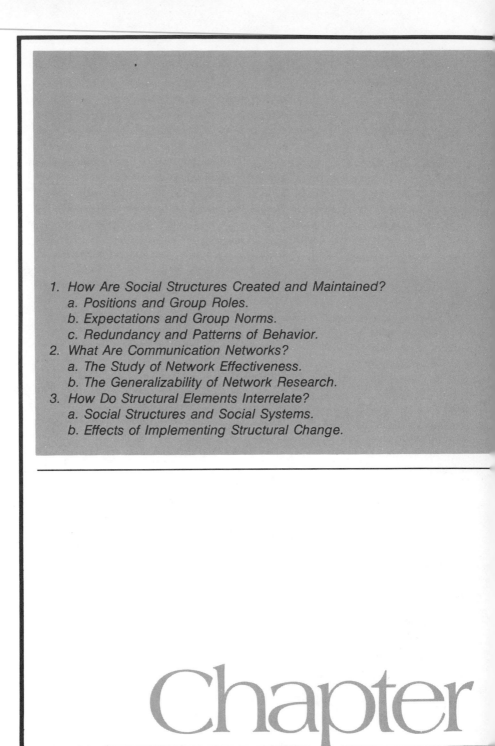

Chapter

Chapter 5 introduced readers to participant-observation and methods observers have at their disposal to sort out various layers of group activity. This chapter's objective is to elaborate on how interaction creates and promotes the melding of group members into a small *social system*. We begin by considering the *social structure* of group-systems. Social structures are created and maintained through interactions, perceptions, and expectations on which relationships between members are based. From our discussion of social structure, we will proceed to examine how group members are joined together by channels of interaction called *networks*.

HOW ARE SOCIAL STRUCTURES CREATED AND MAINTAINED?

A small group is no more or less of a social organization than a company, governmental body, or society in general. The basic differences are attributable to size and complexity but not necessarily to distinctively different human processes. In

communication networks and group social structures

this section, we will review aspects of group behavior and external environments that influence how members organize their relationships into functioning social entities—group-systems. To accomplish this task we will consider three key concepts essential for understanding all human social systems, namely, *positions, expectations,* and *redundancy.*

Positions and Group Roles

The concept *position* can take on a number of connotations (Dobringer, 1969; Monane, 1967). At a relatively simple level, a position is merely the description of what people do in the system. It is their *job* and the responsibilities and privileges associated with it. In most formal organizations, a person's position is structured and seldom changes. In small groups, particularly those which invest a high amount of participatory decision making and influence in all group members, one's position may not be clearly prescribed. A group may be required to develop positions on its own. This is usually thought of as developing a *division of labor* among group members.

Beyond descriptions of what a person does in a position, we can also assess the comparative attributes of positions. Thus, it is possible to *rank-order* positions in a system as to the *amount* of responsibilities and rewards one position carries compared to others. Such determinations produce indices of the *prestige* attached to positions. We usually assume that as the responsibilities, privileges, and rewards associated with a position increase, so will its prestige. Prestige is relatively easy to ascertain in large, formal organizations because the hierarchical arrangement of positions is normally well known and stable over time. Aside from formally delegated leadership positions, small groups seldom evolve a hierarchy of prestige positions.

A concept often used interchangeably for prestige is *status*. We often hear people refer to "high status jobs" and "low status jobs" in a company, or other people referred to as "high status persons" or "low status persons." To avoid possible confusion later on, we shall use *prestige* to mean the formally or traditionally defined duties, prerogatives, and rewards known to be part of a position, and *status* to mean the evaluations and responses *others* give to holders of a position.

It is possible to differentiate between two types of status. First, there is *ascribed* status, which encompasses our reactions to others because of the positions (and prestige) they hold. We adopt certain "appropriate" ways of behaving when interacting with our "supervisors," "parents," "elders," and "professors," because those people *fit* the labels and we have been taught (socialized) to act accordingly. These reactions are based on the ways we have been socially conditioned to act towards people who fall into categories for which we have labels.

In contrast, there is also *achieved* status, which alludes to how others evaluate and react to a person's *performance* in a position or activity. Achieved status is a more complex concept to understand than ascribed status. First, it is based on evaluations of another's performances and such evaluations, even where "objective" criteria exist, are subject to a considerable amount of variation. This variation is due to the fact that no one person will perceive the performances of another exactly the same way. Second, attitudinal or personality compatibilities and other variables like frequency of interaction or interpersonal attraction can affect our perceptions of performance. Generally, the more favorably a person's actions are evaluated, the higher the status the person will achieve.

The concept of status as we are using it here implies that status can be viewed as a continuum ranging from "High Status" to "Low Status." From our point of view, it is not possible to think in terms of "No Status," only gradations along the High to Low continuum. We hasten to add that there is *no necessary relationship* between ascribed and achieved status. For example, your supervisor has higher ascribed status than other group members, but your work group may evaluate supervisory performance as very poor. Therefore, group reactions based on the intrinsic status of a supervisory position are probably different than reactions resulting from that supervisor's achievement of high status in the eyes of group members. A rather humorous analogy can be found in many Hollywood situation comedy plots that employ an inept manager or vice-president in a company owned by "Daddy."

Our discussion of positions, to this point, has not touched on what is usually the most common reference to positions in the study of small and large group systems. This is the concept of group *role*. A role is actually a combination of position, prestige, and status.

Roles comprise a number of different social and psychological factors. There are two general categories of roles, *formal* and *informal*. A formal role is normally thought of as a position and its associated prestige. Formal roles are prescribed by a group, organization, or society (leader, supervisor, father, and so forth). Informal, or *interaction*, roles evolve through association and interaction between members of a group or organization. Thus, we can talk about some members or groups being *opinion leaders* because they are always among the first members to have information and ideas on new subjects of relevance to a group. Similarly, we can speak of *liaison*, or linking, persons in organizations because they seem to help create and maintain informal channels of interaction between members of various groups due to contacts they develop with one or more members (Farace, Monge and Russell, 1977).

Before we leave the subject of group roles, one final point bears mentioning. In small groups where members have relatively undefined formal roles, one's achieved status is usually synonymous with a group role. To determine your role in a group it is often necessary to examine how you interact as a member and how other members react to your actions. Members of groups seldom directly verbalize their reactions about each others' performances to each other during group meetings. They often take one another to task about various ideas or information but seldom confront each other by saying, "You don't have very high status in this group because. . . ." Such feedback is hardly ever that clear or specific. Our roles in groups evolve out of our actions as members, others' perceptions and evaluations of those actions, and the expectations which are formed about how we will act on future occasions.

Expectations and Group Norms

At the basis of all social roles are a number of personal and social *expectations* about another's behavior (see, for example, Goffman, 1959, 1967, 1971; Lindesmith and Strauss, 1969; Rose, 1962). These expectations not only influence our perception of performances but can be used to *evaluate* the appropriateness, correctness, or usefulness of our own performances or those of others. *Norms* emerge when expectations are shared by enough participants to be effectively enforced as codes or *rules* governing behavior.

We are most aware of norms that regulate our behavior as members of society since they are codified into laws. Additionally, we usually understand that certain behaviors are more or less appropriate in particular settings. In conversational settings, we are aware that people expect an opportunity to interact by shifting between talker and listener modes.

One of the best ways to understand normative expectations is to associate expectations with role definitions. Formal or relatively well defined informal roles seldom pose problems for discerning normative expectations. Through stated instructions or regulations, or by informed knowledge of traditions, we usually recognize prevailing expectations for formal roles. In other words, we come to realize the *sanctions* associated with role performances. Sanctions are the positive and negative rewards (benefits and punishments) one receives for correct or incorrect performances. We are generally aware of rewards and costs associated with "poor" performance on our jobs or as parents, for example. The former usually has clearly prescribed *extrinsic* rewards and costs. The latter, however, is more of a blend of both extrinsic and *intrinsic* sanctions. It is usually more difficult to assess the sanctions for being a "poor parent" than those for being an ineffective employee.

Since most small groups do not have formally defined roles for all members, normative expectations are seldom clear at the outset. This is also true of most interpersonal encounters. Recall that a person's group role(s) is determined by the perceptions of other members. The same cycle of interpersonal behaviors associated with role development is also responsible for creating normative expectations. Thibaut and Kelley (1959) point out that normative expectations for interaction are created as a consequence of our decisions to act in one way versus others. Over time, group members arrive at sets of expectations for one another, based on their inferences about behavior, which they developed from past interaction. Hence, we come to expect others to behave in certain ways as a consequence of how we have observed and inferred consistencies, or *patterns,* from their past actions in the group.

We also infer the presence of norms from reactions received from others about our behavior. Feedback, however, is not always clear enough to assess positive or negative reactions. Often members just try to ignore someone whose actions are not positively valued. Other times, groups may make a concerted effort to gain compliance from a normatively *deviant* member. The member usually receives much verbal attention until others are satisfied that group expectations will be met (Schachter, 1951).

Norms seldom evolve as an outgrowth of a group's conscious intent to plan them. A group usually does not sit down and say, "Today we will talk about our group norms." Norms simply emerge through interaction focusing on achieving task related goals. They are used to evaluate member behavior and to justify positive and negative rewards applied to it. They prescribe *ranges* of permissable or undesirable behaviors (Sherif and Sherif, 1969). Small groups particularly have difficulty in consistently managing normative expectations. Sometimes deviations are not recognized as falling outside acceptable boundaries in time to make sanctions timely or effective. There are other instances when a person's group role allows for some behaviors that would usually be considered out-of-bounds (Hollander, 1958).

Redundancy and Patterns of Behavior

To be redundant is to manifest some kind of repetition of thought or action. To assess redundancy, then, we must take account of the frequency with which different behaviors occur. From these observations we can identify *patterns* of behavior within a group. These patterns constitute the observable aspects of a group's social structure. Patterns formed from behavioral redundancy are the *data* from which we make inferences concerning the social structure of a group. The more attuned we are to redundancies and resulting patterns the more information we have at our disposal for understanding small groups. We shall restrict our discussion of patterns to those which are found by observing types and rates of behavior—*content* structures—or preferences for affiliating with other members—*affiliative* structures. The remainder of the chapter is devoted to assessing the *connectedness* of member interaction, the flow of message interchanges, usually referred to as interaction networks.

    Content structures. An observer's task is greatly simplified when there is a clear and efficient way of summarizing group behavior. These summaries provide insights about the *interaction structures* of groups. The term *structure* implies that group participation patterns appear in some form that would not be expected to happen by chance alone (see, for example, Bostroam, 1970; Stech, 1970; Gouran and Baird, 1972). Three kinds of interaction structure patterns can be identified: *distributional, sequential,* and *temporal.*

    The concept "distributional structure" was used by Gouran and Baird (1972) to describe differential frequencies of participation across categories of interaction content. Look briefly at Table 5.1 in Chapter 5. There we were able to count the frequency of content statements for each member. Also notice that the frequencies for each category were summarized in that table. Those frequencies were not evenly spread across members or categories. By looking at these differential frequencies we are able to ascertain *distributional patterns* for both individual members and the group.

    No small group will exhibit a random or undifferentiated pattern of interaction. However, there is little consensus on whether an *ideal* pattern exists. Quite often groups reflect an emphasis on some behaviors. This happens for two reasons. First, at different points in time, a group may have relatively distinct needs for certain types of participation from its members. For example, exchanging information and suggestions about task objectives is more appropriate in early sessions of a group, and exchanging opinions about suggestions may dominate other sessions. Second, members may experience conflicts with each other which lead to unnecessary or inappropriate frequencies for some message categories.

    Participation patterns can also be distinguished by observing categories which follow one another during interaction. Bales (1965, 1970) has dealt extensively with the nature of *sequential* patterns as they relate to personal interaction tendencies. He notes that people in task oriented groups usually enter the flow of interaction with *reactive* statements (such as positive or negative comment) or a question, and, if the person continues talking, will follow with a task statement (for example, give an opinionated statement or information). These extensions after the first entry comment are termed *proactive* behaviors.

A number of communication researchers have simplified and extended the notion of interaction sequences suggested in Bales' research (e.g., Bostroam, 1970; Fisher, 1970; Gouran and Baird, 1972; Stech, 1970). This orientation has focused on assessing nonrandom distributions of categorized interaction sequences in an *act react* framework. Gouran and Baird (1972) labeled these kinds of patterns as the *sequential structure* of a group.

The following are some of the more commonly reported sequences: (1) Requests for information are most often followed by reactions which attempt to provide information or opinion; this general tendency is also found for sequences of seeking and giving opinion or suggestions. (2) Positive and negative social-emotional behaviors, particularly agreement and disagreement, are more likely to follow opinionated statements or suggestions which attempt to orient the activities of a group in some direction. (3) Positive acts are more likely to be followed by other positive acts while negative acts are more likely to be followed by task statements, questions, or other negative acts. (4) Sequential structures appear to vary according to the nature of group purposes for interacting; hence, there is likely to be a difference in structures between groups with relatively specific goals versus groups with less clearly articulated purposes for conversing (such as rap groups or informal group conversations).

What happens in a group is greatly affected by the amount of time members have interacted with each other. *Temporal patterns* are the ways distributional patterns change over time. By examining distributional patterns for similarities or differences between or within group meetings, we are afforded some insight into a group's evolution as a social system. The bulk of research on temporal patterns has focused on constructing and/or testing models of *group development;* these will be the subject of Chapter 9.

Two important points can be made with respect to temporal patterns. First, most groups tend to exhibit *cyclical* changes of interaction within specific sessions of a meeting or between meetings. Philp and Dunphy (1959) noted this tendency in a study of classroom learning groups. Using an early version of the IPA method, they found that interaction patterns differed within and between group meetings. Their results indicated that groups *regressed* from meeting to meeting during their problem solving interaction. Regardless of where problem solving efforts were suspended at the conclusion of one meeting, the beginning of a new session was marked by interaction behavior less typical of where the group left off and more typical of a stage it had passed through before the previous session ended. These groups seemed to "replow old soil" before moving on to pick up where they left off.

A second feature of temporal patterns is their sensitivity to the length of time a group will remain together. Different patterns develop according to constraints placed on a group. Bales and Strodtbeck (1951) discussed such constraints regarding the kind of task demands placed on a group. A task, they proposed, may be *full-fledged* or *truncated*. A full-fledged task is one where group members must produce some kind of integrated action (arrive at total agreement, consensus, on a solution or decision), under conditions that provide sufficiently strong motivation to work together, and may, but not necessarily will, require multiple meetings for task completion. Situations where one or more of these elements are missing are said to produce *truncated* group tasks. Thus, group-system functioning is interwoven with the type of task conditions that are present.

Affiliative structures. As group members interact they develop evaluative images of one another concerning various task performance and social style attributes. They classify and differentiate each other on such dimensions as: Who helps accomplish task objectives? Who is easy to work around? Who have I come to like (or dislike) through working together? How members answer such questions affects the content and frequency of interaction between all participants.

Where communication network channels are potentially open to everyone, group member decisions about affiliating with each other are demonstrated by how members use those channels. Members who rate one another highly may interact more frequently (use connecting channels between themselves more often), send more positive messages supportive of each others' opinions or suggestions, and interact less with other members not perceived to be within the same "circle of friends."

A person's role in a group comprises both structural and emotional dimensions that are not mutually exclusive. Group roles are significantly determined by emotional reactions. Thus, you can be knowledgeable about task demands and provide, from all objective evaluations, insightful and useful contributions in a group; but some members may not like you for a variety of reasons not under your direct control (gender, race/ethnicity, physical appearance, age, resentment of abilities, and so on).

There are many situations where overt behaviors are not readily useful in assessing affiliative tendencies. We are often limited to second-hand information about choice behaviors. This is characteristic of information used by researchers who study the phenomenon of behavioral choices—the study of *sociometry*. The theory and techniques of sociometric analysis were developed, in large part, by Moreno in the 1930s (Moreno, 1960). Sociometric analysis attempts to uncover the patterns of interpersonal choices made by group members. These choices can run the gamut from desires for further interaction to wanting membership in a group led by a particular person. Choices do not have to be positive. If it is possible to determine who group members like the most, it is equally possible to find out who members like the least.

One of the most common techniques for assessing sociometric patterns is by constructing *sociograms*. A sociogram is a graphic representation of group members' choices on some selection criterion. For example, we might ask group members to privately indicate their answer to the following question: "Of the members in this group, who would you most like to work with in another group?" We can tabulate responses to the question and construct a choice diagram, or sociogram, like that in Figure 6.1. We see that Dick is the most frequently chosen person, and that Dick and Ed have chosen each other—suggesting there was some

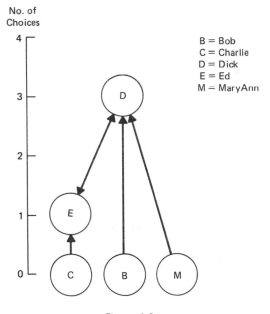

Figure 6.1

mutual attraction between them (at least in terms of wanting to participate together in other groups).

It is possible to make accurate inferences about affiliative choices through direct observation. The content, frequency, sequence of interaction, proxemic behaviors (do some people consistently sit next to each other or across from one another), which members usually support each others' ideas, who argues with whom, and a host of less obvious actions provide some basis for valid inference. Often these patterns reflect the *informal* structure of a group—that aspect of the group's social organization which exists independently of formally ascribed group roles. Informal groups emerge from choice and contact among members of formally composed groups and positions. Some people may be associated with many informal groups, others with only one, and others with none at all. These sociometric groups, often called *cliques,* may wield considerable power and effect the way information is channeled through an organization.

In most small groups sociometric patterns are usually the only operating structures for the group. Small groups have less opportunity for complex informal structures. In most cases, except possibly for a group's leader, group roles are not prescribed and the structure that evolves reflects the interpersonal choices of members. The network characteristics of a group represent those choices and normally constitute the structure of a group, including subgroup coalitions.

Over time, there are likely to be many changes in a group's coalition structures. Members come to distinguish each other on different recurring task and emotional issues. Therefore, on a particular issue, members of one coalition may find themselves pitted against each other. This is both natural and healthy for the group. However, enduring member attractions are also a part of group membership. Some members may find it difficult to switch coalitions and to have to confront a friend. Separating coalitions which emerge over issues from networks based on sociometric choices is not always easy. The two patterns may totally overlap in some groups, while in others, the overlap may not be that complete.

WHAT ARE COMMUNICATION NETWORKS?

Communication networks exist whenever people develop patterns of interaction. These networks can be regarded as maps for channels over which messages are transmitted. A network serves more than a passive channel function for interaction. It becomes a reflection of norms for behavior, affiliations, roles, and coalitions which serves to control and structure relationships among group members. Individuals maintain positions related to one another which, in turn, determine overall interaction patterns. This pattern of linkages is the structural aspect of a group which is regarded as the *communication network.*

A communication network serves to control a situation by setting norms for the form and content of group interaction (Hare, 1976). The junior executive carefully monitors her or his language when writing a

memo to a superior. If someone higher up should be communicated with, a decision must also be made whether to send a message through the normal chain of command or by-pass intermediaries and go straight to the top. If direct contact is necessary, the message may be sent in a formal letter as opposed to the less formal memo normally sent to the next in command.

The issues of *what to say, to whom, in what form,* and *under which specified conditions* relate to prevailing norms that control interaction. Since norms usually condone less carefully controlled interaction between people of similar status or position, communication on an equal level occurs more frequently and carries a higher potential for social exchange and development of interpersonal relationships. By establishing formal and informal relationships through the designation of networks, groups evolve and are maintained (Crook, 1961).

The functional requirements of a group may mandate a *formal structure* by which information can be efficiently channeled (such as, all information about bills and receipts get channeled to the treasurer, all formal motions and agenda items may be channeled through the secretary) as a means of avoiding *information overload* on one person—such as a president. A group may have some control over information flow by establishing a structure of authority, work relations, and spatial arrangements.

Certain social needs and opportunities may permit an *informal structure* to develop outside of the formal structure. If two group members get together to play golf on Friday afternoon, much information may be exchanged, perhaps this opportunity for interaction may establish a friendship bond outside the formal group which, in turn, may facilitate their interactions within the group. An informal network may serve to fulfill certain socio-emotional needs of members, provide a source of satisfaction, influence the degree of individual contributions to the group, and provide an important source of group-related information. An informal network may be synonymous with the formal network or entirely separate from it. In either case, the formal and informal networks play a vital part in the functioning of the group.

Groups generally have a goal of obtaining maximum output with a minimum expenditure of time and energy. A network which permits information collection and decision making by a central source with minimum time lapse may be necessary in a crisis situation. A less centralized network may be used more effectively under different circumstances. The critical concern of a group should be whether networks which have developed are best suited to a task in terms of permitting member satisfaction and accurate, efficient goal achievement.

The Study of Network Effectiveness

Few aspects of small groups have stimulated as much research as the study of channels and interaction networks. Initial study in this area stemmed from rather pragmatic interests about maximizing the effectiveness of large organizational systems. The emphasis was on how *information flow* within and between organizational units can affect production, problem solving, or decision making task outcomes. Such issues are mainly the concern of persons responsible for designing, implementing, and/or evaluating management and supervisory organizational systems. The many studies conducted on communication networks have yielded valuable information on how channel and network utilization affects group productivity and work satisfaction.

Defining communication networks. One definition of a *communication network* is a "set of positions with specific communication channels," with a channel being "the probability that a message can pass in a given direction between two positions (Glazner and Glaser, 1961, p. 1.)" Consider pattern A in Figure 6.2. Each dot represents a person (*a, b, c*) in a three-member group and these people are linked (lines between dots) by two-way *channels* of communication. In this case, *b* and *c* are not linked except through *a*. An example of this pattern might be *a* and *c* are fellow employees. As *a* leaves the office one evening, *c* remarks "Say hello to your wife (*b*) for me." Upon transmitting the message, *a*'s wife responds, "Tell him we will have him over for dinner one of these days." Here we have *b* dependent upon *a* to transmit messages to *c*. In turn, *c* is dependent upon *a* to get the message to *b*.

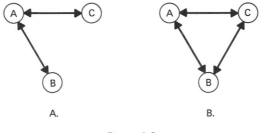

A.   B.

Figure 6.2

One way in which interaction patterns can be described is that they are "the sum of individuals to whom a member has communicative access (Leavitt, 1951, p. 39)." In our example, *a* is in the most *central* position of the network (demonstrates high *centrality*) because he is closest to all other positions. By "closest" we are referring to the distance between one position and another as measured by the number of *communication links*

required to get information from one to another. The sum of distances for a group would be a summation of all the shortest distances (links) from every position to every other position.

Pattern B in Figure 6.2 represents a totally connected network of three group members. In this case all members are an equal distance apart and no single member is central to the group. In most network studies a channel is not determined by whether a person uses it but whether the opportunity for transmission actually exists. Person *a*, for example, may have the opportunity to send a message to person *b* but may elect not to use the option.

A historical overview of network research. Alex Bavelas (1948; 1950) was among the first scholars to write about the potential importance of group communication structures. He described some basic differences between various types of network patterns and discussed their implications for efficient group task accomplishment. Given several communication patterns logically feasible for completion of a task, such as patterns A through D in Figure 6.3, Bavelas questioned whether one pattern would be significantly better than another.

Notice that the four patterns in Figure 6.5 present different interaction opportunities. In pattern A, the Circle, every member (or point) can directly interact with two other members. Only members *b*, *c*, and *d* can do so in the Chain pattern, and only member *c* can interact with more than one other person in the Wheel or Y patterns. The notion of *relative centrality* helps to explain differences in patterns. Member, or position, *c* in patterns C and D possesses high relative centrality because all messages between other positions must pass through (and therefore rely on) that position. Position *c* is highly centralized in these networks. Position *c* is less centralized in pattern B, the *Chain*, while position *c* in a *Wheel* configuration has no higher centrality than any other position.

Bavelas (1950) reported preliminary evidence showing that circle and chain patterns did result in different task outcomes and personal responses. For example, the chain network was more efficient than the circle, and people in central positions were most often chosen as leaders by their coworkers.

Leavitt (1951) studied four types of network structures. His results permitted him to arrange the four structures from most to least centralized—wheel, Y, chain and circle—in descending qualitative order with respect to three variables. First, regarding the *speed* of developing an organization for problem solving, the wheel, Y, and chain developed stability once they were organized, while the circle remained inconsistent. Second, the same order prevailed as to the amount of agreement on group leadership across the patterns. Finally, this order also prevailed in

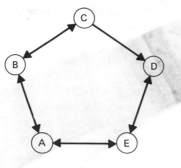

A. Circle

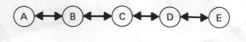

B. Chain

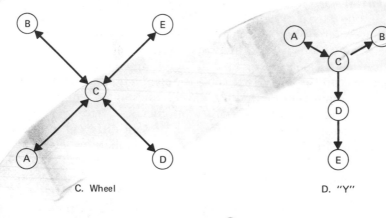

C. Wheel

D. "Y"

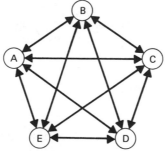

E. All channel

Figure 6.3

regard to member satisfaction with group interaction patterns. In analyzing the effects of positions within a network, Leavitt found that people in the central position sent and received the most messages. These people, in turn, enjoyed their jobs more than those in the peripheral positions.

Applying these findings to real settings, we might conclude that groups with strong leaders who are able to collect and disseminate information will achieve the greatest task efficiency in the shortest time. We might also expect to find leaders gaining the greatest satisfaction and enjoyment from a group while those with the least opportunity to communicate would probably realize the least satisfaction. Reflecting upon your own group experiences, these conclusions probably have a ring of validity. In the classroom setting, students who frequently contribute to the discussion are often the most satisfied with the class and those who rarely contribute are often less satisfied.

Shaw's research vividly demonstrated how the distribution of information affects group behavior (Shaw, 1954a, 1954c). In one study Shaw (1954b) found that while a circle network required more messages per solution than the wheel, it was faster in solving complex problems. However, the wheel was faster than the circle in the solution of simple problems. The implications of these findings are that (1) relatively simple group goals can be achieved more efficiently using a strong leader to organize and control interaction, and (2) more complex task goals require inputs from all members, thus, participation opportunities must be spread across group positions in the network.

Lanzetta and Roby (1956a, 1956b) defined structure according to the specialization and interrelation of jobs in a group. They modeled their network after an air defense center in which members had either (1) a specialized task to be combined with specialized tasks completed by other members to provide "unified task accomplishment," (*vertical* structure) or (2) each member completed the entire task without reliance on others (*horizontal* structure). When members had to depend on others in a vertical structure, they were found to produce more errors compared to autonomous members of horizontal structures. On the other hand, when workloads became heavier, efficiency declined in the autonomous conditions. In general, when a task is not too difficult, it may be better for members to do the entire task themselves, rather than relying on other members. However, when a task is more complex, it may be better to encourage specialization as a means of avoiding errors and inefficiency.

Most researchers now agree that centralized networks are more efficient for solving simple tasks, and decentralized networks are best for solving complex tasks. Moreover, group members located in central positions or having some degree of autonomy will generally gain the greatest satisfaction and enjoyment from working on a task, whereas members who are less central and depend more on other group members for task completion will probably find less satisfaction and enjoyment from group membership.

Perhaps the most prolific researcher of communication networks during the 1960s was Arthur Cohen. Most of his work focused upon the effects of shifting from one network to another during the life of a group (Cohen, 1962, 1964a, 1964b, 1967; Cohen and Foerst. 1968). The conclusion drawn from this research is that a problem solving system developed in a first network will be used in the second network if the first system is more efficient than the second. The problem solving system developed in the first network will not be used in a second network if the first system is less efficient than the system that develops in the second network.

Networks may not be as important to the problem solving ability of a group as is history of a group's prior use of various networks. If a group is accustomed to solving problems in a particular manner, rearrangement of its interaction patterns may not affect the manner in which members proceed to work on a task. For example, assume that the president of a company has established policies and practices in an autocratic, centralized manner for ten years. Then one day he goes to a workshop on new participative management strategies that inspires him to change his style. He decides to let his key staff members have a greater voice in making crucial decisions. To his surprise, he finds they are unable and/or unwilling to assume the responsibility. Whenever a decision is to be made in this newly formed democratic, decentralized network, group members turn to the president for direction just as they have traditionally done in the past. Hence, this problem solving technique still reflects the old mode of operation rather than the newly imposed, "freer," network.

The Generalizability of Network Research

In a summary of his network research, Cohen (1964c) concluded that the following factors contribute to or detract from the likelihood of successful collaboration among members of problem solving groups: (1) a tradition of critical internal evaluation, (2) appropriate sharing of responsibility for developing and modifying work systems, (3) knowledge of alternative work procedures and alternative experience, and (4) a long-range perspective of time and performance. Many factors can intervene to inhibit interaction network effectiveness. In this section we will review some of those factors and their implications.

Leadership in networks. Studies of leadership in networks have concluded that the most efficient communication arrangement will differ for groups with democratic and authoritarian atmospheres. Lyle (1961) concluded that managerial leaders striving for a democratic atmosphere and efficiency should in some way curtail conversation among top staff members but keep channels open and active below themselves and the staff. In a work situation with a more authoritarian atmosphere, leaders should maintain a different communicative setting. They should strive for balance. The more leaders talk, the more they potentially interfere with staff efficiency—but staff morale rises; the less leaders talk, the greater will be staff efficiency—but morale suffers. Another interesting finding from Lyle's study was that the proportion of communication used for feedback from group members to a leader was not related to group atmosphere. However, in cases of feedback denial, morale declined in democratic groups but not in authoritarian groups. It seems group members develop expectations for feedback opportunities in democratic groups which, if denied, result in decreased morale. Apparently authoritarian groups do not develop similar expectations.

Recall that leadership is closely related to, if not synonymous with, centrality. The most centrally located person in a group is generally nominated for a leadership role by group members. More information gets channeled through the person, resulting in his or her satisfaction with and enjoyment in the task and group. Member aspirations for the group are also related to centrality. According to a study by Zander and Forward (1968), people in central positions develop a stronger desire for group success than those in peripheral positions. In general, we may expect a leader to more closely identify with group goals and to develop greater expectations for achievement than those less centrally located.

Fiedler (1964) suggests that *directive* leadership is more effective when the group-task situation is either highly favorable or unfavorable for a leader, whereas *nondirective* leadership is more effective in the intermediate ranges of favorability. Fiedler had five-person groups attempt three tasks under either directive or nondirective leadership. The results indicated a directive leader was more effective than a nondirective leader *only* when the group-task situation was highly favorable for the leader. Thus, under neutral or negative conditions, a leader may find it best to maintain a low profile in the group. Only when the group-task demands are clearly favorable should the leader take a more assertive role.

Personality. The success or failure of leadership is dependent upon characteristics of the task, group structure, member needs, and other factors. One of these factors may well be group member personalities. Several network studies report that various personality traits affect performance (*ascendence,* Berkowitz, 1956; *authoritarianism,* Shaw, 1955; and *population style,* Shaw, 1955) in structured groups.

Cohen and Foerst (1968) sought to determine differences between represser (R) and sensitizer (S) groups in adaptation to communication network and task changes. *Repressers* are those people who attempt to cope with anxiety through repression, denial, and rationalization. *Sensitizers* attempt to cope with anxiety through mechanisms such as intellectualism, obsessive-compulsive behavior, and manifest worry. The findings indicated that Rs develop appropriate problem solving earlier, utilize their systems more efficiently, and exhibit significantly greater leadership continuity in conditions of change. Significant differences were found between R and S groups in times taken to solve problems in the wheel and following network change.

The general conclusion that can be drawn from this and other studies, is that member personalities will have an effect on the output of groups under varying conditions of group structure. This generalization concurs with our perspective in Chapter 2 when we noted that people with certain personality traits are more effective in groups than others. It follows that some organizational networks are more effective than others because of various member personalities.

Embeddedness. Cohen and his colleagues have questioned the applicability of small group network research to field situations. For example, small groups typically perform as subgroups which are parts of, or *embedded* in, larger networks in organizations. The effectiveness of a group may be quite different in isolation than when it is embedded in a larger organization.

Quinn and Kent (1967) noted a potential limitation to the practice of some large organizations to create small subgroups as compensation for the alienating effects of organizational size. Analyzing the attitudes and participation of rank and file members in 113 voluntary organizations, they conclude that members of the *largest* subunits, relative to the total organization, were more likely than others to report success in acquiring information, resources, and recognition from their organizations. Perhaps with the exception of small, executive level committees, larger groups receive more attention from the total organization, resulting in greater member satisfaction.

Another way to view embeddedness is that small groups often break down or decompose into smaller subgroups. A problem with early network studies was that their laboratory procedures did not allow for the natural decomposing of groups. Mackenzie (1967) was able to demonstrate that the four commonly used networks could be further decomposed into smaller subunits embedded within a larger group. The practice of asking group members to carry out specialized tasks or roles is an example of how subgroups emerge within the larger network structures.

When a group is embedded within a larger group we should expect changing pressures, over time, to act on the smaller group. What would happen if a larger group were to add some reinforcement or punishment as a means of improving output? Would some groups better adapt to those pressures than others or would they continue to work at the same level of efficiency? Burgess (1969) found that with the introduction of reinforcement to increase solution rates and reduce errors, wheel networks were no more efficient in solving problems than circle patterns. A wheel is initially faster because communication restrictions reduce organizational problems. Organization is more difficult in a circle network because time is needed to establish some type of relay system. Once the initial transition period is completed, the response rate increases until a steady level is reached. While it takes the circle significantly longer to reach optimum organization than the wheel, the circle is just as productive under conditions of reinforcement once a steady state is achieved.

Size and seating arrangement. In spite of group satisfaction gained from the power and prestige associated with large subgroup membership, greater satisfaction is gained in smaller groups. Member participation and interaction generally increases with decreased size and decreases with increased size. As mentioned earlier, greater enjoyment and satisfaction is derived from increased opportunities to participate. People tend to communicate differently in smaller sized groups. Zimet and Schneider (1969), for example, found that males placed in quasi-therapeutic discussion dyads demonstrated less aggression and greater supportiveness compared to larger groups that exhibited significantly more aggression than support.

The size of a network creates an implicit organizational structure that influences interaction. Another implicit network is the seating arrangement of group members. In groups where members are unacquainted, individuals facing the largest number of members do the most talking and are most likely to be judged as leaders by other group members (Ward, 1968).

Division of labor. Becker and Baloff (1969) found a "division of labor" form of organization to be superior in performance to committee or hierarchical forms of organization in a business game setting. Business school graduate students were organized into three-person teams with the task of estimating demand for four products to be sold at a ballpark concession stand. Based upon estimated demand and variables such as temperature, team standing, attendance, and time of day, groups had to determine how much of each product to buy. Eleven teams were formed into a hierarchical structure with a president and two vice-presidents. Twelve teams were formed into a committee network which required group consensus (unanimous agreement). Thirteen teams were formed into a division of labor network with three vice-presidents (one vice-president was assigned to attendance, one to beer and coffee, and one to hot dogs and ice cream).

The results indicated that the division of labor organization was significantly better than either of the other two networks. The least effective form of organization was the hierarchical structure. In addition, members of the committee and division of labor groups reported less frustration and greater cohesion than the more tightly structured hierarchy. While the division of labor and hierarchy groups reported no difficulty in fulfilling role requirements, six of the thirteen committee groups reported development of a division of labor along the same lines specified for division of labor groups.

The effects of structure on a group were underscored in Becker and Baloff's conclusions. Two variables contributed to group differences: experience and overall group intelligence. Seemingly, experienced and/or "smart" groups can overcome inefficient group structures. Groups with less experienced or intelligent members can be helped or hindered, depending on the type of structural pattern that is employed. One type of structure might prove too complicated and inhibit productivity while another pattern could have just the opposite impact. Task demands and member characteristics need to be synchronized with network structure properties to alleviate ineffective task organizing.

HOW DO STRUCTURAL ELEMENTS INTERRELATE?

Most network studies have been conducted with groups of three, four, and five members. However, we have regarded a small group as roughly three to fifteen members. Is it possible the efficiency of a wheel would break down due to information overload with more than five or ten group members? The answer must be, in some cases, *yes*. The results will largely depend on task complexity, competencies of group members, and capabilities of the central person. You can probably think of some group leaders or administrators who competently handle large amounts of information while, on the other hand, others require strong subordinates to sift through the masses of data before forwarding a concise version of the information.

We agree with Shaw (1964, p. 119) that network research has "demonstrated quite clearly that the pattern of communication imposed upon a group is an important determinant of the behavior of the group." But, we must go one step further than this simple cause-effect relationship. Too many other variables require us to qualify statements such as, "Use a centralized structure when the task is simple and a decentralized structure when the task is complex." As Shaw goes on to conclude, "findings also indicated that the particular relationships between communication pattern and group behavior depends in part upon other variables." Many of those variables have been identified but others remain untested. The interrelationships among variables are endless. Until some fertile mind can put all the pieces together into a comprehensive theory, we are left with a jumble of inconsistent, independent findings. For the time being, we believe that the systems perspective is the most productive approach to the problem.

Social Structures and Social Systems

Whenever a group of people form to work on a mutual objective, they go through a period of organizing themselves in a way that seems to make sense and satisfies the majority of input needs. During this organizing phase, members implicitly learn *whom* to speak to about *what* issues. Some members will inevitably receive more communication than others. These central members will not only be spoken to more often but will speak to others with greater frequency than more peripheral members.

Those people to whom others talk and who talk more frequently will probably experience: (1) satisfaction and enjoyment from the group, (2) identification with group goals, (3) higher expectations than less central members, (4) have a major impact on the satisfaction of other members, and (5) be appointed or elected leaders of the group by other members. We can conclude that the more central members of a group will be assigned higher status than others. Those who are least often talked to and who talk less frequently will probably be lower in status. In essence, the behavior of group members will determine their status in a group.

The relationship between participation and achieved status is not always obvious. In any group, members are aware of how much a person talks and the usefulness or relevance of that talk in terms of group objectives. Judgments members make about contributions usually modify the relationship between quantity of interaction and status. For example, an expert on one phase of a group task may say very little except when the group approaches a personal area of expertise. Yet, the group may assign a high status *leadership* role to that person due to the *quality* of their contributions.

Most groups do not exist in isolation from other groups. Several subgroups may exist within a larger group and may have shared influence. Some subgroup members may belong to more than one group or at least may have close contact with members of other groups. These people create *linking channels* by providing information to more than one group or subgroup. They serve the valuable function of providing a group with information from an outside context. For a total system of groups to work effectively and harmoniously there must be some people who help interrelate the parts.

Individuals or groups without access to external sources of information are regarded as *isolates*. Sometimes they are isolated physically as with a student who is assigned a seat in a corner of the room with no other students near. In other cases, they are psychologically isolated as when a deviate gets excluded from group interaction and is assigned lower status role requirements. External groups or individuals can provide information, reinforcement, or punishment to a group which, in turn, may affect group efficiency. Isolated groups and individuals do not fully share in the advantages of these associations and find it difficult to adjust to changing external conditions or to improve achievement.

It is erroneous to conclude that a centralized network is more efficient than a decentralized network without taking a broader view of the total system. While it is true that simple tasks can usually be accomplished best under a centralized system, a decentralized system can be just as effective once an organizational method is established and if some outside reinforcement is present. In this section we have discussed the *natural* evolution of a social structure within group systems. A knowledgeable group realizes that the natural system of organizing may not be the most desirable. Over time, membership or task demands may change, making a once successful method of operating less than optimally efficient. We have emphasized that a group must pay constant attention to various organizational structures and evaluate their usefulness with changing member and task demands.

Effects of Implementing Structural Change

Changing social structures and interaction patterns is not simply a matter of announcing such changes to a group. Even if the structure is "changed," the group may find it more convenient to continue interacting and working under the former structure. Norms of behavior develop over time and are based on the perceptions of group members. Announcing a change will not necessarily alter norms governing behavior or the thought processes of members. Therefore, careful analysis of a group's history is crucial in planning for change.

A leader or *change agent* must take into account factors related to individual member resistance to change. In general, the known is comfortable, the unknown is threatening. Many are likely to tolerate adverse conditions simply because they fear conditions might get worse with a change in their environment. Individuals will also resist change if they perceive a potential threat to status, prestige, and role relations within a group. A change may carry the implication that an individual was not performing satisfactorily. Under such circumstances, the natural inclination of a member will be to act defensively toward the impending changes.

A rather interesting case of such resistence involved a woman who had performed the role of executive secretary to the president of a small corporation for many years. Over time the corporation grew to the point that the woman had a tremendous work load requiring her to work after hours and on weekends. Perceiving the problem, the president asked four employees, including the executive secretary, to work on a plan of redistributing the work load. After the group had met a couple times, the president was surprised to learn the woman was behaving in a hostile manner toward other members and the group's task. He decided to talk with her on the following day since she was normally a pleasant and cooperative employee. The next day he was dismayed to discover that she failed to report to work and upon further checking he found that she had cleared her desk of all her possessions. Calls to her home were unanswered. The company's most valued employee was lost as a result of trying to make the employee's job easier.

Unless group members can perceive a need for change, request a change, or can forsee positive consequences, resistance may be experienced. Resistance may take the form of decreased group cohesion, increased errors in task efficiency, decreased output, loss of motivation, increased absenteeism, overt hostility, and other negative consequences. The task of the leader, or change agent, is to provide data to the members regarding the need for change and/or the positive consequences of recommended changes. After implementing changes, the leader must regularly monitor group feedback regarding change effects. Finally, someone should rediagnose the situation to determine whether additional modifications and changes are necessary.

While resistance can be anticipated in cases where consequences are not clearly beneficial to an individual or group (particularly in cases where the changes are major), a group does have some potential facilitators of change. A leader's prestige, status, and credibility can provide a positive influence for change. If a leader has the respect and admiration of group members, the person may be more successful than an outsider or less admired member of the group.

Members with sufficient attraction to a group may be willing to endure the hardship of transition and change. If they are cohesive and have a strong feeling of interdependence, the feeling of togetherness may be a positive force (depending upon whether the group as a whole views the change as valuable or harmful). Opposition to change is weakened when those most clearly effected by it speak favorably of such proposals. In general, the group as a total system can be a positive influence upon individual member attitudes and behaviors. Highly cohesive groups that adopt a norm of accepting change are more likely to control individual member resistance.

A final note of caution should be considered regarding the change of a group's interaction network. Any change in part of a system, or a change of a subsystem, will have potential ramifications for the other parts. The consequences may not necessarily be immediate. The changeover from one treasurer to another may go very smoothly, for example, until the year-end report must be filed. A group abolished in a reorganizational shuffle of a larger system may not be missed until some obscure task the group normally completed is left undone.

How much information regarding task accomplishment does a central member of a network store in his or her memory? What happens when that member is replaced or no longer has access to the same channels of information? We might draw an analogy to an air traffic controller who monitors the network of incoming and outgoing airplanes. When the person is to be replaced, the new controller must spend a period of time with the former controller getting a picture of the pattern. The consequences of not having complete control of information in the changeover are obvious. In a similar manner, a group member who changes roles within a group must effectively learn the network potential of the new role so that a smooth transition occurs.

REFERENCES

Bales, R.F. 1965. The equilibrium problem in small groups. In *Small groups: Studies in social interaction,* rev. ed., eds. A.P. Hare, E.F. Borgatta, and R.F. Bales, pp. 444–476.

Bales, R.F. 1970. *Personality and interpersonal behavior.* New York: Holt, Rinehart & Winston.

Bales, R.F. and Strodtbeck, F.L. 1951. Phases in group problem-solving. *Journal of Abnormal and Social Psychology 56,* 485–495.

Bavelas, A. 1948. A mathematical model for group structures. *Applied Anthropology 7,* 16–30.

Bavelas, A. 1950. Communication patterns in the task-oriented groups. *Journal of Acoustical Society of America 22,* 725–730.

Becker, S.W. and Baloff, N. 1969. Organization structure and complex problem solving. *Administrative Science Quarterly 14,* 260–271.

Berkowitz, L. 1956. Personality and group position. *Sociometry 19,* 210–222.

Bostram, R. 1970. Patterns of communicative interaction in small groups. *Speech Monographs 37*, 257–263.

Burgess, R.L. 1969. Communication networks and behavioral consequences. *Human Relations 22*, 137–159.

Cohen, A.M. 1961. Changing small group communication networks. *Journal of Communication 1*, 116–128.

Cohen, A.M. 1964b. Predicting organization in changed communication networks III. *Journal of Psychology 58*, 115–129.

Cohen, A.M. 1964c. Communication networks: In research and training. *Personnel Administration 27*, 18–25.

Cohen, A.M. 1967. A model of group adaptation to organizational change in communication networks. In *Communication: theory and research,* ed. L. Thayer. Springfield, Ill.: Charles C Thomas.

Cohen, A.M. and Foerst, J.R., Jr. 1968. Organizational behaviors and adaptations to organizational change of sensitizer and represser problem-solving groups. *Journal of Personality and Social Psychology 8*, 209–216.

Crook, R.B. 1961. Communication and group structure. *Journal of Communication 11*, 136–140.

Dobringer, W.M. 1969. *Social structures and systems.* Santa Monica, Calif.: Goodyear.

Farace, R.V., Monge, P.R. and Russell, H. 1977. *Communicating and Organizing.* Reading, Mass.: Addison-Wesley.

Fiedler, F.E. 1964. A contingency model of leadership effectiveness. In *Advances in experimental social psychology,* vol. 1, ed. L. Berkowitz, pp. 149–190. New York: Academic Press.

Fisher, B.A. 1970. Decision emergence: Phases in group decision-making. *Speech Monographs 37*, 53–66.

Glazner, M. and Glaser, R. 1961. Techniques for the study of group structure and behavior: II, Empirical studies on the effects of structure in small groups. *Psychological Bulletin 58*, 1–27.

Goffman, E. 1959. *Presentation of self in everyday life.* New York: Doubleday.

Goffman, E. 1967. *Interaction ritual: Essays on face-to-face behavior.* New York: Doubleday.

Goffman, E. 1971. *Relations in public.* New York: Harper & Row, Pub.

Gouran, D.S. and Baird, J.E. 1972. An analysis of distributional and sequential structure in problem-solving and informal group discussions. *Speech Monographs 39*, 16–22.

Hare, A.P. 1976. *Handbook of small group research.* 2nd. ed. New York: Free Press.

Hollander, E.P. 1958. Conformity, status, and idiosyncrasy credit. *Psychological Review 65*, 117–127.

Lanzetta, J.T. and Roby, T.B. 1956a. Effects of work-group structure and certain task variables on group performance. *Journal of Abnormal and Social Psychology 53*, 307–314.

Lanzetta, J.T. and Roby, T.B. 1956b. Group performance as a function of work-distribution patterns and task load. *Sociometry 19*, 95–104.

Leavitt, H.J. 1951. Some effects of certain communication patterns on group performance. *Journal of Abnormal and Social Psychology 46*, 38–50.

Lindesmith, A.P. and Strauss, A.L. 1969. *Social Psychology.* 3rd ed. New York: Holt, Rinehart & Winston.

Lyle, J. 1961. Communication, group atmosphere, productivity, and morale in small task groups. *Human Relations 14,* 369–379.

MacKenzie, K.D. 1967. Decomposition of communication networks. *Journal of Mathematical Psychology 4,* 162–172.

Monane, J. 1967. *A sociology of human systems.* New York: Appleton-Century-Crofts.

Moreno, J.L. et al., 1960. *The sociometry reader.* Glencoe, Ill.: The Free Press of Glencoe.

Philip, H. and Dunphy, D. 1959. Developmental trends in small groups. *Sociometry 22,* 162–174

Quinn, R.P. and Kent, J.T. 1967. Big fish, little fish: A competitive approach to organizational primary groups. *Proceedings of the 75th Annual Convention of the American Psychological Association,* 267–268.

Rose, A.M., 1962. *Human behavior and social processes.* Boston: Houghton Mifflin.

Schachter, S. 1951. Deviation, rejection and communication. *Journal of Abnormal and Social Psychology 46,* 190–207.

Shaw, M.E. 1954a. Group structure and the behavior of individuals in small groups. *Journal of Psychology 38,* 139–149.

Shaw, M.E. 1954b. Some effects of problem complexity upon problem solution efficiency in different communication nets. *Journal of Experimental Psychology 48,* 211–217.

Shaw, M.E. 1954c. Some effects of unequal distribution of information upon group performance in various communication nets. *Journal of Abnormal and Social Psychology 49,* 547–553.

Shaw, M.E. 1955. A comparison of two types of leadership in various communication nets. *Journal of Abnormal and Social Psychology* 127–134.

Shaw, M.E. 1964. Communication networks. In *Advances in experimental social psychology,* vol. 1. ed. L. Berkowitz. New York: Academic Press, 111–149.

Sherif, M. and Sherif, C. 1969. *Social Psychology.* New York: Harper & Row, Pub.

Stech, E. 1970. An analysis of interaction structure in the discussion of a ranking task. *Speech Monographs 37,* 249–256.

Thibant, J.W. and Kelley, H.H. 1959. *The social psychology of groups.* New York: Wiley.

Ward, C.D. 1968. Seating arrangement and leadership emergence in small discussion groups. *Journal of Social Psychology 74,* 83–90.

Weick, K.E. 1969. Laboratory organizations and unnoticed causes. *Administrative Science Quarterly 14,* 294–303.

Zander, A. and Forward, J. 1968. Position in group, achievement motivation, and group aspirations. *Journal of Personality and Social Psychology 8,* 282–288.

Zimet, C.N. and Schneider, C. 1969. Effects of group size on interaction in small groups. *Journal of Social Psychology 77,* 177–187.

Chapter

Many groups have a formally elected or appointed leader who determines the agenda, conducts the meeting, and regulates the flow of interaction. On the other hand, many groups form to work on a specified goal without a formally designated leader. After a relatively brief time, however, one or more members often emerge as dominant forces in shaping the direction of the group. What determines who will emerge as an elected or appointed group leader? What characteristics will help assure successful leadership? If a person aspires to leadership, what should he or she do?

These questions have been a subject of concern and interest for generations. Think how much more efficient group behavior might be if we could determine characteristics of the *best* possible leader for a group. Or, from a personal viewpoint, wouldn't it be nice to know what skills, knowledge, and behaviors a person needs to learn in order to be selected as a leader? Unfortunately, this chapter does not offer an easy formula for success. In fact, we suggest it is useful to think of groups having *multiple* leaders with most members

7
leadership:
power and influence
between group
members

fulfilling leadership roles at various times during the life of a group. We will address this idea more specifically as we examine three major questions: What are the characteristics of leaders? How do "leaders" behave? What makes a leader effective?

WHAT ARE THE CHARACTERISTICS OF LEADERS?

People are fascinated by the ideas and images surrounding leadership. There is a certain quality of glamour and mysticism tied to the subject. Philosophical essays have questioned who is most suited to lead governments; the hero or heroine of literary novels is often embued with proper judgment, handsome appearance, and influential powers. All of us have our personal preferences for certain sports, political, military, and entertainment leaders. As a nation, we are inspired to act upon the words and deeds of our leaders. The glamorous subject of leadership has also caught the imagination of researchers. More studies have been conducted in regard to leaders and leadership than any other area of group behavior.

Trait Approaches to Studying Leadership

Studies conducted during World War I focused on methods of selecting and placing officers for military service. At that time the best method seemed to be to test a candidate's intelligence since intellect was assumed to be an important characteristic of military leaders. However, the single trait of intelligence did not seem suitable to all situations, and researchers continued to search for other character traits that were highly related to directing others. Years later, after a large number of studies had been conducted, Bird (1940) identified seventy-nine traits found to be associated with leadership. Unfortunately, only a small percentage of the traits were common to four or more studies. Representative of early *trait* research were conclusions that leaders are physically larger, somewhat brighter, and psychologically better adjusted than other group members (Shaw, 1976). Conclusions like these resulted in leadership selection tests which attempted to determine whether a candidate was qualified for a position.

The *coup de grace* for trait studies was applied by Stogdill (1948). Upon reviewing the literature, he assessed the predictive strengths of various findings based on the number of studies that reported common results. Two major conclusions were derived from the positive results of at least fifteen studies: (1) the average person occupying a position of leadership exceeds the average group member in (a) intelligence, (b) scholarship, (c) dependability, (d) activity and social participation, and (e) socio-economic status; (2) the *qualities* required of a leader are determined in large part by *demands of the situation*. Positive evidence from ten or more studies also indicated the average person occupying a position of leadership exceeds the average group member in: (a) sociability, (b) persistence, (c) initiative, (d) knowing how to get things done, (e) self-confidence, (f) insight into situations, (g) cooperativeness, (h) popularity, (i) adaptability, and (j) verbal facility.

These findings were so tenuous that Stogdill (1948, p. 64) concluded an "adequate analysis of leadership involves not only a study of leaders, but also of situations." According to Stogdill, "A person does not become a leader by virtue of the possession of some combination of traits but by the pattern of personal characteristics, activities, and goals of the followers." Since goals, membership, and needs change over the life of a group, leadership must be flexible and adapt to meet differing situational demands. However, since physical and personality traits are relatively stable, an individual may be successful in one group but may not be well received in another group situation. Even within a single group, interpersonal relationships change over time, resulting in some initially unlikely choices for leaders emerging to take control.

Additional limitations to the trait approach were identified by Gouldner (1950) who noted that: (1) trait lists seldom distinguished between essential and less important traits, (2) often the traits were not mutually exclusive, (3) studies seldom distinguished between traits necessary for leader emergence and those that enabled the leader to maintain the role, (4) trait studies usually assumed the leader possessed the traits before becoming leader, and (5) studies frequently assumed personality to be merely the sum of individual characteristics, ignoring the dynamic interrelationship of characteristics.

Trait studies generally attempt to determine leader characteristics which are brought to the group. The focus is on leaders as types of persons who can be distinguished from other group members. A more appropriate perspective recognizes the complex interactions between leaders, members, and situations (Hollander and Julian, 1969). Leadership may be regarded as interpersonal influence, involving "an attempt to affect the behavior of others" (Tannenbaum and Massarik, 1968, p. 413).

A leader attempts to move, influence, a group toward perceived goals. Nonverbal and verbal communication acts that facilitate the identification and achievement of group goals are regarded as acts of leadership (Gouran, 1974). This rather broad formulation implies that in a group relationship there is an unequal distribution of power and influence. Group members relinquish certain independent decisions in favor of the leader's position. The power of the leader may be determined by formal authority, law, or implicit consent of the group, but in each case power is vested in the position.

Social Power and Leadership

Leadership depends upon authority which stems from the combination of power vested in a leader and consent of other group members to be led. When a leader performs an act that results in a member's change of behavior or attitude, we conclude that the leader has *influenced* the member. If the leader is capable of influencing members, we refer to the leader's *power* over the members. In other words, power is *potential* influence. Sources of power are often found in resources of a leader and/or the needs of members.

Each person possesses certain characteristics or properties which carry value for other people. For example, a majority of our society may value wealth or material possessions while some people may place a greater value on personal characteristics such as friendliness or honesty. A powerful person is one who possesses one or more properties that are valued by others. Naturally, the greater amount of highly valued properties that a group member has, the more potential influence the person may have over a group.

A team of researchers was able to identify seventeen resources rated "very important" by elementary school children (Gold, 1958). Twenty-one child in each grade, kindergarten through sixth grade, completed a sociometric measure according to the ability of classmates to influence them. Each child was then shown two pictures, one of a student who possessed high power and the other one of a student who possessed virtually no power over the child. Each child was asked whether the two children pictured possessed the seventeen properties and the degree of significance of the properties. Those properties considered as an important resource were generally attributed to high power children. Resources included being: "smart in school," "strong," "friendly," and "nice-looking." The rank of importance varied according to grade, sex of the child evaluated, and sex of the pictured pair. For example, males eight or younger valued other males who had good ideas about how to have fun. Males nine and over ranked "likes to do the same things you like to do" as the most important trait of males.

An interesting issue raised by the study is whether high powered children possess resources before gaining power or whether, as a result of having power, children tended to view the properties of high powered children as resources. Advertisers use the technique of giving products (properties) to powerful people as a means of making the properties desired (resources) by others. Similarly, powerful people may be liked because they are in some ways similar to us, and in those ways in which they are different we may try to imitate their style and resources.

Leaders often achieve a *halo effect* in which all their personal properties become desired by others. Because of a leader's power over others, even those traits that might have been initially derogated by the group become valued. Thus, a star athlete can recommend that we use a certain hair dressing, read a certain book, and behave in prescribed ways since this credibility or charisma carries over from the athletic field to personal life.

Gold (1958) concluded his study of resources in children by noting that values play an important role in transforming certain properties of children into resources which, in turn, determine the relative power position a child holds in classroom groups. This conclusion fails to account for the possibility that a single resource, such as our example of the athlete, may allow the child to gain power. Then, the power of a child's position may alter the values of other children. Assume the boy in third grade who knows how to fight best wears a butch hair cut. Is it because of fighting ability and butch cut that he becomes the most influential boy among the other males? More likely, he becomes influential because of fighting ability, which results in other boys trying to emulate him by cutting their hair in the same style, acting like him, and dressing like him.

These reservations regarding the study of children's resources illustrate some of the problems facing the researcher of interpersonal influence. First, there is a strong possibility that average people do not know who, or what attribute, influenced them to behave in a particular manner. Many bits of information selectively perceived in a situation may cause individuals to accept or reject attempts to influence. Second, the willingness to accept influence is situationally determined. A leader may successfully get the group to work on a task, but may be ineffective in getting the group to accept the proposed solution to the task. Third, there is no reason to think the same resources are consistently important for a group. White (1975) maintains, for example, that former President Nixon possessed the attributes needed and wanted by the American people in 1968. A few years later some of those same traits were considered repugnant by the people who elected him to office.

In spite of methodological problems in the area of social influence, progress has been made on a theoretical level. French and Raven (1968) suggest five bases of *power:* (1) reward, (2) coercive, (3) legitimate, (4) referent, and (5) expert. Each of these depends upon a person (P) perceiving that a power base is within the capability of another person (O). Person O may have little or no actual power, but may exercise considerable influence over the other if person P perceives power in O. Conversely, if O has real power, but it is not perceived or valued by P, then the result may be minimal influence.

An effective leader uses available bases of power to assure potential influence and perpetuation of her or his role-status. Members who support a leader's position may be *rewarded* by special attention, praise, and special favors while those who attempt to reject the influence may be *coerced* by being denied an opportunity to speak, refused favors, and relegated to undesirable positions. Generally, members are more favorably influenced by rewards and can be expected to resist influences when coercive power is used. Rewards also serve to enhance the attraction of O to P while coercion decreases the attractiveness of O.

Legitimate power refers to the right of O to influence P and the obligation of P to accept that influence. Legitimacy may stem from the role of leader. For example, the leader has the right not to call on a member, and the member has the obligation to obey that decision. It may also stem from some interpersonal commitment, for example, the member agreed to support the leader in return for a favor. Legitimacy stems from the social structure accepted by members and the personal commitments made by each individual. Power is usually thought of in terms of *rights*. Thus, a sergeant has the right, or legitimate power, to chew out a private, and an employer has the right to discharge an employee.

According to French and Raven (1968) *referent* power has the greatest range of influence, particularly in uncertain conditions. Referent power is based on identification of P with O, as was discussed earlier in Gold's (1958) study of children. The primary assumption is that an attractive person or group (O) is valued and because P desires to be identified with O, P will assume attitudes or behaviors similar to O.

The final basis of power is identified as *expert* power. Expertness is relative to the individual (O) and to some mental standard held by P. If a leader knows more about a task than other group members, the leader may be valued; however, if group members believe the leader should know even more than is demonstrated about a topic, the leader may be derogated. Expert power may be restricted to a particular topic, in which case members will accept influence on the specific topic but reject attempted influence in nonrelated areas.

In any group situation a leader has one or more bases of power. Successful leadership depends upon a judicious use of these powers. History is strewn with fallen leaders who have relied too heavily upon coercive powers, rewarded their friends with too much favoritism, and depended on legitimate and referent powers when their position no longer satisfied member needs and aspirations. Leaders sometimes kill enthusiasm in a group by using their expert power too frequently. Certainly it is not much fun to be in a group dominated by someone who has all the answers. Overzealous or inappropriate uses of power may lead to the loss of influence; carefully selected and applied powers may assure success.

We recently met the president of a large and prosperous corporation who successfully utilized small degrees of power. His subordinates had more actual power to reward and punish employees and were far more expert in the running of the corporation than the president. A naive observer might conclude that the president wasn't much of a leader. The president had the legitimate power of ownership and little else. Since the corporation is prosperous and growing, and we assume that those are goals of the corporation, is the leader unsuccessful? In our view, he is successful because of his ability to attract and retain the loyalty of an upper management staff who enjoy a sense of responsibility and autonomy. The *role* of leader will be explored further in the section on leader effectiveness but, for the moment, remember that leaders do not always need to use powers available to them as a means of assuring group goals and objectives.

Credibility and Leadership

Perhaps the most important characteristic of leaders in terms of influencing group members is their credibility. This characteristic is also studied under the headings of *ethos* (Aristotle, Trans. Cooper, 1932; see also Anderson and Clevenger, 1963), *trust* (Giffin, 1968; Giffin and Barnes, 1976), *charisma, image,* and *prestige.* Each of these terms refers to an attitudinal bias of P toward O and their significance rests in group member perceptions rather than the leader. If members believe in a leader, it may make no difference whether that confidence is actually deserved.

Aristotle (trans. Cooper, 1932) maintained that the believability of a speaker (ethos) depends however, on an audience perceiving the speaker as having *intelligence* or correctness of opinions, *character* (honest) and *good will* or intentions regarding the listener's welfare. Since a speaker is attempting to influence an audience, a successful speaker is often regarded as a leader. Thus, we believe the principles may hold for the characteristics of group leaders as well. If group leaders can demonstrate intelligence, good will, and honesty they may be effective in influencing group members.

The perceived characteristics of trusted persons in groups were analyzed by Giffin (1968). Three factors appeared to be primary characteristics of persons trusted as group members: (1) expertness, (2) reliability or dependability, and (3) dynamism. *Expertness* can be related to intelligence and expert power. *Reliability* would seem to relate to both character and good will in Aristotle's analysis. *Dynamism* refers to a person's activity, openness, and enthusiasm. This dimension of trust does not seem to be as strong as the other two dimensions and occasionally collapses into the factor of reliability (Giffin and Barnes, 1976). This is not surprising when various groups are considered. In some situations, a decisive and aggressive leader may be needed while in other groups these characteristics would not be well suited to the group.

A similar line of research was initiated by Hovland, Janis, and Kelly (1953). They were interested in what people perceived in a person's "source credibility." Source credibility was considered to be the result of expertness and trustworthiness. Since their early formulations, several studies have disagreed with the perceived factors of credibility. Public speakers have been reported as credible in terms of three factors: (1) *qualification* (or expertness), (2) *safety* (or trustworthiness), and (3) *dynamism* (Berlo, Lemert, and Mertz, 1969–1970). McCrosky (1966) identified five dimensions of audience attitudes toward a speaker: (1) *competence* (expertness), (2) *character* (trustworthiness), (3) *intention* (good will), (4) *personality* (not previously identified, this dimension related to friendliness and pleasantness), and (5) *dynamism*. As Cartwright and Zander (1968) point out, the power of a leader is a combination of member needs and leader resources. Any single dimension or combination of dimensions may be salient enough in terms of member needs to overcome less favorable dimensions.

The effects of power have a strong impact on the attitudes and behavior of group members Hurwitz, Zander, and Hymovitch, 1968). Those who possess power tend to feel satisfied with the group and with role relations in the group. Members lacking power tend to feel inhibited and over time may fail to offer suggestions or to contribute significantly to group goal attainment. When members lacking power speak, they address their remarks to more powerful members and tend to praise behaviors of the power figures. On the other hand, more powerful members tend to address each other or the entire group while devaluing contributions by less powerful members. As a result, leaders of a group are found to speak more frequently, are spoken to more frequently, and enjoy the ego gratification of group membership. All of which serves as an impetus for powerful members to work harder on group goals as a means of achieving even greater satisfaction. To rephrase an old expression, the weak get weaker and the strong generally get stronger (in the dynamics of group relations).

Control and Leader Behaviors

Leadership roles are amazingly gratifying even under contrived conditions of classroom and laboratory simulations. The major advantage of being a leader probably resides in control of one's own actions and the control of others. In a study on why people seek leadership, Hemphill (1961) found a variety of circumstances to motivate people to attempt leadership. People sought leadership if they perceived some reward for accomplishing the task, when they felt they actually could accomplish the task, and when the group was perceived as accepting and supportive of the individual as a leader.

An interesting study of leader emergence by Bavelas, et al. (1965) gave further support to Hemphill's findings. Members of leaderless groups were told that a green light in front of them would signify when trained observers considered a member's comment as valuable. By a programmed sequence of light flashes experimenters were able to manipulate conversational output of members originally low on leader preference ratings. As green light frequency increased, member participation increased. The more members participated, the more likely it was they would later be nominated by others as group leaders.

Interaction dominance, in addition to being a characterization of an individual's behavior, serves as a controlling influence over other members' behavior. As one person talks, others generally are not permitted to talk. Leaders, as we have just seen, tend to talk more than others and also have the opportunity to control interaction of other members through agenda structuring and sanctioning who may talk on what subject for how long.

What happens to those who seek leadership roles but are unsuccessful? They probably will not be satisfied to merely give up their need for dominance, free access to interaction, and control of a group. From a positive point of view, they may seek group influence by asserting their credibility through expert contributions. On the other hand, they may redirect their energies to other groups and withdraw from active participation. Some might become the proverbial "thorn in the side" directing energies against other leaders' attempts to influence. The task of any leader, or group, is to find a way to channel the energies of would-be leaders so that they work for group goals rather than withdrawing or going against the group.

Throughout this section we have primarily referred to a single member role, that of a formally designated leader. Trait and source credibility studies are particularly representative of research focusing on the role and characteristics of individuals designated as group leaders.

Designation of a leader role is also helpful in determining responsibilities. For example, a leader may be responsible for organizing the agenda, directing and monitoring member interactions, and enforcing group norms. The behavioral acts of directing others toward group goals is a function of *leadership* and a sense of responsibility that can be *shared* by multiple group members. "Leader" is generally a label attached to a role, while "leadership" is a function or act of influencing. Leaders do not always need to perform many leadership functions, and leadership may be spread among all members of a group. However, it is the task of those people accepting the label of leader to see that necessary leadership functions are fulfilled by someone. We will now turn our attention to the various ways that leaders may attempt to accomplish this task.

HOW DO LEADERS BEHAVE?

By identifying some of the characteristics of leaders, we have also specified some aspect of their communicative behavior as members. We have noted that a leader is a person who influences others; therefore, any attempt to influence is regarded as a kind of leadership behavior. Leaders talk more frequently, consciously or unconsciously, in attempting to influence others. Moreover, anyone who participates in group task accomplishment is quite likely to fulfill necessary leadership functions at some point in time. In some groups only a few people fulfill leadership functions while in others everyone may play an active part in providing leadership. There are groups where no member is actually labeled a leader, but there are no groups which fail to have at least one person functioning in a leadership capacity. If such a group existed, it would quickly dissipate from lack of action.

Recall that a leader is a person who influences other members. Presumably, influence attempts are aimed at achieving group goals. A single leader, however, *may* be incapable of prompting group action and exerting the control needed to achieve the multiple goals required of a group. At least three overall goals are simultaneously operating within any group: (1) environmental expectations or goals, (2) task related goals, and (3) member goals. One or more of these goal states may have priority for a group at some point in time. The perceived priority of goals affects how members interpret and respond to leadership needs. In short, communicative behaviors of leadership are quite likely to be coordinated with various aspects of goal attainment. It makes sense, therefore, to view leader behaviors in relationship to potential goal states.

Environmental Goals

All groups exist within an environment that will have various influences on leadership and group behavior. If a leader has been appointed or determined by an external agent, strong influences may carefully shape leader behavior. A congressman, for example, is directly answerable to the constituency for legislative behavior *and* social behavior. A foreman may not want to fire one of the workers, but if a superior demands it there may be no alternative. The success or failure of a group is often attributed to the formally designated leader; therefore, the leader is usually the group member most concerned with expectations of the environment.

There are times when environmental demands may run counter to task demands. The leader may rebel against environmental constraints, as in the case of a street gang, or the leader may simply see the task differently than those outside the group. There is a thin line between creativity in task accomplishment and "undesirable" deviation from societal norms and expectations.

An interesting contrast of leader behavior is provided by examining styles advocated by Biddle and Biddle (1968), Alinsky (1946), and Hoffman (1968). All three methods advocate the use of groups to achieve social change. While there may be disagreement as to which leadership style is most effective in achieving long term goals, there can be no doubt that all three styles have been effectively used in specific situations.

Governmental agencies such as the Peace Corps, V.I.S.T.A., and community action programs use the *consensus method,* which seeks change through traditionally approved channels within the environmental system. Sit-ins and marches by labor groups, the poor, and disfranchised represent the *conflict method* in which change is sought within the environmental system but outside necessarily approved channels. The third method works outside approved channels and seeks eventual destruction of the environmental system. War protesters in the late sixties and revolutionary groups today tend to use a *confrontation method.*

In the consensus method advocated by Biddle and Biddle (1968), a leader functions as an encourager motivated by an optimistic faith in human potential. This faith becomes a philosophy of life, giving interpersonal warmth to the leader's relationship with the group. Table 7.1 reports the five-step procedure used by the leader. Two characteristics are noteworthy of the consensus method. First, the leader must have an abiding faith in the group and the system in which it works; second, meetings and discussions are extensive. Conflict with the environmental system is avoided. "Citizen participants should not be predetermined

Table 7.1 Comparison of Consensus, Conflict, and Confrontation Methods of Leadership

CONSENSUS	CONFLICT	CONFRONTATION
1. Preliminary study of history and events in the environmental system	1. Infiltrate community and identify problem	1. Plan a scene
2. Determine the problem and meet with group members	2. Locate the indigenous leaders	2. Publicize and spread rumors
3. Discuss problem, possible solutions, and select course of action	3. Meet with leaders and discuss problem and means of solving it	3. Arrange for free items and props
4. Discuss and act upon the problem	4. Demonstrate to show how power can be used	4. Action—do any thing but don't get caught
5. Discuss related problems and plan continuation of committee actions		5. Act in front of media cameras
		6. Plan another scene

into conflict, lest their opportunities for cooperative development be curtailed." Demonstrations should be used "only when the cooperative steps have proved futile" (Biddle and Biddle, 1968, p. 203).

The conflict method set forth by Alinsky (1946) in *Reveille for Radicals* requires a leader to be "filled with a deep feeling for people." Through a process of identification, the radical leader has a feeling "for and with people" (Alinsky, 1946, p. 14). The four-step conflict method is found in Table 7.1. Two characteristics are noteworthy. First, the leader is expected to be filled with a humanitarian motivation; second, extensive meetings and discussions are avoided. Action is the key to success. "To be static in a People's Organization is to commit suicide" (Akinsky, 1946, p. 203).

Although not as easily identified as the two previous methods of leadership, the confrontation method utilized by Hoffman (1968) gathered a huge following (youth and press) and served to segment the entire nation in the mid-sixties. The six-step method is also found in Table 7.1. Three characteristics of the confrontation method are noteworthy. First, leaders place negative faith in the environmental system. They expect the "establishment" to react against the group. Second, leaders do not expect group actions to bring about immediate results; actions are often doomed to fail from the start. Third, organization, discussion, and planning are held to a minimum.

Leaders in all three methods share a strong personal commitment to the task. Analyzing leaders of the "new left," Keniston (1968, p. 133) noted that the person had to feel "personally responsible for effecting change." Former S.D.S. leader, Mark Rudd, also commented on the concept of commitment. "Radicalization of the individual means that he must commit himself to the struggle" (Avorn, 1968, p. 33). Personal needs and interests must be subsumed under broader group goals.

Proponents of the consensus method allow members to continue their lives as they will. Meetings and actions are conducted in such a way as to allow each viewpoint to be aired. Conflict leaders demand much more from the group. Members are expected to risk themselves to the extent that participation in group activities may result in loss of physical safety, jobs, or community position. A striking worker may risk personal welfare by not reporting to work but is comforted by the knowledge that the cause is just and other group members are willing to share in the sacrifice.

Confrontation leaders demand the most from group members but in some respects have the least difficult task in achieving conformity to group demands. Members to whom this style of leadership appeals often desire to be freed from personal responsibilities. They give their lives to a cause as a means of escape from an unwanted self. According to Hoffer:

> it is this desire that manifests itself in a propensity for united action and self-sacrifice. The revulsion from an unwanted self, and the impulse to forget it, mask it, slough it off, and lose it, produce both a readiness to sacrifice the self and a willingness to dissolve it by losing one's individual distinctions in a compact collective whole (Hoffer, 1951, p. 58).

In seeking to be free from self, a member seeks to identify with others. Unlike consensus and conflict leaders, confrontation leaders must respond to the needs of a selfless membership who expect to be told what to do, how to act, and what to think. The group may take the form of "long-haired, dirty hippies," sedately dressed members of a therapeutic encounter group, or smartly tailored, uniformed armies. In each case, members have given up a repugnant loneliness of individual responsibility in favor of a relatively mindless uniformity of the communal.

Activity develops unity in all three methods. When little is accomplished in the consensus method, meetings turn stale and attendance drops. An effective consensus leader will urge subgroups to do something even if it only amounts to a clean-up period or a social hour. Herein lies the potential advantage of the conflict and confrontation methods of leadership. Alinsky urges leaders to act and discuss it later. Hoffman similarly urges revolutionaries to act. Rehearsals come after the act. The more members do on behalf of the group, the easier self-sacrifice becomes. Increased selflessness allows greater ease of actions and leader influence. Eventually, the member evolves to a state of total commitment to the group and acceptance of group norms and expectations.

The goals of leaders in each method differ significantly. The consensus method leader strives to promote member independence of thought and action in the hope that when the leader eventually leaves a group, members will continue to move towards group goals. For example, a professional scout may organize a community troop but the goal is to develop parent involvement so that scouting activities may continue after the professional has moved on to another group. The conflict leader seeks goal achievement with the group dissolving upon accomplishing the task. A union may continue to exist, but the action or goal for which the leader was responsible will have either failed or succeeded. The confrontation method is totally dependent upon the leader, and since the method is self-denying, actions cannot be allowed to succeed. A classic example is the Chicago demonstrations during the 1968 Democratic convention. If the actions had been "successful," the result would have been anarchy. When the actions failed, as they had to, leaders of the movement could point to the inequities of the system. The role played by Mayor Dailey and his "pigs" shocked the American public and played precisely into the hands of confrontation leaders.

In summary, the three methods reflect different leadership goals toward a common goal of social change. The consensus method permits self-development of the leader and members. Success of a group depends on member involvement and the willingness of an environmental system to cope with the desired goals. A conflict method requires leader commitment and member conformity to leader and group influence. Success is again dependent upon the environmental system's willingness to cope with the desired goals. The conflict method requires total submersion of member goals in favor of group goal conformity. The method requires unity and self-sacrifice. Success will come only with the downfall of the total environmental system.

Task Related Goals

The three styles just described clearly reflect an orientation toward environmental expectations which, in turn, reflect task and member goals. However, a leader cannot be content with simply responding to environmental expectations. Leaders are often selected on the basis of their expertise in a task area. Furthermore, a task will probably be structured according to how the leader perceives it. Often a leader's zeal for a task may result in blindness to environmental and member considerations. Statements like, "Let's get to work!" or "Can we get on with the job?" or "I think we are getting off the track," may keep a group moving toward some goal but may also cause hurt feelings and increased tensions.

In Chapter 5 we discussed the need to be a participant-observer, that is, to actively participate at the same time as you step back and objectively view group processes. This becomes more and more difficult for leaders as they become ego-tied to task activities. Harnack and Fest (1964) note that those characteristics which allow a person to be "elected" leader of a group (such as task expertise or goal commitment) often result in the person not being particularly well liked by group members and in turn not re-elected. We suspect this happens because most designated leaders just cannot attend to both task demands and the affiliative behaviors necessary to satisfy interpersonal need.

Tasks can be viewed from the perspective of actual subject content and from a *process*, or relational, perspective. Hence, an *autocratic* leader will attempt control over decisions related to subject content, while a *democratic* leader will attempt control over decisions related to interpersonal process issues. A *laissez faire* leader will simply sit back and let the group do whatever they want without any attempt to influence.

In a classic study of leadership styles, Lewin, Lippit, and White (1939) compared the effects of authoritarian, *laissez faire*, and democratic leadership. The researchers formed boys' clubs with adult leaders trained to behave in one of the three leadership styles. The styles were: (1) autocratic, where all decisions were made by the leader and boys were required to follow prescribed procedures under threat of strict discipline, (2) democratic, where shared participation was encouraged, group decisions were voted upon, and punishment was minimal, and (3) *laissez faire*, in which the group leader allowed the boys to work and play without supervision or control.

Results from observations showed that an autocratic group accomplished the most work in the presence of a leader but in the leader's absence work related activity drastically decreased. Fights and disagreements reflected the interpersonal tension under autocratic "rule." By contrast, the democratically led group produced less in the presence of the leader but in the leader's absence productivity continued at somewhat higher levels. Fewer acts of aggression suggested a more harmonious and cohesive group. The least amount of work was achieved under the *laissez faire* leadership style. The level of "productivity" measured in this study was the type of interaction carried on by the group rather than an objective measure of actual production. Therefore, the results should be regarded in terms of *communicative* effects.

In a later study, Bradford and Lippitt (1945) concluded that the "hardboiled autocrat" caused resentment and irritability among group members, but lower morale was fostered by a *laissez faire* leader. With such a leader, no one knew what to do or to expect, resulting in a lack of team work and productivity. The democratic leader stirred enthusiasm by shared decision making. In other words, people generally enjoy positive involvement in a task, are willing to tolerate dictatorial task assignments, but are least comfortable and satisfied when they are not sure of what is expected of them.

As noted in a previous section, trait approaches to studying leadership capability have not been very fruitful. However, recent research has detected personality traits which seem to differentiate between persons favoring democratic or autocratic leader styles. Rosenfeld and Plax (1975), in a study designed to assess relationships between personality and professed leadership styles, found that persons favoring a democratic versus autocratic style scored higher on personality trait dimensions describing: (1) achievement through independent action, (2) introspection, (3) nurturance, and (4) sociability. They also scored lower on traits like: (1) abasement, (2) achievement, and (3) aggression. Rosenfeld and Fowler (1976), in a follow-up study which differentiated leader style preferences for females versus males, found that democratic females could be characterized as open-minded and nurturant (a profile closely related to social-emotional aspects of group action) while male leaders were characterized by scores on traits measuring forcefulness, analytical ability, and valuing the love of others (a profile more similar to task related concerns, particularly the first two traits).

An easy, but perhaps misleading, conclusion to draw from these results is that a democratic style of leadership is always the best style to utilize with a group. Morse and Lorsch (1970), Morse and Reimer (1956), and Campion (1968) have reported any advantages of democratic leadership over autocratic supervision are relatively small and situationally determined. Furthermore, in programs of hierarchical (autocratic) supervision, greater profits result from lower labor costs saved by increased productivity. Presumably, it takes less time to produce, or create, certain products when all parties do not engage in joint deliberations about how the work will get done.

One of the situational considerations which may complicate style effectiveness is member needs or personality characteristics. In work settings studied by Vroom (1959, 1960), employees high in authoritarianism performed better under directive leaders. Recall that one of the input variables examined in Chapter 2 was the personality a member brings to a group. Over time, a successful group leader must use a style appropriate for member personalities. Schutz (1958) demonstrated that people differ according to their need to be controlled and to control others. From a slightly different perspective, Harman (1951) noted that people are conditioned to be dominant or submissive. If members have a need to be controlled or submissive, then a more autocratic leadership style may be appropriate.

Arbitrarily prescribing a particular leadership style also fails to account for the leader's needs and personality. Fiedler and Chemers (1974) question whether some people are psychologically able to adapt to various leadership styles. If a leader has a high need to control others, is it realistic to expect the person to give up control in favor of member needs? Conversely, can we expect a humanistically oriented person to operate efficiently in a supervisory role that demands firm, decisive, and rapid decisions? If, as they suggest, leadership styles are relatively enduring behavioral characteristics, regardless of social situations, then "style" is not really distinguishable from personality traits. A logical extension of Fiedler's reasoning is that leaders and managers should be selected and rotated according to task demands and member needs rather than expecting a single leader to adapt to changing contingencies. It may be easier to change leaders than to get the leader to change according to the situation.

Up to a point we can agree with such an idea. However, in the case of emergent leaders, elected officials, and hierarchical promotions, to name a few, determining how contingencies of leader, member, and task situation fit together may be impractical and unrealistic. It is easy to recognize and make adjustments for extreme cases of incompatibility. The autocrat probably should be removed from leader responsibility over task specialists with high needs for autonomy. However, most group situations probably fall in that broad area between extremes. In these cases, we believe that it is realistic to expect a leader to assess environmental constraints, task demands, member needs, and personal orientations as criteria for adopting an appropriate style of leadership.

Member Goals

While discussing task related goals we have strayed into issues related to member goals. Part of the reason for this is that member goals are often synonymous with task goals. In fact, effective leaders will try to assure a close fit. If task related goals are not achieved, member dissatisfaction can be expected. Unless the task is worked on there is no reason for a group to meet. However, we have also noted that tensions, acts of aggression, and other dysfunctional behaviors may arise unless certain member needs receive attention. Among these are needs for recognition, to have an impact, to be pacified in cases of conflict, to receive support from others, social acceptance, and relief from tension. Frequently those closest to a situation are in the worst position to recognize and deal with such needs.

Communicative manifestations of underlying unfulfilled needs include snide remarks, joking, avoiding task related issues, overt hostility or undue pleasantness, curt responses, and so on. Less obvious nonverbal behaviors may be a lack of participation, slumping in a chair, physically pulling back from the group, or fidgeting. Because a formal leader is usually closely tied to a task, the leader may not perceive these behaviors or recognize the significance of their occurrence. For example, if one member offers a suggestion which is rebuffed by a leader as an inappropriate idea, few may be aware of how that member feels about the rejection. Later, however, the member may viciously attack someone else's idea or abruptly leave the room. "What's he upset about?" or "What did I say?" may be comments reflecting a lack of awareness about member needs.

Because a formal leader has responsibility for both environmental and task goals, a second person may need to assume responsibility for monitoring member needs. A *maintenance leader* may say little in regard to task concerns but may be the one to ask whether a particular member understood or was satisfied with a response. Maintenance leaders may offer compromises to member differences, provide salve to wounded egos, crack jokes, tell stories, and make social inquiries regarding personal needs of members. Naturally, this person is accepted by others but may also be regarded as somewhat of a nuisance by a task leader not attuned to interpersonal needs of the group.

When maintenance needs are considered, warm-up socializing that takes place prior to the meeting, coffee breaks, and occasional departures from the agenda take on vital significance for a group. These social functions promote positive interpersonal relationships, develop group cohesiveness and cooperation, and may give members a chance to amend differences under relaxed conditions. We occasionally hear stories of how international crises have been averted by an accidental meeting of U.N. delegates during session breaks or how legislative action is often determined in the confines of a cocktail lounge.

Rigorous taskmasters often regard maintenance issues as frivolous leadership concerns. However, there is a growing awareness that an effective group has interpersonally satisfied members. Some companies even provide centrally located coffee makers in recognition of the vast amount of technical information that is shared during coffee breaks. Workers who stick to the grindstone and never indulge in social activities may be missing a vital part of group functioning—including task accomplishment.

In answer to the question with which we started this section, How Do Leaders Behave?, we can say a leader is responsible for seeing that environmental, task, and member goals are satisfied. This does not necessarily mean a group leader must personally facilitate each of these goal areas. The leader is simply responsible for seeing that they are accomplished. Occasionally, group practitioners maintain that a leader should fulfill specific functions. Stogdill (1974, p. 30) identified six functions associated with *leadership*:

1. Defining objectives and maintaining goal directions.
2. Providing means for goal attainment.
3. Providing and maintaining group structure.
4. Facilitating group action and interaction.
5. Maintaining group cohesiveness and member satisfaction.
6. Facilitating group task performance.

These *process* functions are vital to a group. Note that Stogdill refers to them as associated with *leadership* rather than *the role* of *leader*. The ultimate function of a leader may be to get group members to assume leadership responsibilities. We agree with Homans (1950) when he proposes the responsibilities of a leader are to assume attainment of group purposes and to maintain a balance of incentives to assure member cooperation. At the risk of being prescriptive, in the final section of this chapter, we will address the issue of how a leader may accomplish these responsibilities with maximum effectiveness.

WHAT MAKES A LEADER EFFECTIVE?

In his book *Managerial Psychology,* Leavitt (1972) comments that probably ten percent of all managers have some unidentifiable knack for managing. These lucky few don't know what they do or why, but they intuitively know how to handle day-to-day responsibilities of management. The same may be said for group leaders. Effective leaders often seem to have an uncanny knack for successfully analyzing group needs. For the rest of us, however, consistent success requires study and practice. There are just too many pitfalls to risk muddling by trial and error.

Forms of Leadership

Effective leaders will maximize their capacity to influence others in a group. The *form* of these leader traits and resources will depend upon group values and strengths of the leader. For the leader of a street gang, it may be demonstrating the most daring; for a corporate executive, it may be holding the power to reward and punish. Whatever form it takes, the objective is to draw out the greatest potential effort from each group member.

The form of leadership may be *charismatic, organizational, expert,* or *informal* (Levine, 1974). A charismatic leader depends upon an ability to excite member participation by using personal dynamism, appearance, and emotional appeals. Political appeals on television generally rely upon charismatic appeal to generate votes, contributions, and support. The organizational leader plans for clear role responsibilities, group structure, and administration. The rising young executive is often described as this type of leader. Member feelings may be sacrificed in the quest for planned efficiency. The expert or intellectual leader has been discussed earlier in this chapter. Most of this person's energies are spent on subject content issues at the potential expense of group process and member satisfaction. Levine's fourth type of leader, informal, identifies closely with group members and is sensitive to member needs. This informal type of leader functions in a warm, friendly way and may not even be identified as a leader.

In certain situations each of these types of leaders may be effective. The critical consideration is correct assessment of situational demands. Effective leadership involves matching the characteristic attributes and functions of the leader with the demands and constraints of the situation.

An analysis of over 1,500 behavior descriptions by Halpin and Winer (1952) resulted in the development of a widely used method of measuring leader behavior. Two major factors that emerged were consideration and initiation-of-structure. *Consideration* refers to the degree to which a leader shows concern, understanding, warmth, and empathy for the feelings and opinions of group members. *Initiation-of-structure* includes behaviors such as assignment of roles and tasks within the group, scheduling task assignments, defining goals, setting work procedures and standards, and evaluating member contributions. Notice that these closely resemble task and member goals identified earlier.

Most research relating considerate leader behavior to member satisfaction indicates a positive relationship. One study of a supervisory behavior, for example, found that as consideration increased, employee turnover and grievances *decreased,* but as initiation-of-structure behavior increased, grievances and turnover *increased* Fleisman and Harris, 1962 . However, a study of research and development divisions of organizations found that as structure was added satisfaction increased (House, Filley and Kerr, 1971). The researchers noted that "typical" research and development divisions have very low structure, so additional structure helped clarify role responsibilities and expectations. The contrasting results of these two studies strikingly illustrates the diversity of situational contingencies to which leader behaviors must adapt.

Tannenbaum and Schmidt (1958) have developed a useful model for identifying the degree of control a leader should exercise in a group.

Figure 7.1 graphically shows these varying degrees of control and how they relate to member options for behaving. At the extreme left, virtually all control and responsibility is taken by the leader. At the extreme right, virtually all control is delegated to the group. As a leader assumes control, the group loses control and, conversely, as a leader allows greater member responsibility, the leader gives up some prerogatives of control.

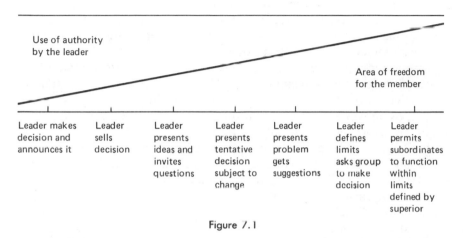

| Leader makes decision and announces it | Leader sells decision | Leader presents ideas and invites questions | Leader presents tentative decision subject to change | Leader presents problem gets suggestions | Leader defines limits asks group to make decision | Leader permits subordinates to function within limits defined by superior |

Figure 7.1

Adapted from: Robert Tannenbaum and Warren H. Schmidt, "How to Choose a Leadership Pattern," Harvard Business Review, *March–April, 1958, (36), 96.*

An effective leader will not follow a rigid pattern for determining degrees of control. Factors such as time allotted to decision making, complexity and relevancy of the task, member needs and capabilities for involvement, and leader responsibilities all have a bearing on what degree of control will be exercised. A decision on whether the group should meet next week may be quickly determined by the leader alone; however, a decision to allocate group funds for a project will probably require member sanction. In some cases a leader may want member input before personally making a decision, but in other cases a leader may permit members to take full control over the decision making process and ultimate decision.

In terms of group influence, the vertical distance from the top to the diagonal line in Figure 7.1 represents the degree of controlling influence a leader will have over process and content decisions. If the leader has correctly assessed a situation, his or her decisions should not cause much dissatisfaction among group members. This does require that leaders communicate their intentions to group members and be willing to justify decisions if they are challenged. It is crucial that leaders explain their role in any given decision. A group's morale can be badly damaged if a carefully considered decision is summarily overruled by the group leader. If a group knows that its level of control is limited to making recommendations, it may then be more willing to accept a higher authority overruling a decision.

Communication Strategies

To say the communicative behaviors of designated group leaders are important is an understatement. Unfortunately, our knowledge of *which* behaviors are important is somewhat limited. One message variable with demonstrated effects on group performance is *orientation*. Orienting message behaviors are those which focus on goal attainment (particularly behaviors meant to "keep the group on the track"), attempt to resolve conflicts between members, or reduce tension. Knutson (1972), using confederates to emit different amounts of orienting messages (high, low, or no manipulation) found that high orientation groups moved closer towards consensus on a discussion task than low or non-manipulated (freely interacting) groups. A subsequent study by Knutson and Holdridge (1975) showed that orientation behavior ratings given by members to each other were significantly related to group consensus. This, however, held true only when more than one or two members received high ratings. Also, orientation ratings and amount of interaction were significantly associated with perceived leadership ratings and observed task leadership interaction behaviors.

In addition to orienting messages, some researchers (Kline, 1970; Gouran, 1969, 1970; Hill, 1976) have proposed that *opinionated* behavior by a leader can affect group outcomes. An experiment by Hill (1976) generated results which support his speculation that groups with nonopinionated or moderately opinionated leaders come closer to obtaining consensus on discussion topic decisions than groups with highly opinionated leaders. The results also revealed that nonopinionated leaders were rated as more competent and objective than opinionated persons.

At best, we have only scratched the surface of probable message behaviors associated with effective leadership. Gouran (1970), using a somewh·t different approach, has attempted to isolate some relevant dimensions of message behavior with probable consequences for group leadership. His findings indicate three distinct clusters of verbal behaviors: (1) goal facilitation, (2) social-emotional behavior, and (3) communication skills. *Goal facilitation* includes such acts as orienting statements and being cooperative or objective. *Social-emotional behavior* encompasses acts of emotional involvement, either positive or negative, in group content concerns. The final dimension, *communication skills,* includes acts such as providing information, clarifying, and being lucid and concise with contributions.

An effective leader clarifies group responsibility and member roles and/or facilitates discussion of these issues to the satisfaction of group members. If members clearly understand their roles, and accept the responsibility of group goals, then a leader should shape his or her style accordingly. If, for example, a group is drawn together for purposes of instruction, and members *know* that they are there to receive instruction, then a leader should have little problem with member confusion or antagonism about group actions.

People generally respond rationally to perceived situations. If leaders can understand how members see the group, they should be able to foster group cohesiveness. Leaders may effectively emphasize if they will: (1) process group activities rather than become bogged down in specific task functions, (2) ask *process* related questions regarding group functioning, (3) facilitate open interaction among participants, (4) be receptive to verbal and nonverbal feedback from members, and (5) encourage member responsibility for group success. The error of many leaders is to assume too much responsibility for group functioning and decision making. If one person were capable of achieving all the environmental expectations and group goals there would be no need for a group.

Communicative actions are the central processes by which leaders influence members. In turn, communication is the primary way leaders can determine whether members are satisfied and whether goals are being met. Communication in a group ties the group together and directs it toward desired levels of productivity and goal attainment.

REFERENCES

Alinsky, S.D. 1946. *Reveille for radicals.* Chicago: University of Chicago Press.

Anderson, K.E. and Clevenger, T.A. 1963. A summary of experimental research in ethos. *Speech Monographs* June, *30,* 59–73.

Aristotle, *The rhetoric of Aristotle.* Translated by L. Cooper. New York: Appleton-Century-Crofts, Inc. 1932.

Avorn, J.L. 1968. *Up against the ivy wall.* New York: Atheneum.

Bavelas, A., Hastorf, A.H., Gross, A.E. and Kite, W.R. 1965. Experiments on the alteration of group structure. *Journal of Experimental Social Psychology 1,* 55–70.

Berlo, D.K., Lemert, J.B. and Mertz R.J. 1969–70. Dimensions for evaluating the acceptability of message sources. *Public Opinion Quarterly 33,* 562–576.

Biddle, W.W. and Biddle, L.J. 1968. *Encouraging community development.* New York: Hold, Rinehart & Winston.

Bird, C. 1940. *Social psychology.* New York: Appleton-Century-Crofts.

Bradford, L.P. and Lippitt, R. 1945. Building a democratic work group. *Personnel 22*, 142–152.

Campion, J.E., Jr. 1968. Effects of Managerial Style on Subordinates' Attitudes and Performance in a Simulated Organizational Setting. Unpublished doctorial dissertation, University of Minnesota.

Cartwright, D. and Zander, A. 1968. Power and influence in groups: Introduction. In *Group dynamics: Research and theory,* 3rd ed., eds. D. Cartwright and A. Zander, pp. 215–235. New York: Harper & Row, Pub.

Fiedler, F.E. and Chemers, M.M. 1974. *Leadership and effective management.* Glenview, Ill.: Scott, Foresman.

Fleisman, E.A. and Harris, E.F. 1962. Patterns of leadership related to employee grievances and turnover. *Personnel Psychology 15*, 43–56.

French, J.R.P. and Raven, B. 1968. The bases of social power. In *Group dynamics: Research and theory,* 3rd ed., eds. D. Cartwright and A. Zander, pp. 259–269. New York: Harper & Row, Pub.

Giffin, K. 1968. An experimental evaluation on the trust differential. Lawrence, Kansas: The University of Kansas Communication Research Center.

Giffin, K. and Barnes, R.E. 1976. *Trusting me, trusting you.* Columbus, Ohio: Chas. E. Merrill.

Gold, M. 1958. Power in the Classroom. *Sociometry 21*, 50–60.

Gouldner, A.W. 1950. Studies in Leadership. New York: Harper.

Gouran, D.S. 1969. Variables related to consensus in group discussions of questions of policy. *Speech Monographs 36*, 387–391.

Gouran, D.S. 1970. Conceptual and methodological approaches to the study of leadership. *Central States Speech Journal 21*, 217–223.

Gouran, D.S. 1974. Perspectives on the study of leadership: Its present and its future. *Quarterly Journal of Speech 60*, 376–381.

Haiman, F.S. 1951. *Group leadership and democratic action.* Boston: Houghton Mifflin Co.

Halpin, A. and Winer, B. 1952. *The leadership behavior of the airplane commander.* Columbus: Ohio State Univ. Research Foundation

Harnack, R.V. and Fest, T.B. 1964. *Group discussion: Theory and technique.* Appleton-Century-Crofts.

Hemphill, J.K. 1961. Why people attempt to lead. In *Leadership and interpersonal behavior,* eds. L. Petrullo and B.M. Bass, pp. 201–205. New York: Holt, Rinehart & Winston.

Hill, T.A. 1976. An experimental study of the relationship between opinionated leadership and small group consensus. *Communication Monographs 43*, 247–257.

Hoffer, E. 1951. *The true believer.* New York: Harper & Row, Pub.

Hoffman, A. 1968. *Revolution for the hell of it.* New York: Dial Press.

Hollander, E.P. and Julian, J.W. 1969. Contemporary trends in the analysis of leadership processes. *Psychological Bulletin 71*, 387–397.

Homans, G.C. 1950. *The human group.* New York: Harcourt Brace Jovanovich.

House, R.J., Filley, A.C. and Kerr, S. 1971. Relation of leader consideration and initiating structure to R and D subordinates; satisfaction. *Administrative Science Quarterly 16*, 19–30.

Hovland, C.I., Janis, I.L. and Kelley, H.H. 1953. *Communication and persuasion.* New Haven, Conn.: Yale University Press.

Hurwitz, J.I. Zander, A.F. and Hymovitch, B. 1968. Some effects of power on the relations among group members. In *Group dynamics: Research and theory,* 3rd ed., eds. D. Cartwright and A. Zander, pp. 291–297. New York: Harper & Row, Pub.

Keniston, K. 1968. *Young radicals: Notes on committed youth.* New York: Harcourt Brace Jovanovich.

Kline, J.A. 1970. Indices of orienting and opinionated statements in problem solving discussions. *Speech Monographs 38,* 282–288.

Knutson, T.J. 1972. An experimental study of the effects of orientation behavior on small group consensus. *Speech Monographs 39,* 159–165.

Knutson, T.J. and Holdridge, W.E. 1975. Orientation behavior, leadership and consensus: A possible functional relationship. *Speech Monographs 42,* 107–114.

Leavitt, H.J. 1972. *Managerial psychology.* 3rd ed. Chicago: University of Chicago Press.

Leavitt, H.J. 1972. *Managerial psychology.* 3rd ed. Chicago: University of Chicago Press.

Levine, S. 1974. Four leadership types: An approach to constructive leadership. In *Small group communication: A reader,* 2nd. ed., eds. R.S. Cathcart and L. Samovar, pp. 381–389. Dubuque, Iowa: Wm. Brown.

Lewin, K., Lippitt, R. and White, R.K. 1939. Patterns of aggressive behavior in experimentally created social climates. *Journal of Social Psycholgoy 10,* 271–299.

McCroskey, J.C. 1966. Scales for the measurement of ethos. *Speech Monographs 33,* 65–72.

Morse, J. and Lorsch, J.W. 1970. Beyond theory Y. *Harvard Business Review 48,* 61–68.

Morse, N.C. and Reimer, E. 1956. The experimental change of a major organizational variable. *Journal of Abnormal and Social Psychology 52,* 120–29.

Rosenfeld, L.B. and Fowler, G.D. 1976. Personality, sex and leadership style. *Communication Monographs 43,* 320–324.

Rosenfeld, L.B. and Plax, T.G. 1975. Personality determinants of autocratic and democratic leadership. *Speech Monographs 42,* 203–208.

Schutz, W. 1958. *FIRO, A three-dimensional theory of interpersonal behavior.* New York: Holt, Rinehart & Winston.

Shaw, M.E. 1976. *Group dynamics: The psychology of small group behavior.* 2nd ed. New York: McGraw-Hill.

Stogdill, R.M. 1948. Personal factors associated with leadership: A survey of the literature. *Journal of Psychology 25,* 35–71.

Stogdill, R.M. 1974. *Handbook of leadership: A survey of theory and research.* New York: Free Press.

Tannenbaum, R. and Massarik, F. 1968. Leadership: A frame of reference. *Organizational behavior and management,* eds. D.E. Porter, et al., pp. 302–322. Scranton, Penn.: International Textbook Co.

Tannenbaum, R. and Schmidt, W.H. 1958. How to choose a leadership pattern, *Havard Business Review 36,* 95–101.

Vroom, V.H. 1959. Some personality determinants of the effects of participation. *Journal of Abnormal and Social Psychology 59,* 322–327.

Vroom, V.H. 1960. *Some personality determinants of the effects of participation.* Englewood Cliffs, N.J.: Prentice-Hall, Inc.

White, T.H. 1975. *Breach of faith.* New York: Atheneum.

The "products" of group action are quite diverse. Typically, we think about group outcomes as "decisions made" or "problems solved." Certainly these are tangible results that may occur. Achieving goals by completing tasks is an important reason for groups to exist. However, there are other important outcomes, or group outputs, which follow as a consequence of group interaction. Members develop unique relationships. They share common bases of experience that are personal and nontransferable. These experiences emerge as members interact and resolve interaction dilemmas. Beyond personal experiences, groups evolve as groups; they develop as unique social entities. Chapter 8 discusses member relationships. Chapters 9 and 10 review group "development" and productive achievements, respectively.

GROUP
OUTPUTS
Part
Four

Chapter

The most obvious output of a group is task completion. When final recommendations are forwarded, reports typed, and action initiated, groups often disband, reorganize, or set to work on new tasks. The *personal effects* of decision making groups are rarely analyzed. There are situations, however, where group impact on members is a *hidden agenda* in decision making groups. Quite often corporate executives get together not only to discuss policy decisions but also to iron out differences and to provide one another with direct feedback. School and law enforcement officials sometimes bring dissidents together for the announced purpose of discussing an issue but, in reality, are attempting to modify behaviors by providing a safety valve for building pressures. Whether member change is a by-product of group interaction, a hidden agenda of group leaders, or a specific goal established at the outset, there can be no question that one of the major outputs of a group is member influence and change.

This chapter explores some of the ways group affiliation and interaction influences individuals. The reader should note that what we discuss here alludes to the *consequences* of

*relationships
between members:
cohesiveness,
conflict and
interpersonal
communication*

interacting. We are dealing with outcomes, or *outputs* if you will, which evolve from interactions with others. This means we must address certain issues related to the interaction, or throughput, dimension of groups. Throughout the chapter remember that concepts like cohesiveness or conflict represent numerous sets of behavioral exchanges between group members. We talk about such processes as having "outcomes" only in the sense that their effects on members are seldom within one's awareness on a moment-to-moment basis and are probably better discussed in retrospect. We will also address alternatives for managing interaction processes, particularly with respect to member conflicts, that may have considerable impact on a group's ongoing interpersonal relationships and task outcomes.

WHY DOES A GROUP HAVE AN EFFECT ON THE INDIVIDUAL?

In previous chapters we have discussed the powerful influence of a group upon individual members. Studies have shown that individuals are willing to disbelieve their own perceptual systems in favor of group opinion (Asch, 1952), go against societal norms (Milgram, 1963), undergo embarrassment (Aronson and Mills, 1959), and endure the threat of physical punishment (Festinger, et al., 1950) in order to behave in ways they believe acceptable to a group. The obvious qualification to this principle is that membership in a group must be important to the individual. The successfulness of group pressure depends on group cohesion and an individual's needs for membership.

Cohesiveness as a Group Outcome

The essence of a group is that a collection of individuals have relationships that make them *interdependent* to some significant degree (Cartwright and Zander, 1968, p. 46). This state of interdependence can be regarded as *cohesion*. The strength of a group depends on the cohesion of its members. People generally desire to remain in a group because of "the attractiveness of the group to its members, their willingness to participate in its activities, and the extent to which they see themselves being rewarded potentially by their experiences in the group" (Moment and Zaleznik, 1964, p. 355).

Fundamental to a group's appeal for an individual is the personal needs and motives of that individual. A group may be very appealing to some people but hold no attraction for others. Each individual brings certain needs and expectations which can be fulfilled by the group. If the group satisfies those needs, the individual will be attracted to the group. The stronger the need or attraction is, the stronger group cohesion will be.

Group cohesion and member reliance upon a group is enhanced by external threats. As an outside force becomes more threatening and difficult for the individual alone to cope with, member needs for the group increase, resulting in stronger cohesion. For instance, as alcoholics accept their own human weakness and acknowledge the powerful threat of alcohol, an Alcoholics Anonymous group becomes an important, if not an indispensable, part of their lives.

All groups have some degree of cohesiveness since the basis for group existence is a common ground of interest. In turn, people tend to be attracted to others who share similar attitudes and experiences (Heider, 1958; Newcomb, 1961). This principle is apparent in groups of friends who exclude or include others on the basis of similar attitudes and experiences. At minimum, every group provides a commonality of attitudes and experiences related to a common objective which, in turn, serves to develop cohesion and to induce liking.

Cohesiveness is also a product of the length of time members have participated in a group (Moment and Zaleznik, 1964). The longer members have belonged to a group, the more opportunities they will have had to interact with one another. They become more alike in their activities and sentiments (Homans, 1950; Heider, 1958), which provides the basis of cohesion. Experimental support for length and frequency of interaction resulting in cohesion was provided in the now classic Westgate Housing Project studies (Festinger, et al., 1950). Residents of older Westgate apartments demonstrated greater cohesion than residents of the newer Westgate West apartments. Not only did Westgate tenants have longer to interact, the housing complex was built in a U-shaped court which was more conducive to frequent interaction than the two-story barrack-like rows of apartments that made up Westgate West.

Opportunities for interaction may, of course, allow members to determine differences and a lack of commonality. If differences are sufficiently strong, a group may disband or individuals deviating from common sources of identification may resign. On the other hand, these differences may be a source of group stimulation, group creativity, member satisfaction, and interest. Life would be rather dull if everyone we encountered had similar views, attitudes, and experiences. A group norm that encourages differences may be an indication of security and cohesiveness. The opportunity for interaction in a group increases cohesion by identifying member similarities and differences. The more members know about each other, the more committed they become to a group, or the more motivation they may have for withdrawing membership. In either case, the end result will generally be a more cohesive group.

Variables influencing group cohesiveness include outside threat, common experience of members, similar beliefs of members, perceived attraction for the group, interaction frequency and length, and task and goal attractiveness. All of these are contingent upon needs of the individual. In order to fit comfortably into a group, the individual member will attempt to influence a group and, in turn, the group will attempt to influence the individual.

The more cohesive a group, the greater influence the group may have on an individual. That is, the more cohesive the group, the more pressure can be brought to bear on an individual (Schachter, 1951). In response, the individual may conform by changing original behaviors or attitudes, or may reject group pressure by psychologically reinforcing an original position. In the latter case, we can expect greater rigidity and strength in the position as a means of defending it against outside pressures. Conformity and deviation both represent a change in the individual's pattern of behavior and attitudes from initial entry into the group. Therefore, the degree of group cohesiveness has a direct bearing on member change.

Cohesiveness and Group Norms

As a group develops cohesion, it establishes standards or codes of conduct to regulate the behavior of individual members. Some norms are explicit, such as "the meeting will start at 9:00," while other norms are implicit, such as "no one will arrive until 9:00 and the group will not get down to business until ten after." Norms are often formed by the group itself but may also be dictated by an outside source. From a societal perspective, laws, regulations, and cultural expectations serve as group norms. Our discussion here is limited to norms developed within the group, but the reader should keep in mind that the environment also provides norms of behavior which groups may support or attack.

Norms are enforced by some form of punishment when individuals deviate. Groups generally seek to maintain normative behavior by communicating and reaffirming norms when deviations occur. Since new members often have difficulty knowing the implicit norms of a group, they generally are advised to initially "sit back and observe..." When President Carter was elected to office he chose not to follow many of the normative behaviors of his predecessors. Some people viewed his deviance from the norms as refreshing, but he was punished by members of both parties for failure to abide by norms regarded as important by Congress. In spite of idiosyncrasy credits gained from the election, Carter was unable to gain approval for some of his key proposals due to norm deviations by him and his staff.

Forms of punishment were discussed earlier in the text and to some degree and tied to situational contingencies. Punishment for President Carter, for example, was failure to get legislation passed. For others, norm deviations may be punished by isolation from group interaction, decision making, and rewards. Perhaps the most powerful sanction available to a group is controlling the opportunity to interact with and influence the group. The more group members desire interaction, the more they will conform—unless members view the group as rewarding deviation by increased interaction.

To answer the original question of why a group has an effect on an individual, we may conclude that in interacting with group members and in seeking group approval, an individual adheres to norms in accordance with the strength of cohesion among members. Even in rebelling against the norms of a group, an individual's attitudes and behaviors are modified by the necessity to build defenses against group pressures. In many therapy groups, for example, members test their ideas and behaviors against other members in order to develop individual strength and self-reliance (Phillips, 1973, p. 84).

HOW DOES CONFLICT INFLUENCE
GROUP PARTICIPATION?

Much attention has been focused on the issue of conflict within a group. When individual members clash in their attempts at group influence, and when members try to change the direction of group thinking, conflict is bound to occur. Everyone has different life experiences, resulting in differences of opinions and attitudes. Given an opportunity to interact, two people will soon discover significant differences regardless of the commonality of their background. These differences actually serve as an impetus to communicate. If it were possible for two people to have identical experiences, attitudes and opinions, there would be no reason to communicate since each person would already know what the other had to say. Perhaps the clearest example of this absurd situation would be the image of an elderly couple married for sixty years, sitting on the front porch of their home day after day. Neither speaks to the other because they have either shared the same past experiences or have already told each other all their jokes, satires, and experiences. Needless to say, the average encounter is a far cry from that scene.

Each time an additional person is added to a small group, more experiences, opinions, and attitudes are added to the interaction pool of the group. Actually, additional people have a *multiplier effect*, rather than an additive effect, since each additional person has not only a personal contribution but also contributes in combination with others in the group. With each additional person, then, there are more possible combinations of experiences, attitudes, and opinions. Is it any wonder that agreement is generally more easily achieved in a ten-member committee than a hundred-member legislature?

The Nature of Group Conflict

The first principle regarding conflict in groups is that *conflict is inevitable*. Second, conflict can be *healthy* and *enjoyable*. It generates interesting discussions, generates critical thinking, and leads to more productive decisions. Lifeless, uninformed discussions may reflect a lack of conflict. Too often a model discussion of a meeting is viewed as one in which everyone is pleasant, polite, and avoids conflict if at all possible.

Doolittle (1976, pp. 7–9) has identified five "myths" about the role of conflict in communication. First, "Individuals are naturally in harmony because of their humanity. Conflicts represent a disruption of this harmony and are, therefore, dysfunctional." As we have previously indicated, groups would profit from recognizing member differences and treating conflict as inevitable. Second, "Conflicts most frequently occur because individuals do not understand each other." This may occasionally be true, but oftentimes members have legitimate differences that cannot be resolved with additional understanding and communication. This leads to the third myth, "Conflict can always be resolved." The different perspectives of labor and management, liberals and conservatives, blacks and whites, will probably never be resolved regardless of the best intentions of both parties. Fourth, "Conflict represents breakdowns in and deterioration of the social fabric" and fifth, "Conflict represents breakdowns in communication" are additional myths relating to the erroneous belief that conflict is undesirable and can be remedied by additional communication and understanding. These myths have probably been perpetuated because people feel uncomfortable with conflict and are aware of its potential destructive, detrimental effects on group behavior.

While conflict is necessary for group interaction, it *can* be destructive to group growth and development. All group members are responsible for working toward constructive rather than destructive conflict. Often the formally elected leader is not in the best position to monitor conflict since the leader is often engaged in the conflict. We have maintained that a participant-observer is in the best position to recognize and influence the interpersonal dynamics of a group. As a semi-detached observer, the participant-observer can monitor *meta-messages* underlying verbal exchanges and can observe the flushed face, muscular tension, and nervous movement often associated with conflict. A more involved participant is often too close to the conflict to recognize danger signs.

A helpful distinction between constructive and destructive conflict has been offered by Fisher (1974, p. 105). *Substantive* conflict involves intellectual opposition to the content of ideas. *Affective* conflict refers to emotional and often personal clashes. Substantive conflicts provide rigor and vitality to constructive group interaction but may lead to affective, often times destructive, conflict. The basic problem is that people tend to invest their egos in their ideas. When their ideas are attacked or questioned, they react affectively as well as cognitively. Thus, it is common for some people to react defensively if their ideas are met with criticism.

Conflict Versus Rejection

There is some justification for group members being ego-tied to their ideas and assertions. Those people whose ideas are accepted by a group gain the immediate ego gratification of having influenced others. Furthermore, a group will probably reward those who are most persuasive with leadership roles and responsibilities. Rejection of ideas often reflects rejection of the person as much as the idea. You can probably recall being in a group that rejected an idea simply because it was not presented forcefully enough or because the presenter was a low status group member. We generally prefer to think that ideas are accepted or rejected on their own merits, but closer examination will probably reveal a strong *affective* component in the decision making process.

The acceptance-rejection concept is closely tied to the notion of winning or losing. If one's ideas are accepted he or she has "won"; rejection indicates "loss." This competitive orientation is not conducive to long-term group development. In the win-lose situation, the loser might react by pretending to be a "good sport," withdrawing from active participation, or counterattacking subsequent issues. All three of these alternatives fail to confront the affective side of conflict directly and may result in reducing the potential inputs of all group members.

Conflict, Cooperation, and Collaboration

In contrast to the either-or condition, conflict that is resolved by allowing all participants to "win" may have the best long-term effects. Deutsch (1949a,b) referred to this as cooperation. However, cooperation often carries the connotation that each member of the conflict gives up something in order to meet the affective demands of a group. Such a practice may result in compromising the best alternatives and solutions. This might be regarded as a *lose-lose* situation where everyone gives away something to achieve group harmony.

There are many occasions where compromise is not needed. All participants can share in "winning" by collaborating on decisions (Giffin and Barnes, 1976, p. 66). In contrast to the potential lose-lose situation of cooperating, everyone strives for the optimum situation of win-win. This requires a pooling of diversity rather than a compromising of differences. Perhaps the best example of the difference between cooperation and collaboration is a marriage contract. In older, traditional marriages the woman was expected to give up her name, career goals, and personal interests in favor of her spouse. In return for food, clothing, and shelter provided by the man, the woman was expected to bear children, clean the house, prepare meals, and so forth. We regard this as a cooperative arrangement since the woman gave up some personal desires to achieve other goals. Many contemporary marriages reflect collaboration in that the man and woman both share in providing a family income, raising a family, and caring for the home. The woman occasionally retains her name and often continues to pursue personal career goals. Failure and success are shared by both marriage partners while each preserves a personal self-identity.

The notion of using collaboration in a group avoids the duality of competition *versus* cooperation. We do not believe it is generally necessary for individuals to "give in to the common good." Nor is it desirable for individuals to feel like they must "win" approval for their ideas at the expense of other group members' ideas. Productive groups involve multiple members in multiple roles. While two people strive for task accomplishment, another may nod approval, and someone else may make a side comment to relieve tension. Each of these people and their functions may be necessary for group success.

When members realize their interdependent role relations, initiation of ideas takes on less significance; or, more properly phrased, each person's role takes on more significance. Collaboration involves recognizing and respecting each person's role in a group. Conflict is not avoided in a collaborative relationship, but it can be productive because members accept the fact that they are interdependent. Conflict occurs because members care about each other and the group as a whole. Differences in experiences, attitudes, and opinions are recognized rather than repressed (Kemp, 1964).

The net effect of collaboration is that participants feel involved in the group. Each member feels that he or she can contribute regardless of opinions held by other members. This involves norms of: (1) acceptance of differences, (2) willingness to risk, (3) mutual trust, (4) flexibility when appropriate, and (5) accurate empathy for others. Patton and Giffin (1973) note that only when members feel comfortable in a group can conflict safely emerge. In a climate of mutual regard, conflict is *issue* oriented. Substantive conflicts will still occasionally give rise to affective conflicts, but under a collaborative condition the feelings can be confronted directly. An implicit norm emerges which encourages members to openly express their feelings as well as their ideas about group issues.

Overt Consensus and "Submerged" Conflict

Harvey (1974) takes the position that consensus may be far more detrimental to group action than conflict. If two people get into an argument they may feel trapped and unable to resolve their differences but at least they, and other group members, are aware that they are engaged in conflict. In contrast, consensus often is a sign of submerged conflict of which no one is aware. Unconsciously, group members avoid responsibility for decision making by agreeing to or accepting ideas that they mildly disagree with or oppose.

In groups where there is little interpersonal regard, destructive conflict often emerges; in groups with high interpersonal regard, consensus often works destructively. If someone you dislike speaks in error, you will probably not hesitate to criticize the statement. If someone you care for errs, you may think to yourself, "she's wrong, but it's not worth mentioning." Or, "If that's his opinion fine, I won't upset him by offering a contrary view." Assume you are in a group that is to determine an important policy. If a friend were to offer an erroneous opinion on the heart of the matter you might be moved to differ. But most major decisions come in small segments. A smaller error might be tactfully overlooked. Furthermore, suppose that the initiator of this erroneous idea is a powerful and knowledgeable person. Despite personal reservations, you may be willing to go along with the idea simply because of the person's status.

Examples of consensus problems are surprisingly frequent but are usually identified only in retrospect. Decisions related to Watergate and the Vietnam War are probably the best known examples of national issues where individual decision makers held private reservations but agreed to actions contrary to their personal beliefs. Millions of Americans have undoubtedly wondered why intelligent, resourceful leaders in the Johnson and Nixon administrations could make such "foolish" mistakes. Most of the key conspirators in Watergate indicated that they privately had reservations about the break-in (see Harvey, 1974). Key members of the Johnson cabinet expressed personal doubts about escalating the war. In both instances these people publicly supported contrary positions.

Harvey (1974, pp. 66–67) identifies six symptoms of groups caught in the mismanagement of agreement.

1. Members privately agree to the nature of the situation facing the group.
2. Members privately agree to steps required to remedy the situation.
3. Members fail to accurately communicate their beliefs to one another.
4. Given inaccurate information, members collectively make decisions contrary to the best interests of the group.
5. As a result of taking counterproductive actions, members experience dissatisfaction and irritation with the group. Consequently, they form subgroups of trusted others and blame other subgroups for the group's problems.
6. Finally, if the group does not directly address the problem, the cycle repeats itself with greater intensity.

At first glance these symptoms seem unlikely to occur. Why would a group of people make decisions to which they are privately opposed? Try to think of a situation where you went along with a group decision only to find out later that it was not in the best interests of the group. One of the authors recalls a high school experience where lack of agreement was not communicated. Word had spread that there was to be a fight in a nearby park. Even though it meant going to the park after curfew, and some youths privately questioned the decision to go, many cars joined in the caravan. The fight failed to materialize; however squad cars did materialize and everyone was taken to police headquarters. Each embarrassed youth told basically the same story, "I didn't really want to go but the others seemed to want to, so . . . ." While examples such as this one probably fall within our common frame of reference, they do not answer the question of why people take counterproductive actions.

Five reasons have been identified by Harvey (1974). First, *action anxiety* stems from fear of acting in accordance with what needs to be done. If required actions are unpleasant, it may be easier to ignore the problem. Many people would be fired if their employers didn't have action anxiety. But why does the anxiety occur? Perhaps because of *negative fantasies* about what will happen as a consequence of acting. A woman who no longer enjoyed living with her marital partner lamented, "I would leave him but I am afraid he would commit suicide." The fantasy about what he might do also provides an excuse from responsibility of having to act. Her lack of action is rationalized in her own mind, as well as in the minds of her friends.

The negative consequences of actions are not only fantasized but are also a *real risk*. Her husband may actually commit suicide. All actions have consequences that may be worse than present conditions. There is some truth to the assertion that we kill the bearers of bad news. In many groups and organizations it may be safer to hide a problem, or just leave if alone for someone else to find, than to be the bearer of ill tidings. Rather than take the risk of actions, groups and individuals often elect the safe path of inaction even to the point of detrimental consequences.

Real or fantasized risk in a group is often based on *fear of separation*. In our discussion of cohesiveness and norms we identified exclusion as one of the most powerful punishments available to a group. Individuals fear ostracism, alienation, and separation. The fear of risking disapproval is grounded in potential separation.

The fear of appearing to be a "sissy" or "disloyal" has a curious consequence. An unwillingness to take risks "virtually ensures separation and aloneness we so fear" (Harvey, 1974, p. 72). According to Harvey, there is a *psychological reversal* of risk and certainty. Members proceed on the assumption that there is no risk in remaining silent and there is a direct risk in rocking the boat. In reality, the risk is just the opposite. When a group decision fails, everyone blames everyone else. The only one who does not share in the blame is the person who risked separation. Those who are promoted or rewarded by a group are those who were most willing to accept separation. Conversely, the failure to act is often predicated on a fear that such actions may result in separation from others. Paradoxically, inaction results in the feared separation. An executive who doesn't want to step on corporate toes by voicing objections may end up losing the job for failure to make substantive contributions to staff meetings.

Managing Submerged Conflict

Problems of consensus can be avoided in much the same way as destructive conflict. When group members feel a sense of acceptance, when they are secure in their role relationships and do not feel the threat of separation, then they should be willing to express opinions and attitudes openly. By openly expressing doubts and reservations, by checking out the validity of inferences regarding others, members should be able to distinguish fantasized risks from real risks. At times members may need to be reminded of the danger of consensus. It is easy and comfortable to sit back while others assume responsibility for decision making. Leaders may need to say something like, "Are you sure this is the direction we ought to be going?" If contrary views are offered, they should be considered seriously. We are reminded of one group leader who habitually tried to draw out responses from group members, then would systemically oppose views that differed from his own. Members soon learned that a request for other opinions was merely a gesture of openness. In actuality, he was closed to any other views.

Destructive conflict can often be avoided by collaborative sharing among equal status members. The same can be said for consensus. Members who are regarded as experts often do not have their opinions tested by others. Nonexperts conclude that "He knows more than I do," or "If I question her it will only result in my looking foolish." Exemption from having one's views tested is, of course, a good rationale for insecure members to establish an image of expertise. By use of name dropping, specialized vocabulary, and jargon, experts build their own fantasies and often escape critical assessment by others.

Occasionally a new group member or nonexpert can bring constructive change of a group by questioning previously established norms. Assume, for example, a group consisted of company officials and experts on labor relations. Given sufficient time to establish their role relations, the experts may have gained enough credibility to offer assertions without having them questioned. Let us assume that the company wants to enact a policy that they fear (fantasize) will meet with union disfavor. The experts feed on the fantasy by testifying that there would be a work stoppage if such a proposal were enacted. Just before the policy is shelved, a new person is added to the group. She looks at the proposal and comments that it "Looks great! Why aren't we implementing it?" The older members smile patronizingly and explain that "If it were enacted the unions would kick up a storm." Our naive new member exhibits a modicum of brashness by asking, "How do you know?" With a little less patience the executives explain that three members of the group who are experts on labor relations have testified to that effect. "How do they know?" she brashly asks. Now she's done it. She has questioned the unquestionable. Nobody's fool, the experts proceed to cite other noted authorities, case histories, and references that led them to their astute conclusions. Most of us would stop right there, thoroughly impressed and somewhat embarrassed at ever having raised the issue. But since this story is fictitious we will make our protagonist quite brash. The next day she schedules a meeting with the union president. "What would you think of this idea?" she asks. In accordance with the expert's predictions, he indicates that he would not be too happy about it, however right now he is involved in some internal conflicts so he would prefer to let the issue slide by. The fantasies are dispelled, the policy enacted, and the committee prospers from having made a correct decision—at least until our protagonist learns to accept the group norm of not questioning the experts.

In the scenerio our protagonist introduced constructive and substantive conflict. She also accepted the responsibility of checking out the fantasized risk. She was not simply playing the role of a devil's advocate. Substantive conflict can, however, be introduced to mask the reality of consensus and to absolve group members of responsibility for their decisions. It has been said that any fool can ask questions and criticize the work of others, but it takes a leader to initiate and to carry out ideas. Questions and comments advanced just to make the initiator of an idea go over hurdles are probably of little benefit. A barrage of questions may permit the cynic to disclaim responsibility for actions, should they fail. Asking questions potentially places others on the defensive while committing the questioner to nothing. Questions can, of course, be coupled with assertions as a more open form of expression. An open form of expression identifies the motivation for the question prior to asking it; this specifies the questioner's position prior to committing the respondent.

The foregoing remarks are not intended to imply that questions and critical comments should not be advanced. Each group member has an obligation to ask sufficient questions to remove doubts about the worth of a proposal. The questions and comments should have a collaborative effect in that members feel the comments aid in the search for the best possible action.

WHAT INTERPERSONAL BEHAVIORS ENHANCE GROUP RELATIONS?

The optimum norm of interpersonal behavior, whether in a decision making group or a therapeutic group, permits free expression of ideas and feelings by all members. Ideas and feelings then become data for the group to analyze. Members are encouraged to openly *own* their ideas and feelings by frequent use of the word "I." In response, other members accept thoughts and feelings as valid for the person who expressed them. Differences are accepted as *differences* without unnecessary evaluation. Feedback is provided honestly and openly as a means of clarifying how members feel about the others' contributions. When everyone shares in the risk of being open and honest with one another, the proportion of risk for any single individual is reduced.

Openness and Group Integration

Openness of feelings and direct feedback are often associated with encounter or sensitivity groups. However, when people propose ideas in any type of meeting they are putting themselves on the line. They are risking rejection, ridicule, and embarrassment by revealing part of their thinking process to others. Openness, or *disclosure,* as we are using the term here, does not necessarily mean revealing deep-seated personal information. We are simply referring to a person's willingness to honestly share inner thoughts and feelings with others (this conceptualization is based upon Pearce and Sharp, 1973). In openly sharing, members are able to compare personal feelings and thoughts with feedback from others.

We enjoy talking with those who accept and understand us. They understand because we reveal ourselves to them in some way. In contrast, failure to openly express feelings and thoughts makes it difficult for other group members to communicate with us in meaningful ways; conflicts may remain submerged, and unwarranted consensus can determine group actions.

Where groups are characterized by acceptance, honesty, and openness, cohesiveness and collaboration should prevail. Of course these are *relationship* characteristics developed by individual behaviors. One act or one person demonstrating honesty does not make for a group norm of honesty. However, the opposite may be true. A significant breach of faith may destroy a prevailing norm of openness. If a group agrees to openness and direct feedback, for example, but when one of the members is punished in the larger organization for something said inside the group, member confidence in sharing may be destroyed.

Rebuilding Openness

Why aren't we more honest in our remarks to others in everyday situations? Partially, perhaps, because we have learned from experience that not everyone can accept feedback or is willing to mutually share information. The group may agree to lay aside these life experiences and expectations in favor of a special condition. However, laying aside well-learned lessons is not easy. Members will typically "test the water" by risking themselves in small ways. Gradually, as they learn that the group can be trusted, they take greater risks. One perceived deviation from agreed upon norms may cause members to think, "Ah ha, now I know what *really* happens when someone believes all this about openness and honest feedback." Groups are generally slow to repair damage done by one perceived indiscretion.

Repairing a damaged group relationship may be most effectively achieved, once again, by the participant-observer. From a semidetached position, developing norms and the effects of norm deviations can be observed. Members more psychologically tied to group processes may not have the perspective necessary to reflect on emerging relationships. Participant-observers may be in the best position to discuss:

1. Direct feelings about group relationships.
2. Observations of nonverbal behaviors, as distinguished from verbal behaviors.
3. Acceptance and concern for member feelings.
4. Willingness to directly confront relationship issues not previously addressed by a group.

In other words, a participant-observer may be better at talking about interaction and group processes than members more intimately tied to the discussion. This is somewhat like the role of a mediator in a labor dispute or an outside consultant to any ongoing group or organization. The significant difference in these two examples is that mediators and consultants are people specifically asked to fulfill the role of participant-observer. A group member who *processes* the group (recounts participant-observation findings) must be careful not to project a "holier than thou" attitude by giving advice. A nonevaluative role of inquiry encourages a group to do *self-analysis* of behaviors and relationships.

Psychological Consequences of Participation

Ultimately, members should feel good about their personal contribution to a group. Members should leave feeling satisfied with relationships established during the life of a group. This is not to be confused with "liking" other members. While we may indeed develop friendships in working relationships, in most cases friendships should be a by-product rather than a goal. Groups that encourage directness, open conflict, respect for differences, honesty in relationships, and sharing personal thoughts and feelings may promote feelings of autonomy. There is a story of Eleanor Roosevelt having visited the Soviet Union. She reportedly argued strenuously with the Soviet Premier. At the end of the meeting the Soviet Premier asked if he could report to the press that they had agreed on some issues. She smiled and reportedly said, "You can tell them that we agree to disagree."

In a similar manner, healthy groups may vigorously debate issues while retaining respect for differences. A satisfied member leaves the group wtih a feeling of completion. Feelings and thoughts have been openly expressed. If a completed task does not reflect the desires of an individual, at least the member has been given ample opportunity to express reservations and dissatisfactions.

If the goal of a group is to change individual behaviors, it is particularly important that each member assume responsibility for personal behaviors as well as changes in other group members. We know of no group process that automatically changes individual behaviors. The fundamental requisite is that individual members assume personal responsibility for their actions. New group members often enter with a "bet you can't change me" or "show me" attitude. This attitude, coupled with an abdication of responsibility, is bound to cause group difficulties and unsatisfactory outcomes. In contrast, a personal willingness to change and to contribute to a group is a healthy sign of eventual success and satisfaction in groups.

In this chapter we have emphasized that members undergo attitudinal and behavioral change as a result of interaction processes and relationships that develop during the life of the group. Member satisfactions may, at times, be more important than concrete task outcomes. If one member feels he or she was not given an opportunity to participate in task accomplishment, the dissatisfaction may be enough to significantly hamper task output in a large organizational structure. Fulfilled members, on the other hand, help achieve acceptance in the larger body and may be the most significant contributors to continued group life.

REFERENCES

Aronson, E. and Mills, J. 1959. Effect of severity of initiation on liking for a group. *Journal of Abnormal and Social Psychology 59,* 177–181.

Asch, S.E. 1952. *Social psychology.* Englewood Cliffs, N.J.: Prentice-Hall, Inc.

Cartwright, D. and Zander, A. 1968. Groups and group membership: Introduction. In *Group dynamics: Research and theory,* 3rd ed., eds. D. Cartwright and A. Zander, pp. 45–62. New York: Harper & Row, Pub.

Deutsch, M. 1949a. A theory of co-operation and competition. *Human Relations 2,* 129–152.

Deutsch, M. 1949b. An experimental study of the effects of co-operation and competition upon group process. *Human Relations 2,* 199–232.

Doolittle, R.J. 1976. *Orientations to communication and conflict.* Chicago: Science Research Associates, Inc.

Festinger, L., Schachter, S. and Back, K. 1950. *Social pressures in informal groups.* New York: Harper & Row, Pub.

Fisher, B.A. 1974. *Small group decision making: Communication and process.* New York: McGraw-Hill.

Giffin, K. and Barnes, R.E. 1976. *Trusting me, trusting you.* Columbus, Ohio: Chas. E. Merrill.

Harvey, J. 1974. The Abilene paradox: The management of agreement. *Organization Dynamics, Summer,* 63–80.

Heider, F. 1958. *The psychology of interpersonal relations.* New York: John Wiley.

Homans, G.C. 1950. *The human group.* New York: Harper & Row, Pub.

Johnson, D.L. and Ridener, L.R. 1974. Self-disclosure, participation and perceived cohesiveness in small group interaction. *Psychological Reports 23,* 361–362.

Kemp, C.G. 1964. *Perspectives on group process.* Boston: Houghton Mifflin.

Milgram. S. 1963. Behavioral study of obedience. *Journal of Abnormal and Social Psychology 67,* 371–378.

Moment, D. and Zaleznik, A. 1964. *The dynamics of interpersonal behavior.* New York: John Wiley.

Newcomb, T.M. 1961. *The acquaintance process.* New York: Holt, Rinehart & Winston.

Patton, B. and Giffin, K. 1973. *Problem-solving group interaction.* New York: Harper & Row, Pub.

Pearce, W.B. and Sharp, S.M. 1973. Self-disclosing communication. *Journal of Communication 23,* 409–425.

Phillips, G.M. 1973. *Communication and the small group.* Indianapolis: Bobbs-Merrill.

Schachter, S. 1951. Deviation, rejection and communication. *Journal of Abnormal and Social Psychology 46,* 190–207.

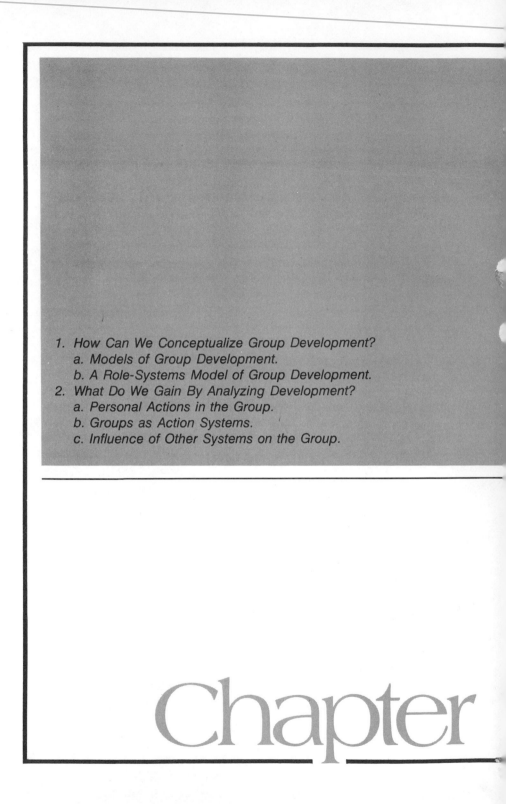

Chapter

W hen I look back to the first meeting of our group eight week ago, I'm really amazed at the things we've done together. First, I never thought we would learn to trust each other—but we did. Second, I (Karen) surprised myself by being assertive. It was a new experience for me. Jim cane out of his shell and, to me, seemed like the real leader of our group. Howard settled down after a few sessions and genuinely tried to be more sensitive to other people's feelings. Most important, I think, was the fact that each time our group met, regardless of whether the session was a "hit" or "bomb," we learned something about each other that we carried with us to the next session.

The fictionalized reaction above is really a composite of true accounts students have written as members of groups. The example is noteworthy because it points out how, over time, members of a group change and adapt to a group, and how experience gained by working with others is something that changes as that *experiential information* accumulates. This chapter discusses ways we can observe and experience group development. In this regard, we will discuss (1) various models researchers have constructed to describe development, and (2) how to use our knowledge of developmental processes in groups to better understand the group as a system.

9 patterns of group development

HOW CAN WE CONCEPTUALIZE GROUP DEVELOPMENT?

Our task in this section is to look at ways group development can be conceptualized. We will focus specifically on what has already been termed *temporal patterns* of interaction structures (see Chapter 6). Group development is usually studied by assessing *how* and *when* certain crucial episodes, or *phases,* of activity emerge as groups strive to complete tasks and to attain goals. Identifying the order of episodes by building *models* helps to explain, in general terms, consistencies of action one might find in many groups. We will briefly review some of the better known models of group development. Ultimately, we will propose a synthesis model incorporating ideas from a number of perspectives.

Models of Group Development

Models attempting to represent group development present a diverse range of perspectives. Some are based on reflection or speculation and others on extensive statistical analyses of observational data or other information. Often models are developed in relation to some method of observing group behavior and are limited by the content and scope of that methodology. Here we will review representative models from the following three perspectives: *psychodynamic, equilibrium,* and *functional.*

Psychodynamic. One of the classic models of group development was devised by Bennis and Shepard (1956). These researchers were human relations training facilitators (guidance and resource persons) conducting a number of "T-groups" at the National Training Laboratory in Bethel, Maine. Observations of groups in which they participated led to the formulation of their model.

Bennis and Shepard worked from a set of assumptions about how personality affects individual participation and group progress. At the core of their theory is the proposition that personality dynamics affect "valid communication" between members. Thus, a person struggling with *intra*personal (personality) conflicts, intensified by situational demands of group membership, will have greater difficulty engaging in valid communication with others than someone without such conflicts.

The *situational demands* of membership are rather unique to T-group settings. First, "encounter" or T-groups may be very unstructured in terms of initial goals and activities. Second, leadership is often diffused among all participants. Designated *facilitators* may intentionally avoid playing leader roles to reduce group dependence on them as authority figures. These and other factors produce a highly ambiguous group setting where the principal "task and goal" is for members to learn how to effectively work with each other to reduce ambiguity.

According to Bennis and Shepard, two primary dimensions of personality may account for the effects of personal behavior on group development. The first dimension relates to a person's orientation toward authority and personal autonomy (freedom). Some people are *dependent* and rely heavily on the control and direction of a group leader (or, in this case, facilitator). Other people are *counterdependent* and harbor a kind of antagonism towards authority figures who might inhibit the free exercise of their own personal action. The second dimension of personality relates to levels of *intimacy* or interdependence needed in relationships with others. Some people can be labeled *overpersonal*, suggesting they need a high degree of intimacy with other group members (possibly higher than the situation permits). Conversely, other members are termed *counterpersonal*, suggesting they desire little personal intimacy with group members (possibly less than the situation demands).

Central to Bennis and Shephard's theory is an assumption that people react to unstructured experiences according to the prominence of one or both personality dimensions. Being dependent, counterdependent, overpersonal, or counterpersonal is a reaction to the uncomfortable feeling of being in an unfamiliar and ambiguous setting. They propose that such personality extremes represent a *conflicted* psychological state for the person vis-à-vis the demands of a group setting. Therefore, a counterdependent reaction that shuns attempts at structuring group behavior conflicts with an obvious situational demand that group members must let themselves be controlled by one another to engage in cooperative group activities. Or, a counterpersonal reaction of avoiding interpersonal closeness may conflict with a situational demand that requires certain amounts of intimacy for building trust.

There is one other type of group member we have not discussed—the *independent*. Independents are persons who seem to make easier adjustments to group membership demands. Presumably, they possess a personality structure which permits them to be unrestrained by authority or intimacy requirements. The independent member unites the group and helps it overcome counterproductive effects of member subgroups based on dependency or intimacy preferences. Independent members emerge as leaders, at least temporarily, to facilitate group progress. However, there is no guarantee that all groups contain independent members. Therefore, some groups may flounder for lack of such unifying persons.

The theory proposes that all groups must attempt to resolve the two basic problems of *dependence* (or authority) and *interdependence* or intimacy). As conceived by Bennis and Shepard, authority relations, how members' orientations dispose them to relate to control or leadership structures, must be tackled first. Only after a group can resolve authority issues can it concentrate on intimacy and ways members relate to one another as unique individuals.

Each primary phase is characterized by "subphases" differentiated by the kinds of member attention given to authority or intimacy issues. The authority phase involves member behaviors aimed at reducing uncertainty regarding responsibility for group action (that is, who will control group activities). Bennis and Shepard speculate there are three subphases of behavior that groups may exhibit en route to resolving authority issues. These are *dependence-flight, counterdependence-flight,* and *resolution-catharis.*

The first subphase stresses group reliance on whomever is acting as a designated group facilitator or leader. This subphase tends to be dominated by dependent members, who are predisposed to look for direction. The group as a whole tries to get its designated facilitator to show them the way.

The second subphase emerges as members begin to polarize into factions over the issue of "who" should take control of the group. Counterdependent members cluster together in opposition to dependent members. Dependent members press for "structure" and attempt to organize group activities (such as form agendas or set up activity committees), while counterdependent members resist the imposition of structure and adopt the status quo as a measure of "group progress" ("Things are fine as they are now.").

The power struggle of subphase two may go on for an extended time. Only when the independents, those members with no vested interest in the struggle, speak out does a resolution-catharsis subphase emerge. This occurs when members begin to discuss how the group might function if the facilitator were not present, or if they just treated the person as "another member." Bennis and Shepard have termed these kinds of discussions as a "symbolic removal of the trainer" because the group begins to focus on developing a sense of responsibility for regulation and control not based on an existing authority figure. Many groups never reach this subphase because they lack strong independent members who can unite the competing factions.

Once a group resolves problems stemming from authority and control, it moves toward overcoming problems related to intimacy. There are also three subphases within the intimacy phase. These are *enchantment-flight, disenchantment-flight* and *consensual validation.* We should reiterate that many groups never reach this phase. After a long series of meetings, many groups will still be trapped in power struggles.

Entry into the enchantment-flight subphase is quite rapid. Members try to submerge the tensions surrounding resolution of authority problems with laughter, joking, and positive feedback. This tends to be a positive overreaction to previous hostility and tension. Norms quickly develop to enforce the light atmosphere and suppress negative emotional displays. After a period of time, the image of solidarity prescribed by these norms can no longer be maintained. Once again members polarize into subgroups characterizing the disenchantment-flight subphase. These subgroups represent member divisions over the amount of emotional involvement and commitment they desire. Overpersonal members push for displays of intimacy and positive emotional support; counterpersonal members seek increasing emotional detachment and a reduction of pressure for maintaining what they believe is a "facade" of positiveness.

Bennis and Shepard (1956, p. 433) summarize these two subphases saying that they are "marked by a conviction that further group involvement would be injurious to members' self-esteem." A resolution of the interdependence dilemma may take place. A last subphase, consensual validation, can emerge to unify overpersonal and counterpersonal factions. The emergence of consensual validation is closely tied to other pragmatic aspects of group existence. These groups, toward the end of their laboratory existence, are urged (sometimes forced by classroom procedures) to go through a period of group and individual evaluation in connection with the total experience. At this point, independents can stimulate group action in terms of summarization and evaluation concerns. The principle task is usually a kind of "reality testing" where members obtain feedback from one another about their respective roles in the group. Time pressures may cause this subphase to be severely curtailed. However, most groups will perform some sort of closing activity even if time or faction conflicts produce only superficial results.

To summarize the psychodynamic model proposed by Bennis and Shepard, they view group maturity as a process of establishing valid communication between members. Two major personal attributes of members may block progress—orientations toward authority and intimacy. Groups progress through two primary phases that focus on concerns for authority and intimacy, respectively. Some groups experience difficulties of such magnitude they never overcome these obstacles. This usually happens in groups where members are experiencing inner conflict between situational demands for behavior not compatible with their personal orientations.

Equilibrium. A social systems equilibrium model is the result of Bales' (1950, 1953) sociological assessment of small groups as *microcosms* of larger social organization. The interaction theory approach embodied in Bales' research focuses on the interplay between group members and a group's functioning as an *action system*—a unit of people who perform together in some interrelated manner. Bales assumed that activity in small, problem solving groups simulates processes found in larger social systems such as companies, governmental agencies, or social institutions. Thus, he was interested in constructing a theory for how social systems adapt and change in the course of producing tangible outcomes from internal activities.

Bales chose to simulate conditions of system adaptation and change by constructing small, "leaderless" groups of students assigned to solve various problems with the condition that members had to reach consensus regarding a final decision. Bales and his colleagues used structured observations of verbal interaction between group members to build their theory, which was the forerunner of the IPA observation method discussed in Chapter 5. Direct observation of group behavior plays an integral role in the development and validation of Bales' theory.

Bales' central assumption about group-system behavior was that all social systems (regardless of size) are continuously engaged in managing external and internal pressures (or tensions) about social action. External pressures emanate from the larger system in which a group is embedded and to which the group is accountable. For example, a team of researchers responsible for testing the safety of company products is a group that might be found in a larger division responsible for research and development. Likewise, a subcommittee of the Senate Foreign Relations Committee is subsumed under a larger committee unit. The activities and demands of larger groups provide structure and direction for smaller subgroups. Their demands for subgroup action constitute *external pressures* on the group.

Internal pressures emerge from the interaction among group members as they strive for cooperative action. Many of the concepts reviewed in previous chapters (personality attributes and effective personality, task aptitude, attitudes, power, status, and so on) create internal pressures, or *strains*, on a group. Internal tensions are created as members simultaneously try to build viable interpersonal relationships necessary for effective group work and to meet external demands.

Bales applied the term *equilibrium* to those activities groups engage in to manage internal tension states. In essence, his theoretical work was directed at explaining the processes involved in a group's attempts to obtain and maintain some point of harmony. The assumption is that group-systems are continuously engaged in activities that minimize internal tensions yet are responsive to external demands. The "point of harmony" groups seek may be thought of as a state of equilibrium. This balance point may shift as behavioral needs appropriate to harmonious group relationships change over time. Thus, the equilibrium states are *dynamic* as groups attempt to find and maintain these various points.

Bales and Strodtbeck (1951) proposed that, in the course of working on a specific task, groups manifest three primary phases of activity— *orientation, evaluation,* and *control*. These phases are distinguished by the relative amounts of certain verbal behaviors members exhibit. They assumed these phases were indicative of a group's attempts to establish or maintain an equilibrium between internal and external demands.

The phases are characterized by the kinds of task-oriented behaviors, and positive or negative social-emotional behaviors, that peak or decline at different points in time. Think of a group session divided into approximately three equal and sequential time segments. The first segment, or orientation phase, is so named because members tend to seek and give information. These information exchanging actions are intended to assist members in orienting themselves to task concerns. Information exchanging behaviors are most frequent in the beginning of group sessions and gradually decline (but do not end) over time. Within this phase social-emotional activity begins to increase slightly. This holds for both positive and negative acts—although positive acts are more frequent than negative acts, usually by a ratio of approximately three to one.

The second phase, evaluation, is marked by the "peaking out" of opinionated acts which denote member evaluative actions. There is also a significant rise in negative activity. Evaluative acts, asking for and giving opinions, enable group members to deliberate over alternative courses of action. Logically, negative action increases during this time as members disagree over alternatives while positive acts rise less dramatically.

The final phase, control, is so named because of the amount of direction-related activity found at this time. Group direction is manifested in acts which seek or give "suggestions." Suggestions can involve specific decision alternatives, or procedural issues. Control refers to group attempts at *acting on* suggestions. The control phase is characterized by the peaking of directive activity, the leveling off of negative acts, an increase in positive acts, and a slight decrease in opinionation. These behavioral patterns make sense, occurring as they do in the final segment of activity. Groups must get their members to reduce deliberations on alternatives (opinionation) and settle on one final decision. This may take some prompting, thus increased direction via suggestions seems necessary. Settling on a final decision that would result in task completion requires general group support which can be seen as positive behavioral acts. While positive acts increase, negative acts decrease as the group moves toward a final solution or decision.

The model of developmental progression sketched by Bales and

Strodtbeck provides insight into how behavioral fluctuations represent a group's strain toward equilibrium. The orientation—evaluation—control phase sequence, coupled with positive and negative reactions to task operations, appear in many groups varying in task expectations and member attributes (see, for example, Heinicke and Bales, 1953; Philp and Dunphy, 1959; Psathas, 1960).

    Functional models. "Functional models" are those designed to delineate *how* groups behave. Contrasted to psychodynamic or equilibrium models, functional models are less theoretically based in the sense that developmental patterns are not prescribed by some set of prior assumptions. Such models are easier to describe since a lengthy background rationale about theoretical assumptions is not necessary for understanding each model. We will discuss here a communication based model of *decision emergence.*

    Fisher (1970) devised a method for analyzing types of verbal interaction groups use in deliberations of various *decision proposals.* A decision proposal typically takes the form of member statements about preferred group action (such as, "I think we should advise the council to spend two million dollars on a new solid waste recycling plant.") His intent was to trace communicative behaviors associated with group progression toward consensus. He labeled this progression "decision emergence." Similar to Bales' method, Fisher used interaction analysis results to derive what he believed to be significant phases in group movement toward consensus. The four phases are identified from the results are *orientation, conflict, emergence,* and *reinforcement.*

    The orientation phase is characterized by high frequencies of ambiguous verbal acts (neither supportive nor nonsupportive of proposals), a pronounced tendency toward agreement with diverse ideas, a marked tendency to reinforce unfavorable attitudes toward ideas, and emphasis on attempts at clarification. In other words, groups appear to be searching for ideas to build on or a direction to pursue. Fisher views this behavior as caused, in part, by member uncertainties about other members' status and viewpoints. As he indicates, "Characteristic of the first phase, then, is getting acquainted, clarifying and tentatively expressing attitudes" (Fisher, 1970, p. 61).

    Following the orientation phase (which may be relatively long for some groups) is a conflict phase. Behavior in this phase is typified by disagreement fostered by increasing "polarization of attitudes" over proposals. There is less ambiguity in verbal statements in this phase. While disagreement increases, so do agreements supporting specific proposals. Members exhibit less inhibition about voicing support or opposition to proposed decisions than in the orientation phase. We might add that such interaction patterns are characteristic of groups where members have a sense of confidence or trust in one another. According to Fisher's data, the conflict phase is shorter than both orientation and emergence phases.

As conflict typical of the previous phase subsides, a third phase can be determined. Fisher identifies this as an emergence phase, a time when ambiguity increases and supplants part of the conflict. Fisher (1970, p. 63) maintains that ambiguity functions differently here than in the orientation phase, taking the form of "modified dissent" rather than indecisiveness.

Fisher's point is that as groups deliberate on a task, successively fewer proposed decisions gain support until only a few (possibly two or three) have withstood emotional and logical tests. At the time, members must begin to move towards a final decision, if for no other reason than to meet external demands. This movement may require modification of previously held attitudes (which may have been publicly stated) in favor of a group proposal. Such changes are seldom sweeping and members begin these changes by substituting ambiguous statements for definite positive and negative reactions voiced during the conflict phase. That such a process of change goes on in this phase is evident by the continuation of relatively high amounts of favorable and supportive statements—though probably for fewer proposals—and a longer period of duration than other phases.

Fisher points out that significant group movement toward a final decision actually takes place in the emergence phase. With movement in the direction of a final decision comes increasing member commitment to an impending decision. Identification with the final proposal is articulated in a *reinforcement* phase. As the label implies, this phase is dominated by verbal statements in support of the proposal. Verbal ambiguity decreases as opinions shift toward concrete agreement. The function of this phase is to provide an appropriate time for members to show group solidarity and agreement with the decision. Hence, the reinforcement phase serves to bond members together in a state of positive-definiteness contrasted to the negative-definiteness found in the conflict stage or uncertainty in the orientation and emergence phases.

A Role-Systems Model of Group Development

To say a group "develops" implies that members change their perceptions of and behaviors toward one another. These changes occur as external and internal demands influence interpersonal relationships between members and the group-system. Attempting to understand developmental tendencies in groups requires that all group action be observed and assessed cumulatively. The observer must discern how clumps of behaviors seem to form into patterns of action and whether different patterns appear to occur over time.

Models of group development attempt to place meaningful labels on these patterns. Some models rely only on observed behaviors (such as Bales and Strodtbeck) while others blend experienced observation with "educated guesses" about the internal states of group members (such as Bennis and Shepard). The objective of all such models is to provide a coherent explanation of behavioral patterns that signify changes in a group's mode of activity.

The model of group development we will describe in this section is a blend of two group behavior perspectives. We started with Bales' perspective on relationships between personality and perceived group roles (discussed in Chapter 2). Next, we adopted an equilibrium-type model of group system functioning (first put forth by Parsons, Bales, and Shils, 1953; and later modified by Hare, 1971, 1976; and Mabry, 1975.) The end product of the model building effort was a *Role-System Model* (or RSM).

The guiding assumption behind the RSM is that group development is best understood as a series of shifts in the relationships between group members over a period of time. These shifts are assumed to be more or less observable as one assesses group members' verbal and nonverbal message content. Shifts in member interaction content reflect group attempts at constructing a functional social unit. In other words, a *unit* that integrates personal needs with task demands and environmental influences, forms a social structure by establishing shared expectations for group action (norms, roles, and patterns of interaction between members) ultimately creates goal oriented outcomes.

Conceptual components of the RSM. We recall Bales' (1970) proposed that there were three dimensions to a person's perceived personality: (1) the extent of power and influence a person needs *over* others or needs *from* others, (2) personal orientations toward achievement—either traditional or unconventional, and (3) the amount of affection (emotional attachment) desired in one's interpersonal relationships. We called these dimensions "effective personality" because they allude to how we perceive the behaviors of group members in terms of *inferences* we make about their personalities. Effective personality relates to the *effect* a person's behavior has on our preceptions of him or her and subsequent predictions we make concerning his or her future behavior.

One of the intriguing aspects of Bales' position is his assertion that dimensions of perceived personality are the bases for group roles. According to his framework, members evolve into roles depending on how their behavior is perceived by others. Also of importance is the fact that roles (1) are significant aspects of a group's total social structure, (2) can endure if other aspects of a group remain relatively stable (such as membership and task/environment), and (3) can change as a consequence of group influence that emerges during interaction. Group roles are not an "all or nothing" proposition. Our perceptions are a matter of degree and can change over time.

We are less concerned with specific role judgments than the way effective personalities and task environment factors converge during interaction. We can then consider group development in terms of simultaneous group experiences related to meeting *internal* and *external* demands. Internal demands arise as a consequence of interpersonal relationships and role emergence; external demands are pressures placed on a group from other elements of its environment. The two sets of demands are not independent. External demands can create internal demands, and internal demands can create new external pressures. Saying the two "converge" during interaction implies that both demand types effect the group *as a group*. It is this effect that is observed when we arrive at decisions concerning group development. The notion of stages or *phases* of development implies successive changes in *group response styles* that indicate differing impacts of external and internal demands.

Let us change our perspective about individual response styles and consider each effective personality dimension as a *group* response style. We can then identify significant points in group maturation based on the relative frequencies of certain behaviors in those three dimensions. Each unique combination of effective personalities (behaviors) defines both interpersonal relationships and group attempts to comply with external demands. In short, the same dimensions we use to make inferences about individual role development may be generalized to account for group development. Thus, we may speak of a period in which group attention focuses on power and achievement demands versus another period that focuses on power and affection.

This discussion has covered the RSM's *role behavior* components and proposed that different behaviors will be distributed over time in such a fashion to suggest unique points of development. Let us now turn to the second set of components of the RSM, its *sequential* aspects, and suggest a rationale for ordered occurrences of behavior over time. We are interested in labeling significant shifts in group behavior and showing how behavioral components relate to both internal and external demands.

Our method of combining behavioral components and changing behavior states employs a modified version of a model created to explain how social systems (at any level of size or sophistication) adapt and change. The model was formulated by Parsons, Bales, and Shils (1953) and has theoretical assumptions similar to those of the equilibrium model described by Bales and Strodtbeck.

In this model, four phases explain system actions: *adaptation, goal-*

attainment, integration, and *latent pattern-maintenance.* The model is referred to as the AGIL model in accordance with the sequence of phases. Adaptation relates to initial definition and structuring of external system demands. Goal-attainment refers to a system's decision about action believed to be the best solution to external demands. Integration is the attempt to resolve negative feelings resulting from goal-attainment and to reinforce commitment to the decision and the system. Latent pattern-maintenance is a period of individual reinforcement which takes place between system responses to external pressures; a time when members maintain solidarity and commitment to system goals and values.

Developmental phases in the role-systems model. Responses to demands on a group are shaped by personal needs and desires, which are observable as parts of effective personality. Similarly, group responses to external and internal demands are shaped by individual member needs and desires. A group experiences marked behavioral changes as it attempts to *control* two kinds of internal and external demands during the process of task completion. The first set of demands is for *adaptation.* A group must adapt to personal demands arising from previous member interaction or from ambiguity that exists when a newly formed group of people begins working together. Simultaneously the group must process task environment inputs. The second set of demands is for *resolution.* Groups must resolve personal member demands emerging from internal and external adaptive processes and must accommodate demands from external sources.

Implicit in the above description of group control are four areas of action. These areas form four phases of group development proposed in the RSM. Figure 9.1 provides a pictorial representation of the phases, how they are sequentially related, and the behavioral dimensions characterizing member reactions in each phase. While all phases describe member interactions, the first two deal with adaptations and the latter two describe resolutions. The *Latency* and *Integration* phases are concerned more with internal demands while *Adaptation* and *Goal-Attainment* deal with external demands.

The first phase of the RSM involves personal adaptation to a group by its members. We call this period of adjustment *Latency.* Member reactions to one another are, at this point in a group's history, a product of past group experiences with the same members (in the case of ongoing groups) or impressions about groups in general that members carry to a situation from past experiences in other groups. This phase is best understood as one in which member familiarization takes place. Regardless of whether group members have met before, every group engages in an initial period of interaction highlighted by more or less positive *affective*

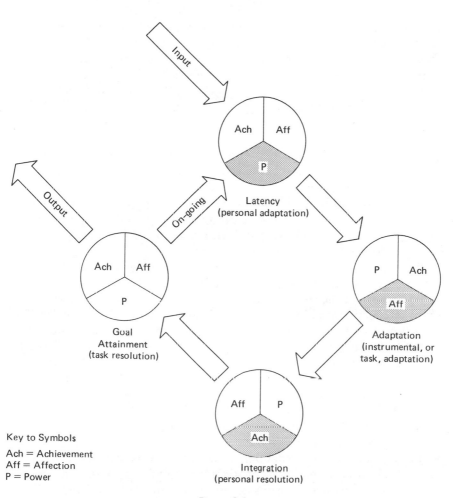

Key to Symbols

Ach = Achievement
Aff = Affection
P = Power

Figure 9.1

reactions, which help to establish tentative perceptions of interpersonal closeness, and *achievement* oriented reactions, which provide insights into individual perceptions of the task environment. In groups with relatively clear task objectives and a history of meeting together, only a few minutes may be taken up with this kind of interaction. Its value, however, is not diminished, and a wise group leader recognizes the importance of this activity as an entry into the often harder task of assimilating external demands. Groups like human relations training groups may dwell on this phase for many sessions before members are ready to move to another phase.

Personal adaptations give way to the second phase of *Adaptation.* Here members focus on obtaining shared understandings of what is expected of their group and how they should proceed to satisfy those expectations. Behavioral emphasis is on group *achievement,* including which member or members will exercise the most influence or *power* over the group. Comparing adaptation and latency phases, a critical behavioral distinction between them rests with the emerging importance of member status and power that can affect task definition and pursuit of task alternatives.

Adaptation to external demands requires both definition of expectations and formulation of alternative courses of action. Information and opinion exchange (indicative of group achievement) and suggestions (indicative of both achievement and power) are prominent in this phase. Behaviors characteristic of positive or negative interpersonal affect are less salient (although they are present) but will increase in frequency as the group nears the next phase.

Adaptation involves generating alternatives for group action. These alternatives stem from the ways members believe the group should proceed. Group conflict is generated by clashes between members about which alternative should be adopted. The conflict involves both choice reduction and status building because as choices are eliminated, the choices remaining reinforce the influence of members supporting them. This period of interaction is essentially a "power struggle" between members; a time when the question of "Who will lead?" is implicitly or openly confronted.

The third phase represents "personal resolution," and is labeled *Integration.* Integration connotes group recognition of a status structure based on responses to external demands. Every time a group begins to adapt to and resolve external demands, member influence is calculated on the basis of each member's contribution to group goals. Some members will appear more desirous of influence than others. Eventually, a few members will be recognized as supporting the position most likely to obtain final acceptance.

Integration is directly related to power and interpersonal affect. There are at least three reasons why prominent affective responses re-emerge during this phase. First, defending one's claim for group influence requires *negating* claims of other members. Second, seeking the support of other members requires heightening their personal regard for you. Third, showing support for the position or attitudes of another also requires positive social-emotional behaviors. Integration may be a relatively short phase when the number of alternatives are few or when a status structure exists that has carried over from other group projects. It might, however, be prolonged when a group is relatively large, new and/or the number of alternatives are many.

A group may not be totally successful in formulating an acceptable status structure. However, a point comes in even the most disagreeable groups when members must accept some form of influence and direction toward goal attainment. The alternative is group dissolution. Few groups disintegrate before some form of task related output is produced—even if it is of poor quality. Most groups are able to obtain control over external demands and engage in "task resolution."

This point of control signals the fourth phase labeled *Goal-Attainment.* It is a terminal point of specific group activity marked by an output related to the group's task environment. All three behavioral dimensions are prominent in this phase. There is a convergence of ascendency, achievement, and affect (usually more positive than negative) because the group has a means of rewarding itself as an action unit. The rewards are recognition of task resolution, knowledge that group efforts may have a desired impact on the task environment, and at least a temporary respite (maybe only a few minutes or a day) from other pressures for performance.

WHAT DO WE GAIN
BY ANALYZING DEVELOPMENT?

The Role-Systems Model, or any other model for that matter, is useful only to the extent it can be applied to a group and facilitates the understanding of group processes. We will conclude this chapter with an assessment of how the RSM can be used to gain insights into individual behavior within a group and group-system operations as a unit.

Personal Actions in the Group

Members of a small group compose one cluster of "inputs" to the small group system. As we saw in Chapters 2 and 3, every member is a unique component of the group in that each person has a slightly different personality, set of attitudes, and history of social experiences. We have also seen that a particular group of people may be more or less similar in terms of these personal attributes. High similarity, or *homogeneity*, can, under certain task conditions, be an asset for a group; however, low similarity, or *heterogeneity,* can also be beneficial. Knowing the personal characteristics of members can be important in understanding how and why a group behaves in certain ways. Unfortunately, we seldom have enough of this information in real life settings to make accurate prediction possible. We must rely on observations of personal behavior to assess why members react as they do. The RSM may be of assistance in these observational tasks.

Stability and change in personal behavior.   Any group setting presents a set of potentially unsettling consequences to its members. Each person must work to satisfy a number of demands: (1) on the group as an action unit, (2) as a member who must contribute to group action, and (3) as an individual who must find ways of satisfying personal needs and expectations. Of particular concern for each individual is figuring out where he or she "fits" in relation to other group members. For the most part, people assume that past relevant experiences can be *generalized* to new situations (Rotter, Chance and Phares, 1972). Personal behavior that "worked" before is likely to be used again. In groups with relatively clear task goals and members who have previously worked together, personal adjustment is not difficult and past behaviors reappear in the new setting. When members have not worked together, or when task goals are unfamiliar or ambiguous, actions that were satisfactory in past group settings may not prove beneficial in the new setting. Groups act differently; they spend more, or less, time on different phases of development depending upon the adjustment demands placed on group members.

Some personal characteristics predispose members to act and react similarly regardless of other group members or task demands. People with high needs to influence the outcomes of interpersonal settings will react in ways to satisfy those needs. Similarly, persons with low commitment to achievement through traditional means (possibly viewed as radical or backward), may react that way regardless of other member or task demands. As groups work together, overall styles of behavior and perceptions of behavior shift. Different kinds of behaviors are likely to occur more frequently at some times than others, and members will be more receptive to perceiving certain behaviors one time than at another time. Thus, personal orientations toward control or achievement may not have the same impact in the Latency phase as they do in the Adaptation phase.

Every group member can be expected to react differently to the group at different points in time. Everyone tends to exhibit behaviors associated with the three role dimensions. However, members seldom lose or dramatically change their personal styles of behavior. While we all engage in some amount of ascendent activity, express positive and negative affection, or participate in task achievement, we are not likely to react in ways totally uncharacteristic of our personal disposition. What this means for the observer is that identifying a probable phase of group maturation is important in making accurate assessments of individual behavior. It is easy to misconstrue a person's natural adaptation of "where a *group* is at" to be an inference about "where the *person* is at." Personal styles and group actions often converge at certain points of development.

Understanding and predicting personal behavior requires constant attention to the person and the group. Seldom will we be able to give this kind of attention without giving up part of our personal involvement and spontaneity. The importance of consciously trying to adopt a participant-observer orientation lies in the fact that we all make inferences about other members during the course of group work. Therefore, it seems beneficial to apply a more systematic framework, like the RSM, to our natural tendencies in order to attribute motivations for personal behavior. It is important, for example, to distinguish between a person's desire for control *because* the person values a particular means of goal achievement in contrast to a general desire to control others. In the former case, a person's ascendent behaviors may not arise until the group nears an integration phase. For the latter case, however, we may notice ascendent actions (such as numerous suggestions or tendencies to disagree with differing alternatives) almost from the outset of group work. Ultimately, our understanding of, and attitude toward, other members will depend upon these kinds of distinctions.

Misobservations. Quite often an individual may *misread* group expectations. For example, you may have observed occasions when certain members of a group assumed that one style of behavior was expected when, in actuality, this assumption was incorrect. Many instances of faulty assumptions can be found in reactive interactions with others. Judgments of people who have acted on faulty assessments of group expectations subsequently affect their ability to relate to others and to contribute to a group. This is not an easy circumstance to rectify. Sometimes there will be no resolution of the misunderstanding. However, such difficulties can be overcome to the extent that: (1) a person has freedom to change in the eyes of others, (2) inferences about a person are not rigidly adhered to by other members, and (3) a group has sufficient time to gain new experiences.

Groups As Action Systems

In Chapter I we introduced the idea that small groups can be viewed as particular kinds of social systems. A social system exists where some identifiable set of components (such as people) are linked together (for example, through interaction) for some mutually desired goal (such as task accomplishment). Small group systems depend on the communicative links between people. These links are established when members interact. Links can be behavioral, as in communication networks, or they can be impressionistic, as in sociometric networks. Regardless of how we conceptualize the links, they are present and constitute the *action* that a group generates. The end results of action, making a decision or changing one's attitude, for example, are consequences of communicative interchanges between members. In a similar fashion, the development of a small group is the result of group action in the form of communicative interchanges.

The Role-System Model, based on behavioral dimensions of communication which influence member perceptions of one another, is intentionally stated in general terms. Therefore, we expect the RSM to hold for *most* groups in *many* settings. It is presumptuous to assume the model will *always* predict developmental tendencies. Our reservation is due to the various ways groups adapt to their task environments. Groups with a relatively long history of interaction and members who have frequent contact outside the group may combine Latency and Adaptation phases or skip the former altogether (Effrat, 1968). Other groups, particularly those with highly ambiguous goals and limited member experience with one another, may enter an Integration phase before completing a fully recognizable Adaptation phase. These are *possible* alterations of the basic model. Assessment of previous research, coupled with personal experiences in a wide range of small group settings, suggests the most applicable sequence of developmental stages approximates the RSM.

Ultimately, the value of any model is determined by its usefulness. By "usefulness" we mean the extent to which it can help participant-observers expand their awareness of group functioning. The RSM is useful only to the extent that participant-observers can account for behavioral dimensions and sequential changes of group actions.

Behavioral dimensions. We have not yet provided a precise description of behavioral categories associated with the RSM dimensions. It is a difficult task because behaviors observed in one context may have a different impact (perceived meaning) when observed in another context. We are limited to some tentative *estimates* of behavioral categories which appear more closely related to one dimension than another. As a means of providing an estimation, we will use IPA categories described in Chapter 5 and suggest what we believe to be the *most relevant* behavioral dimensions. The "most relevant" qualifier is intended to suggest that such categories represent only approximations of the behavioral dimensions and may not be powerful definers of dimensions in all situations.

Table 9.1 demonstrates relationships of IPA categories to RSM behavioral dimensions. The ascendence, or power, dimension is composed of statements or requests for suggestions as well as agreements and disagreements. This is the only behavioral dimension where task and social-emotional behaviors are combined. Providing direction (by making suggestions) is only one form of ascendent behavior; the other as-

Table 9.1 Proposed Relationships of Interaction Process Analysis Categories to RSM Behavioral Dimensions

ROLE-SYSTEMS MODEL DIMENSIONS	INTERACTION PROCESS ANALYSIS CATEGORIES
Ascendence (Power) *Orientations:*	Giving Suggestions, Asking for Suggestions; Agreement; Disagreement.
Achievement (either by traditional or radical means):	Giving Opinions; Giving Information; Asking for Opinions; Asking for Information.
Affect (either positive or negative):	Seems Friendly; Dramatizes Shows Tension; Seems Unfriendly.

cendent activity is voicing agreement or disagreement with reference to the thoughts of others. Whether these acts connote a desire to control group activities or a desire to have some other member take control is not directly ascertainable.

The achievement dimension may be identified by questions and responses concerning information and opinions. Such interaction content is typically the substance of goal oriented exchanges in a group (Bales, 1950, 1970). Whether someone is high or low in traditional means of achieving group goals is a matter of *what* the person says.

The affect dimension is probably the most straightforward of the three dimensions. With the exception of agreement and disagreement, as identified with ascendence, social-emotional categories seem appropriately associated with this dimension.

Developmental dimensions. The intent of the RSM is to identify phases of development in groups. These phases are characterized by the three behavioral dimensions. A dimension may partially define a phase *without* marked increases or decreases in the incidence of behaviors which define that dimension. You will certainly find fluctuations, but they can be quite subtle and increases in one dimension may not result in large decreases in another dimension. The inference process can be further complicated by tendencies for certain categories to remain relatively frequent over time. For example, categories like "gives opinion" and "gives information" account for a large amount of any group's total interaction. A related consideration is that overall *rates* of interaction may change through time, thereby permitting some categories to display increases while others may remain relatively stable.

Table 9.2 Expected Activity in Behavioral Dimensions at each Phase of the Role-System Model

PHASES	BEHAVIORAL DIMENSIONS		
	Ascendence	*Achievement*	*Affection*
Latency: Length varies considerably from group to group; may be difficult to discern as a phase distinct from Adaptation.	Both agreement and dis-agreement are low; proportionately fewer suggestions than requests for suggestions.	Requests for information and opinion frequent; incidence of both high, with opinion highest.	Incidence of affection low to moderate with a bias toward positive acts.
Adaptation: Under most circumstances this will be a clearly identified period of activity for a group.	Proportion of suggestions to suggestion requests widens; agreement and disagreement increase, with agreement higher.	Giving opinion begins to increase at a faster rate than giving infor-mation; requests for both are stable.	Positive and negative acts increase proportionately.
Integration: Quite often difficult to discern; may be short, protracted, or merely a period of ambiguous conversation; tends to appear like Goal-Attainment when of short duration.	Both suggestions and requests decrease; agree-ment and disagreement increase with rate of increase for disagreement higher.	Incidence of giving and asking for information decrease; giving opinions increases as requests for same drop.	Positive and negative acts highest at this point; differential between positive and negative drops to its lowest point.
Goal-Attainment: Normally an easy phase to sense; may be of short or long duration; often its initial entry point is a group's only Integration period.	Suggestion behavior remains low; agreement increases as dis-agreement decreases.	Opinionation stable; tendency for informa-tion to increase slightly.	Overall frequency decreases; positive vs. negative differential increases.

Table 9.2 is a *guide* to assist participant-observers in using the RSM. The table contains brief descriptions of verbal activity for each behavioral dimension in the four RSM phases. These descriptions are meant to be "reference points" on which an observer can compare group actions as a means of forming initial inferences about a group's place in the sequence of development. The phases are identified in terms of the ease or difficulty an observer may experience when attempting to observe them.

As mentioned earlier, some groups may not *appear* to go through the RSM phase sequence. Whether or not a group progresses in the prescribed manner is often a matter of whether or not the progression is perceived. If the observer has access to accurate observational information and does not find clear indications of transitions, one may reasonably infer the group has digressed and should attempt to explain why that could happen by examining input, throughput, or output dimensions of the group. Perception of developmental sequences is neither easy nor always accurate—even if a group behaves in an exemplary manner.

Influences of Other Systems on the Group

Developmental patterns are determined by the nature of a group's task environment. Any task environment is a product of some broader, more encompassing, social system of which a group is involved. External systems affect the task environment either directly or indirectly, depending on a group's relationship with such systems.

Direct influences are usually found in situations where a group is part of a larger organizational system. The way a group develops, specifically the distinctness of its phases over time, often corresponds to the nature of external demands placed on a group. A group faced with a clearly defined task of moderate difficulty, under heavy pressure for task completion, may not exhibit the same differentiation of developmental sequences as one with unclear goals, high difficulty, and only moderate time demands for goal attainment.

The responsiveness of other systems to group action is tied to the impact such action is perceived to have. Take, for instance, a group working on a promotional campaign. If the group is only one of several competing teams responsible for completing a proposal, anxiety over task completion might be particularly informative. Approached another way, suppose the team represents a group responsible for planning the promotion of all products for a company. Their actions may directly effect a number of other groups whose productivity is tied to the planning group's decisions. It is not inconceivable to expect the group to be under a variety of noncomplementary pressures to (1) create a "successful" campaign, (2) finish planning, so a media production team can begin working, (3) stay within budget projections, (4) complete the task phase in one week, and so forth.

This illustration demonstrates that a group's interrelationship with other components of a system determines its impact on the system and, in turn, the system's attempts to create an impact on the group. Members of small groups are usually aware of demands on their group. As a participant-observer you will find it difficult to separate yourself from those demands, but you must do so. Reactions toward other groups or systems may obscure valuable information about *your* group's behavior as an action system. Then too, your group may act in ways that are detrimental to the group's ultimate objectives. A group may also disassociate itself from other units in a system that can be of assistance in a task. *Inter*group cooperation requires that groups know how they interrelate and how they can work together toward optimally beneficial actions. In order to assess these interrelations, group members must carefully observe and analyze.

REFERENCES

Bales, R.F. 1950. *Interaction process analysis.* Reading, Mass.: Addison-Wesley.

Bales, R.F. 1953. The equilibrium problem in small groups. In *Working papers in the theory of action,* eds. T. Parsons, R.F. Bales and E.A. Shils, pp. 111–116. Glencoe, Ill.: The Free Press of Glencoe.

Bales, R.F. 1970. *Personality and interpersonal behavior.* New York: Holt, Rinehart & Winston.

Bales, R.F. and Strodtbeck, F.L. 1951. Phases in group problem solving. *Journal of Abnormal and Social Psychology 46,* 485–495.

Bennis, W.G. and Shepard, H.A. 1956. A theory of group development. *Human Relations 9,* 415–437.

Effrat, A. 1968. Editor's introduction (Applications of Parsonian theory). *Sociological Inquiry 38,* 97–103.

Fisher, B.A. 1970. Decision emergence: Phases in group decision-making. *Speech Monographs 37,* 53–66.

Hare, A.P. 1971. Editor's forward (Sensitivity training). *Sociological Inquiry 41,* 125–132.

Hare, A.P. 1976. *Handbook of small group research.* New York: Free Press.

Heinicke, C.M. and Bales, R.F. 1953. Developmental trends in the structure of small groups. *Sociometry 16,* 7–38.

Mabry, E.A. 1975. Exploratory analysis of a developmental model for task-oriented small groups. *Human Communication Research 2,* 66–74.

Parsons, T., Bales, R.F. and Shils, E. 1953. *Working papers in the theory of action.* Glencoe, Ill.: The Free Press of Glencoe.

Philp, H. and Dunphy, D. 1959. Developmental trends in small groups. *Sociometry 22,* 162–174.

Psathas, G. 1960. Phase movement and equilibrium tendencies in interaction process in psychotherapy groups. *Sociometry 23,* 177–194.

Rotter, J.B., Chance, J.E. and Phares, E.J. 1972. *Applications of a social learning theory of personality.* New York: Holt, Rinehart & Winston.

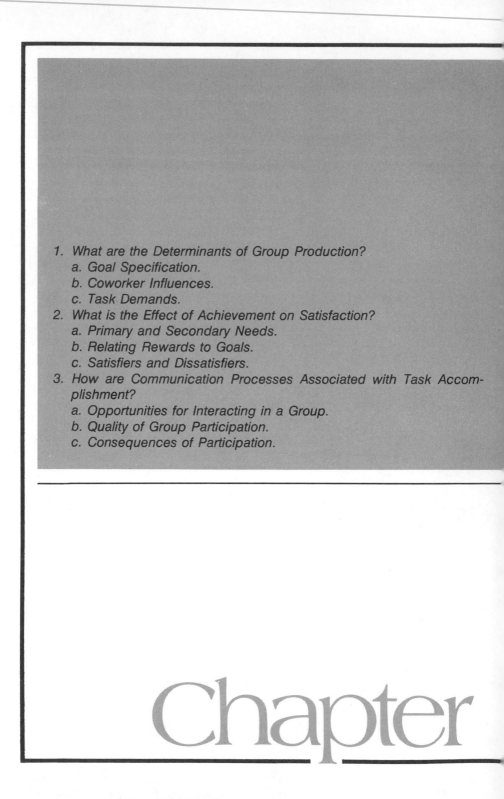

1. What are the Determinants of Group Production?
   a. Goal Specification.
   b. Coworker Influences.
   c. Task Demands.
2. What is the Effect of Achievement on Satisfaction?
   a. Primary and Secondary Needs.
   b. Relating Rewards to Goals.
   c. Satisfiers and Dissatisfiers.
3. How are Communication Processes Associated with Task Accomplishment?
   a. Opportunities for Interacting in a Group.
   b. Quality of Group Participation.
   c. Consequences of Participation.

Chapter

The preceding chapters were designed with the intent of dissecting communicative processes and social-psychological factors responsible for transforming groups into social entities. Implicit in our discussions is the assumption that groups function for some *purpose(s)*. The common denominator shared by all groups is that *something must happen.* Groups, regardless of their drives, must achieve a desired goal.

WHAT ARE THE DETERMINANTS OF GROUP PRODUCTION?

The "bottom line," so to speak, for any group is "what did you accomplish?" Suppose you answered an advertisement for production workers in a manufacturing firm. You are instructed to report to work the next day. Upon arrival, the manager opens the door to the production room and tells you and your five coworkers to "go in and get to work." The door closes and you are faced with an array of raw materials, machines, and tools—*but no instructions.* All you know is that

10 group production and achievement

you will be evaluated upon completion of the work. For a while you would probably wander around looking at everything, straightening piles of materials and perhaps testing some of the machinery. After tiring of these activities you would probably turn to some of your coworkers and say something like, "What do you think we ought to do?" As a group, you would probably determine your goals, tasks to accomplish goals, role responsibilities, and set some standard by which to gauge your task accomplishments. In the ensuing hours, problems of production and personal relationships might arise and be dealt with by group members. Undoubtedly, you would develop friendships with some members and dislikes for others. Some members loaf, while others do more than their share. At the end of the day, some members might look with pride at all that has been accomplished, while others grumble. The manager may then walk in the room, survey the results and comment, "Nice job; you really got a lot done today." You brighten and smile. Or, he may say, "Not bad, but I've seen a lot better." Then you feel more weary and irritated than before. Whichever form the manager's comment takes, the group will probably temper their evaluation of group relations and development according to his final evaluation of production and achievement.

Let's review this hypothetical group from a systems perspective. Initially, you were placed in a new environment with five other individuals and an unorganized collection of resources. Furthermore, you were confronted with certain constraints—you had to accomplish some kind of work in a room with a fixed quantity and quality of resources. This can be regarded as an *entropic* (chaotic) situation. By entropic, we mean you have little *information* at your disposal to help clarify expectations about your behavior. Because of this high degree of ambiguity, there are any number of ways that "work" can be accomplished. Solution multiplicity, or *equifinality,* is quite high because there are many tasks to be performed and members have almost unlimited options for structuring their work.

As a means of bringing order out of chaos, interaction (*throughout*) began regarding the goals and attendant tasks required of each member. However, each objective and task represented a decision point at which other objectives and tasks were dismissed. As members discussed which alternative to select, tension and stress were created by the uncertainty of whether a decision was in the best interests of accomplishing group goals. The tension was probably reduced by experience and feedback during the throughput stage of group life, but it could be resolved only by the manager's final standard of measurement.

Relationships and roles formed and developed over time, resulting in stabilized group *output.* All of the decisions were made on the basis of the eventual assessment. The degree to which you were satisfied with other members, the decisions, and work was influenced by assessment of task accomplishment. With that assessment came removal of uncertainty and stress.

Our example may seem rather contrived since production workers or group members are rarely faced with so much ambiguity in their jobs. Objectives and tasks are generally specified by external authorities. However, it does serve to illustrate that groups work under varying degrees of stress according to the clarity of their objectives, tasks, and standards of performance. The more ambiguous the constraints, the more stress the group may experience. In this chapter we are going to examine some of the determinants of group production and the effect of achievement upon member satisfaction.

As the reader might have sensed from our example, group productivity rests on (1) *goal specification,* (2) *coworker resources,* and (3) *task demands.* The *process of group interaction* represents the ways a particular group of people deal with these factors. Hence, communication behaviors are the crucial elements in the process of group interaction. In this section we will look more specifically at goal specification, member resources, and task demands.

Goal Specification

Goals may determine tasks or tasks may determine goals. In either case, goals should be designed to increase clarity about group performance. The goal of determining a budget for the coming year implies certain task responsibilities such as committee budget requests, anticipation of income potential, and balancing of the previous year's books. The task of "balancing the books" may also involve specifying a goal of getting balance sheets to the auditor by a certain date.

Goals are relevant to the degree they reduce equivocality for a group or an individual. If people are clear in their minds about what to do and when to do it, there should be an increase in productivity (Weick, 1969). A field study of telephone operators found that operators worked more efficiently when the goal and goal path was clear than when it was ambiguous (Cohen, 1959). Operators also felt more highly motivated and more secure with clear work responsibilities. In general, productivity and satisfaction should increase as equivocality decreases.

However, the correlation between goal clarity and satisfaction cannot be extended indefinitely. Frederick Taylor (1911) and Henry Ford are often credited with having spawned an era of *scientific management* in which "time and motion" engineers controlled and clarified workers' task responsibilities. Tasks became so specialized that workers were asked to work, not think. The overriding concern of this approach was efficiency of operation. Costs were kept at a minimum by planning the worker's every move. Efficiency was based on the idea of "one best way" (Churchman, 1968). Workers soon gave way to machines since, if the one best way is known, a machine can be designed to do the task faster, cheaper, and more reliably than humans. In the case of decision making groups, decisions once made laboriously by committees can now be made instantaneously by computers.

The fatal flaw of scientific management is its failure to allow for human reactions. In the race for efficiency, human needs, motivations, and intellects are often ignored. People want control over their behavior; removal of control results in motivational deterioration. Workers have been found to produce more when they can vary the rate of a production line than if it remains at a steady rate (Steiner, 1972). Workers are more responsible and responsive when charged with the control of machines rather than being controlled by machines. In general, group members need creative control over their behaviors or illegitimate behaviors emerge to decrease productivity. Managerial philosophies developed by Blake and Mouton (1964), Likert (1967) and McGregor (1960), among others, have argued that workers can be highly productive when given an opportunity to establish their own goals and production tasks rather than having them dictated by others.

When individual and group goals collide, group functioning is hampered. If members privately hope a group will fail, or if they are working for objectives incompatible with overall group goals, the result may resemble a pair of horses trying to pull a wagon in separate directions. *Homogeneity* of group and individual goals can facilitate productivity. When group members individually strive for the same goals as the total group, cooperation should result. A large number of studies dealing with the effects of "mixed motives" (conflicting goals) have demonstrated that groups perform more effectively when the situation requires cooperation rather than competition (Deutsch, 1949; Shaw, 1958).

A limitation of the cooperative goal is that tasks requiring *high* cooperation have been found to take four times as long as tasks having lower cooperative requirements. Groups have also been found to make five times as many errors when given high cooperative requirements (Shaw and Briscoe, 1966). In general, cooperation increases coordination problems, which reduce the quality of group performance.

Ultimately, the challenge for a group is to develop goals that all members are willing to accept and which will be explicit enough to give direction to individual member contributions. However, groups often encounter a number of problems in the formulation of goals. Group goals are often stated for public appeal rather than actual group interests. For example, a teacher association might publicly state a goal to be in the interests of children, when the actual goal is to increase salaries.

Goals are often vague and ambiguous. In order to avoid injuring anyone's feelings, groups transcend individual differences by stating goals that will offend no one and, we might add, will aid no one. Vague goals also avoid the embarrassing test of achievement. In order to move from vague goals to more precise goals, the group may need to develop specific measures of performance. Methods of measuring achievement are not always easy to determine and are often open to criticism. How does one measure the quality of a decision or discussion? If goals remain intentionally vague, it may be impossible to tell if the group ever fails to meet its objectives. Of course, vague goals may also rob some groups of measured success.

There is often pressure to get on with task accomplishment rather than discussing goals. Groups often develop out of an immediate need and are so busy working on immediate tasks that they overlook broader objectives. At times, goals may seem so obvious as to not warrant making them explicit. In other cases, goals are difficult to articulate because they are based upon implicit and sometimes hidden motivations. In either case, members may want to get *to* the task rather than talk *about* the task.

Another problem with goal formulation is the distance between goals of an organization to which a group belongs and the goals of the group. Or, from a narrower prospective, goals held by individual members compared to the goals of a group. Here we are not concerned with homogeneity, but with the ability of individuals to see how their personal goals relate to the totality of all goals. If the path between the two sets of goals (such as organization and group, or group and individual) is clear, a group or individual may be more motivated to work for the wider objectives. Galbraeth (1968) argues that a company should formulate goals in such a way that individuals begin to see themselves as an extension of the company (for example, "I am an IBM person"). In this way individuals begin to view their lives as service for the company. At a group level, if individuals begin to see the group depends on their personal inputs, they may work harder to achieve success for the group.

The following check list is a means of assessing whether a group has effective goal specifications:

1. Are goals of the larger organization, of which the group is a part, identified and written?
2. Are group goals identified and written?
3. Are goals of the larger organization clearly related to group goals?

4. Are the goals of individual group members specified?
5. Are individual goals clearly related to group goals?
6. Are individual, group, and organizational goals measurable in terms of achievement?
7. Are rewards and penalties directly related to achievement?
8. Are environmental influences weighed in regard to achievements?

It is critically important for members to participate in formulating group *and* individual goals. Participation promotes identification with and acceptance of goals. As group members communicate with each other about group and individual goals, they become psychologically committed to those goals. This commitment is then translated into production and satisfaction. To further assure active participation, rewards can be tied to achievement of goals.

Standards of measurement become more important when rewards are tied to achievements. Organizations and groups certainly don't want to reward those who do not perform up to expectations; it seems only fair to let groups and individuals know what they must do in order to achieve rewards. Some organizational leaders believe it is their function to provide a critical check on group activities. Therefore, they only raise questions and concerns about group accomplishments and never provide direct rewards for achievements. You can imagine the impact this has on morale.

Clear and understandable goals and goal paths reduce equivocality. When groups lack structure and direction, members experience stress, which drains productive energy. Distressed group members do not make productive workers. Lack of productivity creates dissatisfaction with a group (Harris and Harvey, 1974). Dissatisfaction hinders productivity even more, resulting in a potential breakdown of the entire group.

Goals, standards of measurement, and reward structures can be effective tools for a satisfied and productive group. There is, of course, the possibility that a group or individual may fail to achieve specified goals. Obviously that is demoralizing as well. However, assume that you are in a 1500 meter race and your goal is to complete the run in less than five minutes. After each 500 meters, a person with a stopwatch tells you how you are doing in terms of the goal and spectators cheer your performance. Unfortunately, you fail to achieve the five minute goal. Contrast that situation with running 1500 meters without an objective, without any feedback regarding your success in meeting some standards, and without any type of rewards for your efforts. After the race, you don't know whether you have run well or poorly. Which situation seems preferable? Which situation do you think would give rise to a better performance? An unfortunate number of groups fail to achieve their potential for precisely the same reasons.

Coworker Influences

Ideally, groups make better decisions than individuals because with the presence of other members: (1) higher quality work is stimulated, (2) individual resources are pooled, (3) more people means a greater chance that a person with superior resources will influence a decision, (4) mistakes are identified in the group, (5) discussion stimulates ideas, (6) errors cancel out by chance, and (7) there is pressure to make justifiably risky choices (Johnson and Johnson, 1975). It takes very little group experience to learn that these principles do not always work. Performance is *sometimes* facilitated by the presence of others. Group members are more highly aroused by the presence of others. Increased arousal produces behaviors high in an individual's response hierarchy. Thus, high arousal facilitates performance when the best decision or behavior is well learned. When the task requires new or poorly learned responses, however, arousal will have an inhibitory effect (Zajonc, 1966).

Limitations to the social facilitation principle include cases such as a lazy person who is motivated to work in the presence of peers, or well-learned responses that are forgotten in the presence of evaluators. Anxieties due to potential evaluation are powerful feelings which may facilitate or inhibit ask performance. They generally facilitate behaviors that are well learned or are likely to evoke favorable attitudes, but they may have inhibiting effects upon task behaviors that are poorly learned or likely to elicit adverse evaluations.

Members often model their behaviors after fellow members. This is most likely to happen when coworkers seem to be making progress on task assignments or appear to be receiving rewards for their efforts (Bandura and Walters, 1964). Assuming the model behavior is positively directed toward group goals, and it is the best possible behavior for group purposes, the behaviors of coworkers will enhance production and achievement.

A group's productivity is also influenced by the composition of its membership. The resources, attitudes, and dispositional properties that members bring to a group determine how well the group will meet task demands. When tasks require highly specialized roles it is generally desirable to have a diverse membership; When everyone must do exactly the same task, a homogeneous group is usually ideal (Davis, 1969).

Although dispositional qualities of coworkers affect member ratings of satisfaction with group experiences and outcomes (Heslin, 1964), evidence concerning the impact of such variables on productivity is not clear. If a task has one best solution, a heterogeneous membership may be appropriate in order to get diverse input. In a classic study of group productivity, Marjorie Shaw (1932) provided groups and individuals with a problem of logic in which one best answer could be determined.

She concluded that one of the major advantages of a group over an individual is the opportunity for members to correct each others' errors. Using an abstract task with one best answer, her conclusion is probably valid. However, when we examine types of task demands more carefully in the next section, some limitations may be noted.

Task Demands

In Chapter 4, we introduced the four major task dimensions identified by Shaw (1963). To review, they included *difficulty, solution multiplicity, cooperative requirements* and *population familiarity*. We have already touched on population familiarity and cooperative requirements as they affect achievement. Difficulty will be addressed next, then solution multiplicity.

Research by Zander (1971) and others indicates that: (1) group success is followed by a willingness to engage in a more difficult task, while failure is often followed by selection of an easier task; (2) the more members desire group success, the more likely they are to request tasks of intermediate difficulty; (3) the more members desire to avoid group failure, the more they prefer tasks at the extremes of the difficulty range (that is, they prefer very easy tasks in order to assure success or very difficult tasks in order to guarantee an excuse for failure). In other words, success tends to be rewarding and reinforces group aspirations, failure is punishing and tends to force a group to seek tasks that will be more rewarding.

It is not surprising to learn that Shaw and Blum (1966) found group performance, as measured by time and errors, decreased in quality with increased task difficulty. As task demands increase, group members give less attention to each aspect of the task, resulting in reduced quality of performance. When the challenge of a difficult motor-reaction task is presented, however, groups generally respond by working more quickly (Zajonc and Taylor, 1963). Group performance on a difficult task is also facilitated by the opportunity to communicate feelings of satisfaction about a group's progress. Furthermore, in groups where members are encouraged to express differences, performance is often superior in comparison to groups that are less receptive to an open exchange of differences (Maier, 1970).

Solution multiplicity refers to the number of alternatives available to a group, and the extent to which a solution can be tested for correctness or appropriateness. According to Steiner (1972), solutions can be viewed as *disjunctive, conjunctive, additive,* or *discretionary*.

Disjunctive tasks require only one solution at the expense of all other contributions. The most obvious example of this is a task that involves a

mathematical or logical calculation with only one possible answer. "When a task is disjunctive a group's potential productivity is determined by the resources of its most competent member" (Steiner, 1972, p. 27). Failure to achieve success as a group can be attributed to: (1) lack of members who possess necessary resources to solve the problem; (2) failure of members with necessary resources to solve the problem; (3) failure of members with necessary resources to convince other members that they have the correct answer; (4) failure of members with necessary resources to communicate the correct answer; (5) failure of members with necessary resources to use their skills to solve the problem; and (6) failure of the group to accept the contribution of resourceful members.

In general, a group may fail to reach its potential productivity because of inadequate *processing of information*. The processing of information involves the communication skills of group members. Members must be able to listen objectively to all contributions offered. They must weigh contributions on their own merit rather than because the majority favors one particular answer. Members must be sensitive to the verbal contributions of all, regardless of the skill with which they are contributed. Members must try to resist the temptation to reject ideas contributed by low status members without giving them a full hearing. And finally, members must individually strive to present ideas as convincingly and effectively as possible so that the ideas may receive a fair hearing.

Some solutions are of the *eureka* type. That is, when the solution has been determined it is obvious to all. Members exclaim, as the name implies, "Eureka, we have it." Whenever a task is not of the eureka type, the chance of ineffective information processing *increases* since the correct answer will not necessarily be obvious.

Conjunctive tasks are those in which rules prescribe that one member will determine the group output. The *critical* member is generally the weakest contributor to the group. For example, if a group of workers was measured by the least productive worker in their group, the task would be regarded as conjunctive. Teachers often gauge their assignments and lectures by the least productive class members in order to communicate with the entire class. Teams on an assembly line cannot go any faster than their slowest members. Almost any division of labor has some degree of conjunctivity. Everyone depends on everyone else to fulfill their responsibilities and is hampered by the least productive members. One member who does not understand the instructions, or who is unmotivated to work, may limit productivity.

Conjunctive and disjunctive tasks depend on a single group member. Disjunctive tasks are solved by the *most* resourceful member and conjunctive tasks are determined by the *least* resourceful member. In both cases communication among group members is vital to success. Failure

to effectively communicate group needs and information will cause a group to fall short of its productive potential.

Additive tasks involve the contributions of all group members. A group's achievement is measured by combining the contributions of all members. A group norm that encourages equal contributions by all members represents an additive approach. The danger is that not all members may have equal resources, motivations, and attitudes to warrant being given equal weight in a group. An additive task runs the risk implied by the saying "too many cooks spoil the broth." Coordination problems and extended socio-emotional episodes are common in these tasks since members are directly tied to each others' contributions.

Tasks that permit group members to select their own weightings and combination rules are regarded as discretionary tasks (Steiner, 1972). Members may select their most resourceful person to determine the answer to a problem, or they may choose any other combination of members they deem appropriate. Within limits, members are free to process information in any way that they see fit. Naturally, when that much discretion is left to a group the chosen process becomes critically important to group success. Generally, groups have two potential courses of action. Assume that you are given two tasks. In one, you are required to throw a ball as far as you possibly can. In the other, you are required to throw the ball as near to a mark as possible. The first task could be regarded as *maximizing* since it would require your maximum effort. The second task would require your most accurate toss and could be regarded as *optimizing*. A group's use of its member resources often resembles one of these two tasks. The decision to maximize versus optimize is not always easy to make.

Tasks that can be broken into specialized subtasks and performed by different members are regarded as *divisible*. The group's problem is to match resources of its members to task requirements. Motivational problems may be encountered if subtask requirements are either too easy or too difficult for the matched member. Those tasks which cannot be broken down are regarded as *unitary* and usually carry higher cooperative requirements. If a task is unitary, a smaller group is at an advantage since it has fewer problems of coordination than a large group. If a task is divisible, larger groups have a potential advantage in that task responsibilities can be broken down among a sizable pool of members. However, a large group still has the problem of matching member resources with subtasks and coordinating efforts of greater magnitude than in a small group. Assuming a task could be broken into a variety of different subtasks, high group productivity will reflect the best possible organizational decisions regarding a system of division and matching. If members are dissatisfied with their responsibilities, group performance will, correspondingly, fall below its potential.

In this section on task demands we have introduced sixteen possible combinations of tasks. Disjunctive, conjunctive, additive, and discretionary tasks refer to *which member(s)* may determine the *level of productivity* in a group. Disjunctive and conjunctive tasks involve a single member, additive tasks involve all members and discretionary tasks are left to the determination of a group. The type of *task objective* may be either optimizing or maximizing. Optimizing tasks require a group to strive for an optimal standard, while maximizing tasks require the greatest possible effort from group members. Tasks may also be unitary or divisible.

A group of Senators responsible for determining a public policy would probably engage in a task of preparing legislation that could be labeled discretionary, optimizing, and divisible. Any combination of Senators could provide input into the group, and, in turn, the group could weigh the contributions of each individual. The task would require providing the best possible type of legislation, not necessarily the longest legislation. Undoubtedly, work on the bill would be broken into subsections in order to spread the workload. The manner in which the task was subdivided, assigned and treated will be reflected in the quality of achievement.

WHAT IS THE EFFECT OF ACHIEVEMENT ON SATISFACTION?

A fundamental aspect of human nature seems to be that people will do those things for which they will be rewarded—or believe they will be rewarded—and avoid those activities for which they will not. The difficulty comes in specifying rewards that will work for a particular individual. An opportunity to participate in a small group may be a reward in and of itself for some people while for others it may be perceived as very unrewarding.

Primary and Secondary Needs

There are two broad classifications of needs to which people seem to respond, *biological* and *social-psychological* (Berelson and Steiner, 1964). Biological needs are regarded as primary since they relate to life sustaining elements such as food, water, oxygen, and protection from the environment. These needs may be fairly well satisfied at any given time, but social-psychological needs are never fully met. Needs related to the mind and spirit are regarded as *secondary*, or higher order, needs since they have much greater influence on behavior after primary needs have been met.

Consider a group of laborers and management executives working together on a profit sharing plan. Let us assume the laborers barely make enough money to meet their basic needs, and the executives make enough money to live quite comfortably. In this event, we might expect laborers to advocate a direct payout of as much of the company profits as possible. The executives might argue for as much of the funds to be plugged back into capital improvements as soon as possible so the company will make even greater profits in the future. Or, they might contend that funds should be set aside in a pension program to be withdrawn after retirement when they are least affected by income tax deductions. Both groups favor having profits returned to the parties that achieve the profits, but they are approaching solutions associated with different types of needs. The laborers are totally concerned with satisfaction of primary needs while the executives are concerned with more long term needs.

Groups composed of members with primary needs can effectively reward participation with material goods such as money. In a similar vein, physical products of achievement may be more appealing to such people, particularly if some reward is attached to the output. Maximizing tasks may be more appealing than optimizing tasks since the latter often demand a qualitative judgment. Groups composed of members whose primary needs are satisfied will be much more susceptible to rewards of recognition, prestige, and social affiliations. These groups may be rewarded by praise of achievements and may enjoy having done a task effectively.

This division of *reward appeal* is not as easy as the previous remarks would indicate. Basically, people seek that which they are in need of or lack. Therefore, a poor person may enjoy the benefits of good social relations and a job well done. There are many examples of starving artists who continue to paint. However, identification of primary and secondary needs is a useful place to begin. People will be more responsive to task responsibilities if they can see some payoff in terms of their needs.

Relating Rewards to Goals

Many manufacturing companies use some form of profit sharing for their employees as an incentive for efficient production. The success of such programs may be tied to whether the employees know that the rewards are a direct result of their behaviors. One successful program uses bulletin board displays, company newsletters, and union newsletters to inform its employees of quarterly paid profit shares, and uses memos to inform employees of how innovations or errors in production affected profits on a weekly basis. Profit sharing funds are distributed according to salary levels. Therefore, the more workers have contributed to profits the more they receive. Sales commissions are often paid on a similar principle. However, the link between company profit goals and individual sales goals is often ambiguous. If salesmen could also receive an extra dividend that links commissions to company profits and losses, the interrelationships would be more apparent.

Satisfiers and Dissatisfiers

Groups often depend on *esprit de corps,* cohesion, and member enthusiasm to produce results. Undoubtedly, pep talks have their value but they are not a good substitute for member resources and needed payoffs. Frederick Herzberg (1959) has developed a "motivator-hygiene" theory that makes a useful distinction between *job satisfaction* (motivation) and *dissatisfaction.* He maintains that people seek two types of goals which affect behavior in different ways. The opposite of job satisfaction is not dissatisfaction, it is simply *no* satisfaction; the opposite of dissatisfaction is simply the *absence* of dissatisfaction. The significance of the distinction is that the types of satisfaction are caused by entirely different sets of factors.

Factors having the greatest effect upon job satisfaction include achievement, recognition, work itself, responsibility, and advancement. All of these relate to what a person does. A completely different set of factors are regarded as job dissatisfiers: company policy and administration, supervision, salary, interpersonal relations, and working conditions. These are extrinsic to the nature of the work since they describe the environment of the job. In other words, intrinsic rewards relate to the task itself (they are satisfiers) and extrinsic rewards relate to environmental constraints. This formulation suggests that group members could be satisfied with their achievements while dissatisfied with their fellow group members, the leadership of the group, and the system in which the group is embedded.

The satisfier-dissatisfier distinction helps reduce the "needs" dilemma discussed earlier. Herzberg's theory suggests that groups need to satisfy both the intrinsic and extrinsic needs of members. It is possible to have members who are not dissatisfied with a group *per se* but are not satisfied with the product of their achievements. Conversely, members may gain a great satisfaction from having done a job well but may be quite dissatisfied with group composition.

According to Herzberg, if we want to motivate a group to make greater efforts we should focus on task-related issues and payoffs. On the other hand, *hygienic* environments prevent dissatisfaction, but cannot contribute directly to member satisfaction and happiness. Imagine a classroom with a "nice" teacher who serves snacks each day and enjoys "rapping" with the students. Assume that the subject to be covered (for instance, organic chemistry) is important to your future success as a student and employee. In this situation you might not be dissatisfied with the class as a social environment but also might not be satisfied with task achievement. The error of the teacher may be in trying to buy the satisfaction of the class when motivation cannot be bought.

Herzberg (1968, p. 67) contends that, "A motivated man will do things of his own volition that far exceed what he could be made to do by offers of food or money. The strongest kind of motivation is self motivation." Leaders and parent organizations of groups can do much to aid group motivation by providing praise and recognition of achievements. Feedback can help the group achieve a sense of personal satisfaction with the product of their efforts.

Finally, in respect to payoffs, we should recognize the difference between optimizing and maximizing tasks. If a group cuts out paper dolls for an hour, they can look at the stack at the end of the hour and gain a sense of pride in the product of their efforts. If a group discusses a problem or issue for an hour there is often no tangible record of achievement. When a traffic planning board works on a new intersection, how can it be certain those efforts have created an *optimal* traffic flow? Eventual approval by a city council and actual traffic reports after implementation may provide some degree of delayed satisfaction, but immediate gratification may not be forthcoming. In this case, the group may need to rely on the degree to which members found such experience and achievements personally satisfying.

Maier (1970) proposes that task accomplishments can be measured by the quality of an outcome (presumably judged by some predetermined criterion) and the degree of acceptance of an outcome by group members. Group functioning can be facilitated by an opportunity to express those feelings of satisfaction among the membership (Shaw, 1976). The degree of acceptance can be measured as the extent of member commitment to enact decisions, to defend decisions with others, and to publicly express satisfaction with decisions.

HOW ARE COMMUNICATIVE PROCESSES ASSOCIATED WITH TASK ACCOMPLISHMENTS?

Most, if not all, group activities require some amount of communicative behavior between members. While it would be presumptuous to think a group's success or failure hangs on every sentence or nonverbal cue, it's reasonable to assume group productivity and goal attainment require effective message exchanges and interpretations of feedback cues (both verbal and nonverbal). As we have said throughout, communicative behaviors influence and are influenced by a number of social and psychological factors. In this concluding section we intend to focus specifically on relationships between communicative behaviors and productivity.

Since the content and flow of communication between group members may be both cause and effect of task accomplishment and goal attainment, we can approach our discussion with two distinct considerations in mind. First, we must recognize that communication processes can facilitate or impede task accomplishments. These potentialities were discussed at some length in Chapters 6 and 8. Second, task accomplishment may, by itself, affect communicative behavior. Each person's own satisfaction with group actions, either through direct influence on, or identification with, those actions is a major determinant of subsequent communicative behaviors in a group. From each member's perspective, there seem to be three issues associated with group interaction that have some bearing on personal satisfaction with membership and overall group effectiveness: (1) opportunities for participation; (2) effectiveness or *quality* of participation; and (3) perceived consequences of participation.

Opportunities for Interacting in a Group

Most people assume that group membership guarantees the opportunity to participate. This may or may not be the case. Such variables as the type of leadership style used, spatial or other environmental factors, a person's place in an existing group network, how likeable or attractive others perceive an individual to be, the person's known status in other groups (that is pertinent or relevant to members in that particular group), and so on, are also influential. Another component of "opportunity" however, is an individual's motivation to interact based on the perception that a group can provide satisfying or rewarding feedback. Hence, opportunities for interacting in a group are the result of factors a member may or may not directly control.

Since we have devoted a number of chapters to those variables less easily controlled by a single member (group social structures and networks, leadership patterns, and so on), additional attention to personal motivations seems appropriate. Clearly, any group member's motivations for participation are never solely the individual's responsibility. At minimum, personal motivations for group involvement are stimulated or suppressed by the kind of task(s) a group works on, and the magnitude of member rewards contrasted against negative consequences (or risk) of group failure.

In a summary of literature on group and member aspirations for achievement, Zander (1968) distinguishes between two kinds of motivations, desires for successful group achievement and desires to avoid group failure. On the surface, these sound almost synonymous. Certainly the two motives can operate simultaneously for a member or group. The difference, however, can be explained by assessing the phrases "successful group achievement" and "avoid group failure."

According to Zander, attention to group success creates motivational impetuses for approaching (wanting to work on) certain tasks because successful completion appears highly probable. Individuals (or groups as a whole) who have strong needs for successful work experiences tend to prefer tasks (find them most attractive) that are of *intermediate* difficulty. Members (or groups) with strong desires to avoid failure, however, do not usually manifest the same task preferences. Those who wish to avoid failure tend to prefer tasks that are either more or less difficult than those of intermediate difficulty.

The consequences of needs to attain success or avoid failure seem important in understanding opportunities for group participation. Consider the person with a high need to avoid failure who perceives a group's task definition as too simple, while others perceive it as appropriate, a "sure bet" to succeed, and a source of reward for the group. The deviant member's attitudes toward the task will meet opposition from other members. This source of conflict, should it emerge, draws attention away from task involvement. Members favoring a task definition must spend additional time defending their position and trying to convince a deviant member that the task is worth the time and effort. Should such persuasive attempts prove unsuccessful, the deviant member may find resistence to further attempts at interacting. Viewing the group as a system, its effectiveness is diminished because the system's human resources are not fully applied to task accomplishment. In theory, if members have an opportunity to express their ideas, opinions, and attitudes they should be more satisfied with the final product of group efforts. By contrast, dissatisfied members may place lower value on group achievements and be less productive or involved in group interaction.

Quality of Group Participation

Aside from the effects of personal motivations, communicative skills of group members can weigh heavily in determining both the quantity and quality of group achievements. Unfortunately, while we are intuitively aware that productivity depends on the nature of communicative inputs to a group, knowledge concerning exactly how inputs are related to productivity is limited. We know how people behave in certain situations but do not know much about how three or more people will respond to one another over a prescribed time period to produce collective action.

Part of the reason for the "fuzziness" surrounding the relationship between communication and productivity is that, while we can identify certain behaviors occurring in a group, there are many other thoughts, attitudes, and behaviors that escape detection. This point was made in Chapter 5 with respect to the complexity of relevant behaviors a participant-observer can profitably perceive, interpret, and use while monitoring group interaction processes. However, as we indicated in that chapter, Bales has pointed us in the right direction with his analyses of task behavior. The potential for that kind of approach can also be found in our discussion in Chapter 7 of how the use of orienting types of statements can affect leader and group effectiveness.

There have been a few attempts to assess the association between communicative inputs and group outcomes. Studies focusing on *orientation behavior* have investigated its impact on task completion variables, like quality of group solutions. Where this has been done, however, the results were inconclusive. A study reported by Leathers (1972) did address this issue directly. He composed experimental laboratory groups in which a confederate was instructed to provide messages intended to either "facilitate" or "disrupt" discussion between members. A third set of groups was composed without the presence of a confederate and served as control groups representative of "natural" interaction. Judges were asked to rate the *quality* of communicative messages and task outcomes as groups in each condition attempted to attain consensus on a task. Results of the study indicated there was a positive relationship between quality of communication and rated quality of task outcomes. Facilitated groups were rated higher on quality of communicative content and task solutions than were natural or disrupted groups. The notion of communication *quality*, though somewhat ambiguous, can be thought of as messages which keep a group focused on task relevant concerns.

The nature of messages exchanged between members is only one dimension of group-system communication. Many of the remarks made earlier in this text relate to communication behaviors and interaction processes beneficial to productive groups. In general, open, free flowing interaction among group members is essential. Such interaction should not only focus on task-related issues but on the social-emotional aspects of a group as well. Members need to feel comfortable in relating both thoughts and feelings to the group.

Groups also need to step back and assess the quality of interaction and the effect of emerging relationships on productive results. A group needs to determine whether each member has had an opportunity to fully and completely express ideas. When expressing ideas, did members keep their remarks relevant to the group? Were the remarks succinct enough to retain group attention but elaborate enough to receive adequate interest from other members? In responding to contributions of others, did group members allow the contributor to be understood before offering contrary opinions? Did the group maintain an open mind about ideas and opinions? Did they give recognition to the contributor as a person regardless of whether the idea was accepted? In terms of the group process, could the group take an objective view of itself in process? Could members talk about their differences in addition to simply differing? And, finally, did the group give recognition to all the contributors rather than focusing only on the assigned leaders?

Consequences of Participation

As members of a group, we are usually aware of others' reactions to us. We also possess some impressions about how a group is reacting as a system. Whether we can always verbalize these impressions will vary greatly from meeting to meeting and group to group. This awareness or sensation is a "feeling" we have about a group, other members, and our orientations to both. Johnson (1977) proposes these "feelings," and the labels we can attach to them, represent our interpretation of a group's *climate* at that moment. Hence, we can describe a group as tense, easygoing, defensive, supportive, cold, friendly, and so on. These labels are used to interpret our perceptions of an underlying theme (or themes) we draw from content and process levels of interaction.

Perceptions of communication climates are a natural outcome of any sustained period of group participation. Moreover, the types of climates that evolve appear to have a substantial impact on productivity and satisfaction. This assumption has, in fact, been influential in the analysis of behavior in complex organizations and the development of management strategies in these settings. Organization analysts such as Likert (1967) have argued that the way complex organizational systems structure and implement communication flow (upward or downward), accuracy, employee receptivity (of directive messages from hierarchical superiors), superior-subordinate disclosures, and the amount and opportunity for superior-subordinate cooperativeness and sociable interaction, are crucial components in a productive organizational climate.

Probably the best known report on communication climates in small

groups was that of Gibb (1961). Using information from a program of research on small group productivity started in the mid-1950s, he concluded that small groups were more productive under conditions of *supportive* versus *defensive* communication climates. Supportive climates are characterized as nonjudgmental, cooperatively interdependent, spontaneous, reinforcing participative planning and actions without status biases, empathic, and willing to experiment with new ideas without preconceived prejudices. Defensive climates, which are more or less at the opposite end of the spectrum, reflect high amounts of evaluative or judgmental reactions (positive or negative) toward others, attempts at controlling or changing another's behavior, manipulation, emotional neutrality (or failing to express concern for the feelings of others), superiority or status-seeking, and dogmatic or competitive behaviors.

Gibb's analysis provides a subjective composite of labels which distinguish groups that facilitate or impede task accomplishment and satisfaction with participation. A somewhat different approach has been proposed by Mabry (1976), using questionnaire responses from participants in over fifty small groups having various sizes and tasks. He found four dimensions associated with participants' perceptions of their groups' communication climate, *participation, identification, power,* and *personalness.*

The participation dimension relates to how well members share task responsibility, the amount of interaction in a group across all members, and how effectively a group functions as a unit. Identification is the label given to members' perceptions of how *meaningful* or *pleasurable* their group's work experience was to them. The power dimension describes questionnaire statements about the distribution of influence between members (concentrated in a few members or spread rather evenly across members), and the existence of cliques or coalitions on issues. Personalness, the fourth dimension, describes the extent to which members engaged in socializing, disclosing information about themselves, and felt the group permitted positive or negative interpersonal attractions to develop.

We must emphasize that this is a descriptive approach. Unlike the position presented by Gibb, these dimensions of a group's communicative climate are not prescriptive (good versus bad). Although it is rather safe to assume that maximizing participation, heightening group identification, balancing the distribution of influence, and facilitating sociability, friendliness, or the exchange of affective responses between members may be desirable, there can be exceptions to such behavioral dimensions that might increase the effectiveness or productivity of par-

ticular groups. Also noteworthy is the fact that these dimensions have not as yet been correlated with measures of production quality and quantity or group satisfaction. They do provide a relatively concise set of descriptors for the kinds of behavioral contingencies we all face as members of small groups.

REFERENCES

Bandura, A. and Walters, R.H. 1964. *Social learning and personality development.* New York: Holt, Rinehart & Winston.

Berelson, B. and Steiner, G. 1964. *Human behavior: An inventory of scientific findings.* New York: Harcourt Brace Jovanovich.

Blake, R.R. and Mouton, J.S. 1964. *The managerial grid.* Houston: Gulf Publishing.

Churchman, C.W. 1968. *The systems approach.* New York: Dell Pub. Co., Inc.

Cohen, A.M. 1959. Stiuation structure, self-esteem, and threat-oriented reactions to power. In *Studies in social power,* ed. D. Cartwright. Ann Arbor, Mich: Institute for Social Research.

Davis, J. 1969. *Group performance.* Reading, Mass.: Addison-Wesley.

Deutsch, M. 1949. An experimental study of the effects of co-operation and competition upon group process. *Human Relations 2,* 199–231.

Galbraeth, J.K. 1968. Motivation and the technostructure. *Personnel Administration* Nov.–Dec., *31,* 5–10.

Gibb, J.P. 1961. Defensive communication. *Journal of Communication 11,* 141–148.

Harris, B. and Harvey, J.H. 1974. Self-attributed choice as a function of the consequence of a decision. *Journal of Personality and Social Psychology 31,* 1015–1019.

Herzberg, F. 1959. *The motivation to work.* New York: John Wiley.

Herzberg, F. 1968. Motivation, morale and money. *Psychology Today 1,* 42–45 and 66–67.

Heslin, R. 1964. Predicting group task effectiveness from member characteristics. *Psychological Bulletin 62,* 401–407.

Johnson, B. McD. 1977. *Communication: The process of organizing.* Boston, Mass.: Allyn & Bacon.

Johnson, D.W. and Johnson, F.P. 1975. *Joining together: Group theory and group skills.* Englewood Cliffs, N.J.: Prentice-Hall, Inc.

Leathers, D.G. 1972. Quality of group communication as a determinant of group product. *Speech Monographs 39,* 166–173.

Likert, R. 1967. *The human organization.* New York: McGraw-Hill.

Mabry, E.A. 1976. The effects of task frequency and task type on perceived communication climates in task-oriented groups. Paper contributed to the Interpersonal Communication Division program, International Communication Association Convention, Portland, Ore., April 1976.

Maier, N.R.F. 1970. *Problem solving and creativity in individuals and groups.* Belmont, Calif.: Brooks/Cole.

McGregor, D. 1960. *The human side of enterprise.* New York: McGraw-Hill.

Shaw, M. 1932. A comparison of individuals and small groups in the rational solution of complex problems. *American Journal of Psychology 44,* 491–504.

Shaw, M.E. 1958. Some motivational factors in cooperation and competition. *Journal of Personality 26,* 155–169.

Shaw, M.E. 1963. Scaling group tasks: A method for dimensional analysis. Technical Report No. 1 ONR Contract NR 170–277, Nonr-580 (11), University of Florida.

Shaw, M.E. 1976. *Group dynamics: The psychology of small group behavior.* 2nd ed. New York: McGraw-Hill.

Shaw, M.E. and Blum, J.M. 1966. Effects of leadership styles upon group performance as a function of task structure. *Journal of Personality and Social Psychology 3,* 238–242.

Shaw, M.E. and Briscoe, M.E. 1966. Group size and effectiveness in solving tasks varying in degree of cooperation requirements. Technical Report No. 6 ONR Contract NR 170-266, Nonr-580 (11), University of Florida.

Steiner, I.D. 1972. *Group process and productivity.* New York: Academic Press.

Taylor, F.W. 1911. *Principles of scientific management.* New York: Harper & Row, Pub.

Weick, K.E. 1969. Laboratory Organizations and Unnoticed Causes. *Administrative Science Quarterly 14,* 294–303.

Zajonc, R.B. 1966. *Social psychology: An experimental approach.* Belmont, Calif.: Brooks/Cole.

Zajonc, R.B. and Taylor, J.J. 1963. The effects of two methods of varying group task difficulty on individual and group performance. *Human Relations 16,* 359–368.

Zander, A. 1968. Group aspirations. In *Group dynamics: Research and Theory,* 3rd ed., eds. D. Cartwright and A. Zander, pp. 418–429. New York: Harper & Row, Pub.

Zander, A. 1971. *Motives and goals in groups.* New York: Academic Press.

Small groups are complex social units. Our approach to studying communication in small groups focuses on roles communication plays in the formation, maintenance, or change of human groups. Preceding chapters have dissected group processes and discussed their relationships to communicative action. We realize it is easy to forget the total picture while examining component parts. We dedicate this final chapter to a brief re-examination of communication in group systems.

REFLECTIONS ON SMALL GROUP SUBSYSTEMS

In Chapter 1 we presented a model depicting relationships among input, throughput, and output components. The model has operated as our conceptual and organizational "blueprint" throughout the text. Each chapter has elaborated on concepts and behaviors associated with components and how they fit together. Figure 11.1 contains an "expanded" version of the original model. It summarizes key concepts in

11

a final look at communication and small group systems

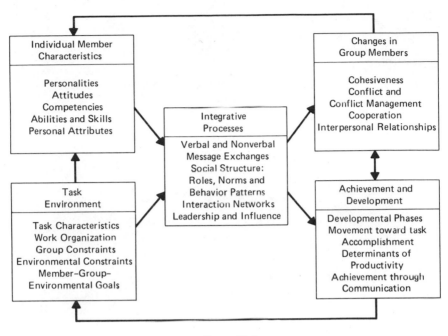

Individual Member Characteristics		Changes in Group Members
Personalities Attitudes Competencies Abilities and Skills Personal Attributes	Integrative Processes	Cohesiveness Conflict and Conflict Management Cooperation Interpersonal Relationships

Integrative Processes

Verbal and Nonverbal
Message Exchanges
Social Structure:
Roles, Norms and
Behavior Patterns
Interaction Networks
Leadership and Influence

Task Environment

Task Characteristics
Work Organization
Group Constraints
Environmental Constraints
Member–Group–
Environmental Goals

Achievement and Development

Developmental Phases
Movement toward task
Accomplishment
Determinants of
Productivity
Achievement through
Communication

Figure 11.1

the model's component parts and should assist your review of that material.

As you can see, we have covered a wide range of concepts and behaviors. In spite of all this "information," our understanding of how these components function to create a group-system is still limited. There are just too many groups and situations where generalizations fail to predict expected outcomes. Throughout the text, prescriptions and directions about ways group members, or groups, "should" act were usually avoided. Instead, we focused on explaining how different thoughts and acts are interrelated and how they contribute to complex social processes that constitute small group functioning. We have advocated the desirability of stepping back to look at the total system. We will heed our own advice in this section and take a more encompassing perspective while reviewing small groups as communication systems.

The Input Subsystem

A group is composed of members, a task presumably related to member goals, and an encompassing physical and social environment where members interact. Selecting the attributes, characteristics, and competencies of its members may or may not be a group's prerogative.

Groups designated through agencies of higher authority seldom control membership. An environmental context of a "workplace," for example, constitutes a larger organizational system that controls many facets of group membership and member characteristics. Informal "friendship" groups developing within that environmental context, however, can be more selective. Harry in the shipping department may never gain acceptance into a group composed of people from the sales and accounting departments, while Shirley, who works in plant operations, might be a sought after member.

Inclusion in or exclusion from a group might not be related to environmental controls at all. How we perceive others is a potent factor influencing personal reactions and attitudes. Harry may not be invited to join the group from sales and accounting—even if they want to meet people in shipping. Members of the group might think Harry is a "social nothing" and avoid him.

The same factors operate in groups composed by higher authorities. Picture a group composed of managers assembled to evaluate a company's management training program. There are many similarities between members. They are all managers who, presumably, understand the needs and problems of managers. All have experienced management training programs, been through and/or used the one they are evaluating and probably have useful insights to contribute. Do these similarities insure that members will eagerly seek out each other? Attach equivalent importance to their contributions? Work efficiently and effectively together? Resolve conflict? Promote cohesiveness? Produce an unbiased and helpful program evaluation? Not at all!

What will determine group processes and outcomes? Here are some possibilities: (1) members' existing attitudes toward each other; (2) Individual attitudes and beliefs about the task generally and specific task related issues; (3) how members perceive the behaviors of other members (effective personality); (4) members' personal competencies as social communicators; (5) the amount of time they have to complete the evaluation; (6) how detailed their result must be; (7) the availability of necessary resources (such as data from intermediate program analyses, research assistance, secretarial help, and so forth); (8) whether members are free from other duties or interruptions by subordinates during meetings; (9) methods members use to organize group sessions for working together. All of these factors, and many more, influence how the group functions and what it accomplishes. Together, personal characteristics and environmental influences combine and contribute to definitions of purpose, significance, personal regulations, and reward that members negotiate during face-to-face interaction.

Groups influence and are influenced by their environmental contexts.

The environment determines constraints and resources for a group. Some environmental contexts, as in the case of a parent organization, create a group and its membership. Rewards and costs (or punishments) are often provided as a stimulus and measure of success. The results of group production are fed into that social context which, in turn, determines the group's future. An organizational system needs the groups it creates (or it wouldn't create them in the first place) and demands the product of group accomplishments. In turn, a group's existence depends on the organization's demand for its products and services.

Our frequent examples of groups embedded in organizational systems should have alerted readers to the relationship between individual small groups and their encompassing social contexts. It is also apparent by now that groups and contexts mutually influence each other. In the past, laboratory research simulations have often failed to realistically include or assess *interdependent* relationships between groups and their environments. We could substantially upgrade our understanding of all group processes by increasing our awareness of small groups as minimal social systems and components of larger system contexts.

The Throughput Subsystem: Integrative Processes

The interplay between input, throughput, and output subsystems is virtually impossible to observe and analyze in its entirety. We can do no better than make "educated guesses" about most relationships between component parts. Human systems are complex, and this complexity is a major barrier to complete observation, analysis, and understanding. We have stressed that communicative action should be the focal point of our attention. Why? By observing behaviors that bring and keep people together we have a better chance of understanding linkages between inputs and outputs. Communication is the basic ingredient of all integrative processes. Other essential elements of human integration like social structures (norms, roles, networks) or social influence processes (power, leadership behaviors) exist because group participants interact with each for reasons of personal and group enhancement. Portraying how various human intrapersonal and interpersonal factors blend into something called a "small group" has been this text's basic objective.

We have maintained that communicative acts influence and are influenced by member personalities, attitudes, resources and environmental demands, interaction networks, leadership characteristics, patterns of group development and member relationships. Communication is not only a prerequisite to achievement, it is the essence of group existence. Without communication a group would be no more than the sum of its human parts. Communication processes transform a collection of individuals into a social system we call a small group.

Whether participant-observers perceive a group as a system or merely a collection of individuals working on a task depends on the psychological distance from which they view it. Observe a single ant or group of ants and you fail to find the significance of their actions. Observe a colony of ants inside a glass farm and their actions manifest a sense of purpose and meaningfulness. Individual members of a group are interdependent components responsive to one another and the outside influences. A group survives only as a consequence of *inter*action rather than individual action.

Participant-observers are part of the system they choose to analyze. There is a constant strain between getting too involved in task issues to maintain objectivity and being so psychologically removed from a situation that important behaviors go undetected. These problems are compounded when participant-observers must use the same interactive processes they are attempting to influence. A group is one of the few systems (although computers are narrowing the gap) that has the capacity to evaluate and reorganize its collective behaviors.

What we label as "human communication" is not limited to strictly observable sense data in the form of symbols. There are many emotional, subjective, and nonverbal elements that influence our relationships. Outside observers and mechanical recorders may not be sensitive enough to detect some elements of communicative processes. Because they can be sensitively attuned to subtle differences in a group, participant-observers are in a better position to weigh such elements.

Participant-observers also have the advantage of long term involvement in developing group relationships. Development is reflected in patterns of interaction over time. A single slice of interaction noted by an observer may well distort and deflect the process. Participant-observers use more than their eyes and ears. They use their intuitions and feelings as well as their minds. They let their total awareness supplement sensory data. Of course these perceptions are open to bias and incorrect inference. Communication serves as a means of checking the accuracy of subjective perceptions. Feedback about this data opens up a group and permits opportunities for discussing the implications and consequences of interactive processes.

Members share the fate of a group. Problems associated with one component of a system can alter or adversely affect other components. For the process to function, members must *react* as well as act. Message senders require message receivers; influencers require influencees. One dissatisfied member can destroy the efforts of ten satisfied members.

This is particularly true in cases of problem solving or task oriented groups.

Groups are *functionally interdependent* when a goal cannot be achieved without the involvement of all members. A disjunctive task, for example, requires the most competent or resourceful member to provide an acceptable solution. That member can succeed only when members are willing to accept the individual's influence. In many cases production and achievement depend on "wise action" by some members and "prudent inaction" by others. Even a group of friends, to remain a group, depends on willing interaction and expectations of personal restraints shared between members.

Task performance is often attributed to the success or failure of a single individual designated as a leader. Losing teams don't fire the players, they fire the coach. A huge volume of leadership research has failed to identify the "ideal" leader or leadership style. We propose it is useful to look at leadership responsibilities necessary for a group and that leadership may be spread throughout its membership. Interdependent role responsibilities force shared acceptance of group achievements. Influence is not merely one-way, as in the case of a single dynamic leader, it is multidirectional.

If a group operates as a system, the same person is not always going to dominate its actions. Each member adjusts to the needs and potentials of other members. Aggressively dominant members often pay the price of receiving negative feedback to suppress their actions. Those who lead must adjust to demands and pressures of those they wish to lead. At times we may legitimately ask, "Who is influencing whom?" We have suggested that a productive approach for guiding groups as systems is to identify role differentiations among members. It makes no difference whether a formally appointed leader reduces tensions between members, for example, as long as *someone* does it when necessary. If a designated leader concentrates on task demands, someone else may need to satisfy social-emotional demands. Each role is essential to group functioning. Groups often promote role specialization and, at the same time, can be complemented by a heavy interdependent relationship between holders of specialized roles.

The Output Subsystem

Member interactions result in many things. The results of integrative processes were discussed as *outputs*. Outputs are both tangible and intangible consequences of group-system integration. Often, tangible outcomes are what we look for as bench marks of successful group interaction. Making or assembling a piece of machinery, writing a re-

port, suggesting a new course of action or implementing such suggestions, or in specialized groups, observing changes in our personal behavior or the behavior of others, constitute tangible outputs. These, and others, are usually tied to immediate or long range goals associated with various rewards.

Most of us are probably near-sighted when it comes to assessing group outcomes. We usually think in terms of tangible results or extrinsic rewards. Indeed, keeping our jobs or getting a bonus are tangible outputs. Sometimes intrinsic rewards are important. A sense of accomplishment or ego satisfaction that comes with the completion of a project is important—particularly when extrinsic rewards are not present. The consequences of interacting with other people are not always obvious even when tangible outcomes are easily observed. Its probably impossible to engage in group interaction without experiencing some personal changes. Such engagements, at the very least, provide basic social learning experiences. The "storehouse" of information about our social world increases. Also, we probably come away from a group with modified attitudes about self, others, and certain social issues—especially those tied to task-related interaction. These are usually intangible outputs of a group. They are seldom observed and rarely looked for by ourselves or others.

Intangible outputs can be associated with a number of factors: cohesiveness, conflict and its resolution, tangible outcomes and attaining goals, and a small group's changing patterns of activity, (or development) as a purposive social entity. How communicative behavior affects each member, or the group, is not always clearly indicated by output variables. That any group output, to an extent, depends on some kind of communicative action is unquestionable. Some impacts are immediately recognizable, as in the case of decision making tasks requiring cooperation in face-to-face exchanges. In other settings communicative impact is usually hidden from surface observation. Members of a four-person assembly group may never talk directly to one another as they build something. The instructions they receive from their supervisor and how the supervisor gives praise or criticism will affect each member. The impact of that supervisor's communicative behavior, although administered to each individual member, may explain the group's rate of production, morale, or many other aspects of performance and satisfaction. Though not a type of small group setting we have focused on in the text, our point for the example is straightforward: small groups as we know and study them depend on communication to engage in purposive action. If we consider the supervisor as another group "member," and describe the group's interaction network as a "wheel" network, the point is even clearer.

CONCLUDING REMARKS:
SMALL GROUPS AS COMMUNICATION SYSTEMS

A "systems approach," like the one we have used, places some unusual burdens on readers. Most obvious among these burdens is the demand to think about something normally viewed as relatively simple and ordinary as complex and problematic. Second, those complexities of explanation were divided into what may have seemed to be arbitrary thought units. Finally, we have demanded that readers take our organizational scheme, which divided everything up, and use it to put everything back in order. This, we are sure, has not been a trifling set of demands.

Our primary purpose and text design has revolved around this fundamental assumption: the study of small group communication is actually an endeavor that explores how communication *creates* small groups. The plan of this text has worked toward articulating this point of view. Various chapters and chapter sections discussed issues associated with both our basic position and concepts related to small groups in general. These efforts resulted in an eclectic assessment of small group communication. Groups are more than the sum of their human parts. Communicative action, meaningful, symbolically translatable behavior, is also more than the sum of its parts. It seems only fitting that such complexity be combined to, hopefully, enhance our knowledge of these two important social processes.

Our final chapter gives us an opportunity to reinforce the text's central theme: communication binds the elements of small group systems into functioning social entities. Modes of communicative action are both causes and effects of group members' attempts to work with each other. Input, throughput, and output variables are inseparably interwoven within the content and patterns of group interaction. Chapter 11 offers an expanded model of small group systems and discusses relationships between communication and system processes.

CONCLUSION

Part
Five

Chapter

Absolute personality. Those personal mental attributes of members that show up on measuring instruments.

Action anxiety. Fear of acting in accordance with what needs to be done.

Acts. The smallest discernible segments of verbal or nonverbal behavior to which an observer can assign a classification.

Additive tasks. Achievement is measured by combining all member contributions.

Affection. One of the three needs and orientations identified by Schutz. Members vary in their need to express and receive close personal relationships.

Affective conflict. Emotional, and often personal, clashes.

Ascendant tendencies. Those personal attributes of members' personalities that lead them to assert individual prominence and control of a group.

Assembly effect. The result of combining people with certain personalities.

Attitude. A predisposition to behave in a favorable or unfavorable manner toward a person, object, or idea.

Autocratic leader. Attempts control over decisions related to subject content.

GLOSSARY

Authoritarianism. A personality trait of group members perceived to be less sensitive, less equalitarian, and more autocratic.

Balance theory. An unbalanced mental state produces psychological tension and generates motivational forces to restore balance.

Behavioral contract method. Involves specifying member goals and responsibilities for the group. Usually identified with therapy related groups.

Behavioral flexibility. An individual's ability to adapt new ways of behaving as a means of obtaining desired goals.

Biological needs. Primary life-sustaining needs for food, water, shelter, etc.

Cathectic oriented groups. Groups which primarily have social-affiliative objectives.

Coalitions. Minority or majority subgroups of similar opinion on certain issues.

Cohesion. Group member interdependence obtained through rewarding group experiences.

Collaboration. Members pool their diversity in order to arrive at the best group solution.

Communication. A social process that involves the simultaneous exchange of symbols or behaviors (translatable into symbols) between two or more people.

Comparison level. The minimum level of reward/cost ratios members use to make decisions, such as maintaining membership in a group.

Compatibility. In regard to personal needs or personality traits, the extent to which two or more people possess needs or traits that complement one another and lead to satisfying interpersonal relationships.

Conflict. A clash of opposing forces.

Conflict method. A leadership style that seeks change outside approved channels but within the environmental system.

Confrontation method. A leadership style that seeks eventual destruction of the environmental system by working outside approved channels.

Congruity principle. When a change in attitude occurs, it occurs in the direction of increased agreement with the prevailing frame of reference.

Conjunctive tasks. Those tasks in which the weakest contributor to the group determines group output.

Consensus. A state of task completion where members arrive at a mutual decision or acceptable solution related to goal objectives.

Consensus method. A leadership style that seeks change through traditionally approved channels within the environmental system.

Content. Verbal and nonverbal messages that are sent and received.

Contriently interdependent goals. An incompatibility between individual and group goals, where the attainment of individual goals impedes attaining other individual or group goals.

Control. One of the three identified needs and orientations by Schutz. Members have a need to express and receive power relations with others, by either dominating others (expressing) or being submissive in a power relationship (receiving).

Cooperation. Each member of a conflict gives up something (compromises) in order to meet the affective demands of the group.

Cooperatively interdependent goals. Those goals in which members find the realization of individual or group goals contribute to attainment of goals held by other members.

Credibility. An attitudinal bias of one person toward another. Generally thought to be based upon expertness, trustworthiness, and dynamism.

Decision-emergence model of group development. A model designed to reflect progression toward consensus.

Defensive climate. Group atmosphere characterized as evaluative, controlling manipulation, emotional neutrality, superiority, and dogmatic or competitive behaviors.

Democratic leader. Attempts control over decisions related to interpersonal process issues while promoting group input on task issues.

Dependability. Members are expected to conform to some generally accepted definition of their appropriate role in a group. Members are either self-reliant and responsible or unconventional.

Descriptiveness. The clarity and concreteness of feedback we give to others.

Developmental sequence model of group development. A set of speculations about how groups behave over time in regard to task and interpersonal relationship issues.

Direction of attitude. A favorable or unfavorable evaluation of a subject or person.

Discretionary tasks. Tasks that permit group members to select their own weightings and combination rules for determining a solution.

Disjunctive tasks. Require only one solution at the expense of all other contributions.

Dissonance. The existence of nonfitting relations among cognitions that motivate changes in attitudinal sets. It is a negative drive that occurs when a member simultaneously holds two cognitions which are inconsistent.

Distributional structure. Differential frequencies of participation across categories of interaction content.

Divisible tasks.   Tasks that can be broken into specialized subtasks and performed by different members.

Doppelganger effect.   The tendency of leaders to surround themselves with key assistants who look and think like them (doppelgangers).

Dyad.   A two-member interaction system.

Dynamic equilibrium.   Members show acceptance of, and attraction toward, others who they believe are acting in their best interests as a measure of engaging in reciprocal and mutually satisfying interaction.

Dynamism.   A person's activity, openness, and enthusiasm.

Effective personality.   Those behaviors we attribute to the personalities of others as we perceive them during social interaction.

Embeddedness.   Small groups exist within (are embedded in) larger organizations and groups.

Emotional relationships.   Positive and negative attractions members have toward each other.

Emotional stability.   Personality traits related to consistently appropriate emotional reactions toward others.

Empathic communication.   The ability to perceive how other people react to our communicative messages.

Entropy.   A high degree of ambiguity.

Equifinality.   Multiple options for structuring task accomplishment.

Equilibrium model of group development.   Those activities groups engage in to manage internal tension states. Group-systems are continuously engaged in activities that minimize internal tensions yet are responsive to external demands. The point of harmony is viewed as a state of equilibrium.

Eureka task.   A task in which the solution is obvious to all.

Exchange theory.   A small group perspective that explains group behavior in terms of interlocking behavioral transactions. An exchange theorist believes group behavior is best understood by assessing how members develop and nurture consistency in their interactions with each other.

Fear of separation.   Real or imagined fear of being removed from a group as a consequence of acting.

Feedback.   A controlling response to a stimulus.

Field theory.   A small group perspective that makes the assumption that group behavior is an interplay between individual goals and constraints placed upon fulfillment of individual goals by the goal(s) of the group or external environment.

Forward-backward.   One of the dimensions in Bales' model relating to group achievement and definition of group goals and procedures. A forward member is perceived as task oriented, analytical, and easily adapted to problem solving demands. A backward member is perceived to propose unconventional goals and is generally at odds with the definition of group activities accepted by forward members.

Functional models of group development. Those models which attempt to determine how groups behave in some specific task environment.

Goal-definition feedback. Focuses attention on the relationship between what the group is doing and its stated objectives.

Group. A network of people who have intentionally invested part of their personal decision making power in the authority of a larger social unit (a group) in pursuit of mutually desired but separately unobtainable goals.

Group development. Maturation of group member relationships and group movement toward a desired goal.

Halo effect. When one characteristic or property valued by others carries over to other characteristics and properties of an individual.

Hidden agenda. An undisclosed topic or attitude a member elects to keep to her/himself.

Identification feedback. Is typified by comments that relate to the development of group identity or a sense of groupness.

Idiosyncrasy credits. The process of accommodation that takes place when group members permit deviant behaviors by members who have gained group favor.

Inclusion. One of the three needs and orientations identified by Schutz. Members have a need to express and receive satisfying social relationships with others as indicated by being included in activities of others and including others.

Influence. An act of leadership resulting in a member's change of behavior or attitude.

Informal structure. A group's social organization which exists independent of formally ascribed group roles.

Inputs. Group members (their personalities, social status, etc.), the nature of the tasks, and physical/social environment.

Intensity of attitude. Strength of sentiment.

Interaction process analysis (I.P.A.). A classification scheme developed by Bales for analyzing verbal acts.

Interaction theory. A small group perspective that maintains a social structure exists when some set of expectations develop between participants in regard to their role relationships and interpersonal reactions to each other.

Interacts. Two-message sequences of verbal acts.

Interchange compatibility. The extent to which two or more members have needs that are similar (for example, both have high needs to give and receive inclusion).

Interpersonal orientation. The tendency to behave toward others in a manner consistent with how we conceive of ourselves as social communicators.

Isolates. Members or groups without access to external sources of information.

Job dissatisfiers. Environmental influences external to the job such as salary, supervision, working conditions, and interpersonal relations. Extrinsic rewards related to environmental constraints.

Job satisfiers. Motivators for task accomplishment such as achievement, recognition, and responsibility. Intrinsic rewards related to the task.

Kinesics. The study of body movement.

Laissez faire leader. Lets the group do whatever it wants without attempt to influence.

Leader. A role in which a person attempts to move and influence a group toward perceived goals.

Leadership. Interpersonal influence involving an attempt to affect the behavior of others.

Liaisons. Persons in organizations who help create and maintain informal channels of interaction between members of various groups.

Linking pins. People who provide information to more than one group or subgroup (see Liaisons).

Maturation (groups). The stages a group goes through as members work with each other.

Maturation (group members). The ways people adjust to working with their fellow members.

Maximizing tasks. Task outputs are measured by the greatest quantitative effort.

Meaning context. A point of reference which is used to interpret the symbols and behaviors of others.

Negative fantasies. Fear of what might happen as a result of acting.

Networks. Maps of repetitive channels over which messages are transmitted, which set norms for the form and content of interaction.

Nominal group technique. Problem solving method which structures interaction of participants: (1) round-robin, nonevaluative session with members contributing ideas; (2) discussion and clarification of all contributions; (3) rank ordering of three to five best items by member balloting; (4) discussion of most frequently chosen items; (5) balloting for top choice.

Nominal interaction. Group participants are observed by others.

Norm. Constraints on members as to how they must behave in a group and the attitudes to be held toward the group.

Openness. Willingness to honestly share inner thoughts and feelings with others.

Sociogram.   A graphic representation of group member choices on some selection criterion.

Status.   Evaluations and responses others give to holders of a position.

Status agreement.   The extent to which group members agree on the amount of status each group member has in the group.

Steinzor effect.   Members' verbal participation is typically directed toward members furthest away from one another.

Strain toward symmetry.   The motivation for agreement among group members who are attracted to one another.

Structural feedback.   Refers to the way responsibility, authority, and power are allocated among group members.

Structural relationships.   Role relationships with other group members.

Substantive conflict.   Intellectual opposition to content of ideas.

Supportive climate.   Group atmosphere characterized as nonjudgmental, cooperatively interdependent, spontaneous, which reinforces participative planning without status biases.

Systems theory.   A small group perspective that systematically puts together relationships between sets of social processes or variables.

Tasks.   The work responsibilities of a group.

Task behaviors.   Consist of questions and answers for messages of information, opinion, and suggestion.

Task oriented groups.   Groups that primarily have work related objectives.

Temporal patterns.   The ways distributional patterns change over time.

Throughputs.   Those elements of behavior that facilitate or impede progress toward a goal. The primary element is communication between group members.

Traits.   Characteristics of members. Can be physiological or psychological, and can be actual or ascribed by others.

Unitary tasks.   Tasks that cannot be broken into subtasks or performed by subgroups.

Upward-downward.   One of the dimensions in Bales' model similar to an ascendant tendency. A person perceived as upward is oriented toward success and power. Downward members are likely to devalue themselves.

Reciprocal compatibility. The extent to which one or more members' needs satisfy other members' needs (i.e., one person has a high need to control others and others have a high need to be controlled).

Redundancy. Repetition of thought and action.

Reflective thinking process. Involves (1) definition of terms/issues; (2) analyzing the major aspects of the problem; (3) determining possible solutions; (4) selection of the most desirable solution; (5) assessing the validity of the chosen solution.

Resources. Personal properties of members valued by others.

Roles. Group related identities based on responsibility or styles of behavior.

Role-systems model of group development. A model designed to trace maturation according to shifts in role relationships over time.

Saliency of attitude. The degree to which the subject or person is important to an individual.

Sanctions. Positive and negative rewards for correct and incorrect performances.

Scientific management. A philosophy of management based upon the assumption that there is one best way of working on a task.

Self-disclosure. The voluntary giving of personal information about oneself to others.

Sequential structure. Distributions of categorized interaction sequences.

Small group. Exists if (1) its members are able to conduct their affairs together in a face-to-face interaction; (2) members become associated with one or more roles related to group activities; (3) it is small enough to function without dividing itself.

Social-emotional behaviors. Positive and negative acts involving friendliness or unfriendliness, dramatization or tension, and agreement or disagreement.

Social-facilitation principle. Group members are more highly aroused by the presence of others. High arousal produces behaviors high in a member's response hierarchy.

Socialization. The transmission of parental attitudes and values to the child.

Social-psychological needs. Secondary needs related to the mind and spirit.

Social sensitivity. The tendency to understand others—member feelings and behaviors.

Social structures. Are created and maintained through communicative consistencies, perceptions, and expectations upon which relationships between members are based.

Optimal maturation. Maximizing achievement of task objectives in ways as to attain the highest level of satisfaction possible for group members.

Optimizing tasks. Task outputs are measured by quality of effort.

Originator compatibility. The extent one member is able to provide expressions of affection, control, or inclusion commensurate with the needs of another.

Output. Task accomplishments and member changes.

Owning feelings and thoughts. Accepting responsibility for our reactions rather than blaming others.

Paralanguage. Nonlanguage vocal expressions.

Participant-observer-orientation. The ability to be simultaneously involved in the task role responsibilities and ongoing observation and analysis of behavioral elements which make up a group's communication system.

Participatory cointeraction. Typical group-type activities where members work and talk together.

Participatory noninteraction. Assembly-line-type of co-work with limited opportunities for communication.

Personal feedback. Is intended to let other people know how you feel about them as individuals.

Position. A description of what a person does in a group.

Positive-negative. One of the dimensions of Bales' model. Positive members appear friendly and sociable and tend to treat others as equals. Negative members are viewed as unfriendly, disagreeable, and "self-concerned."

Power. Potential influence available to leaders.

Prestige. Formally or traditionally defined duties, prerogatives, and rewards known to be part of a position.

Process. Interpretation of relationships between group members depending upon awareness of message frequencies, flow, and sequence across members and time.

Program evaluation and review technique (PERT). Involves the following seven-step problem solving method: (1) state desired outcomes; (2) specify the necessary group behaviors to reach the goals; (3) assign an operating sequence to each behavior; (4) estimate the amount of time for each operation; (5) separate each operation into a distinct "subsystem" and operationalize it using procedures 1 to 4; (6) assign action priorities to the sequentially ordered operations; and (7) allocate available resources by priority.

Proxemics. The study of how people use space.

Psychodynamic model of group development. Group maturity is viewed as a process of establishing valid communication between members.

Slater, P. 1955. Role differentiation in small groups. *American Sociological Review 20,* 300–310.

Smith, M. 1968. The self and cognitive consistency. In *Theories of cognitive consistency,* eds. A. Abelson, et al., pp. 366–372. Skokie, Ill.: Rand McNally.

Strodtbeck, F.L. and Mann, R.D. 1956. Sex role differentiation in jury deliberation. *Sociometry 19,* 3–11.

Tagiuri, R. 1958. Social preference and its perception. In *Person perception and interpersonal behavior,* eds. R. Tagiuri and L. Petrullo, pp. 316–336. Stanford, Calif.: Stanford University Press.

Thibaut, J. and Kelley, H.H. 1959. *The social psychology of groups.* New York: John Wiley.

Zajonc, R. 1960. Balance, congruity, and dissonance. *Public Opinion Quarterly 24,* 280–296.

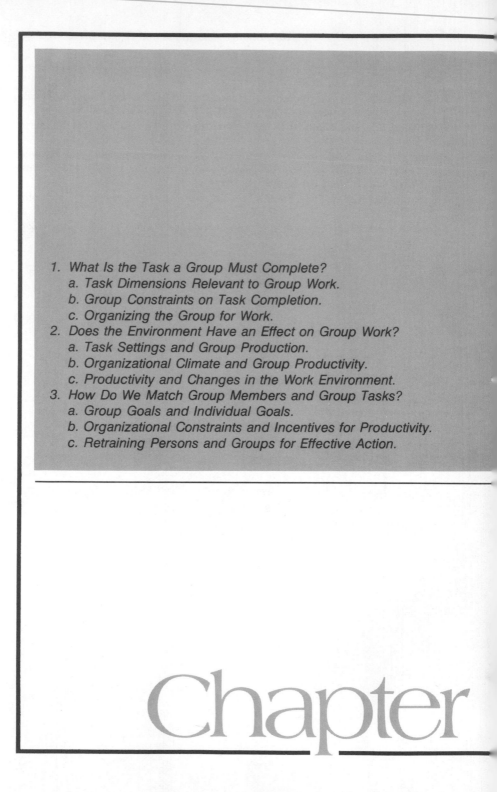

Chapter

author index